# PRISONS &
# PUNISHMENT

2ND EDITION

# PRISONS & PUNISHMENT

## THE ESSENTIALS

## DAVID SCOTT
## NICK FLYNN

Los Angeles | London | New Delhi
Singapore | Washington DC

Los Angeles | London | New Delhi
Singapore | Washington DC

SAGE Publications Ltd
1 Oliver's Yard
55 City Road
London EC1Y 1SP

SAGE Publications Inc.
2455 Teller Road
Thousand Oaks, California 91320

SAGE Publications India Pvt Ltd
B 1/I 1 Mohan Cooperative Industrial Area
Mathura Road
New Delhi 110 044

SAGE Publications Asia-Pacific Pte Ltd
3 Church Street
#10-04 Samsung Hub
Singapore 049483

Editor: Natalie Aguilera
Editorial assistant: James Piper
Production editor: Sarah Cooke
Copyeditor: Solveig Gardner Servian
Proofreader: Lynda Watson
Indexer: Martin Hargreaves
Marketing manager: Sally Ransom
Cover design: Wendy Scott
Typeset by: C&M Digitals (P) Ltd, Chennai, India
Printed and bound by CPI Group (UK) Ltd,
Croydon, CR0 4YY

© David Scott and Nick Flynn 2014

First edition published as *Penology* in 2008. Reprinted 2010, 2011 (twice) & 2013
This edition published 2014

**Library of Congress Control Number: 2013950939**

**British Library Cataloguing in Publication data**

A catalogue record for this book is available from the British Library

MIX
Paper from responsible sources
FSC® C013604

ISBN 978-1-4462-7346-3
ISBN 978-1-4462-7347-0 (pbk)

# CONTENTS

# ABOUT THE AUTHORS

**David Scott** is senior lecturer in Criminology at Liverpool John Moores University. David has published widely on prisons, punishment and critical criminology. Recent book titles include *Controversial Issues in Prisons* (Scott and Codd, 2010), *Critique and Dissent* (Gilmore, Moore and Scott, 2013), *The Caretakers of Punishment* (2014) and *Why Prison?* (2013). David is a former co-ordinator of the European Group for the Study of Deviance and Social Control and is a member of the steering committee of the Reclaim Justice Network. He is also an associate editor of the *Howard Journal of Criminal Justice* and is on the editorial board of *Criminal Justice Matters*.

**Nick Flynn** is senior lecturer in Criminology and Criminal Justice at De Montfort University. Nick has published widely on prisons, rehabilitation theory and practice, and environmental criminology. His most recent book is *Criminal Behaviour in Context: Space, Place and Desistance from Crime* (2010). Prior to teaching, Nick worked as a freelance researcher on criminal justice issues and as a campaigner for penal reform. He is on the editorial board of the *British Journal of Community Justice*.

# COMPANION WEBSITE

*Prisons & Punishment: The Essentials* is also accompanied by a companion website, which is accessible at: www.uk.sagepub.com/scottandflynn

The website, which contains resources for both lecturers and students, intends to complement and build on the material here presented and includes the following material:

- Links to government reports
- Links to related websites and blogs
- Links to free journal articles
- A glossary

# PART I
# PENOLOGY

# 1.1 THINKING LIKE A PENOLOGIST

**Core areas**

introduction to the book
running themes in penology
'fugitive thought': a brief introduction to penology
thinking outside the box

**Running themes**

- Social divisions
- Power
- Imagination

## INTRODUCTION TO THE BOOK

Welcome to *Prisons and Punishment: The Essentials*. Many people are drawn to the study of punishments, crime control and other means of responding to wrongdoing and social deviance. Those who harm, and how we should best respond to those harms, fascinate us. This focus on punishment and penal institutions, such as the prison, and their possible justifications is the remit of what is called 'penology'. Students can approach penological subject matter from various academic disciplines, such as philosophy, history, social policy, or the social sciences. The study of penology is a fast-growing area in many universities and, while there are many specialist books and introductory textbooks, it is difficult for those who are new to the subject to decide what best to read and in what order. The intention of *Prisons and Punishment: The Essentials* is to provide you with a one-stop, easy-to-use reference guide that covers the main themes of prison and punishment modules.

The book is not intended to act as a replacement for lectures, textbooks, journal articles or specialist contributions in the field, but rather as a complement to such materials and activities. In short, the aim of the book is to help you to get the most from your studies. If this text can clarify and make sense of a complex penological debate, stimulate your interest, encourage you to look at issues in more depth, or help you use your imagination to start thinking more creatively about how social problems can be conceived of or addressed, then it will have achieved its aim—and perhaps much more.

The book introduces some of the common principles and concepts of prison, community sanctions and punishment. It provides hints, tips and handy summaries of the main themes and issues; and, ultimately, it aims to enhance your understanding of, and ability to use, penological knowledge. It should help you to structure and organise your thoughts, and it should enable you to get the most from your textbooks and the other reading that you do as part of your course. We also hope the book appeals to the general reader who is looking for a straightforward introduction to, and summary of, penology that is easily digestible and can be read relatively quickly. Overall, *Prisons and Punishment: The Essentials* should help you to challenge common-sense and populist assumptions about prisons and punishment, and to think critically about the subject matter.

To support you in your studies, the book provides bullet points of key arguments and debates. Alongside this, it uses the following unique features to help you develop insights into penological thought.

- *Core areas and running themes* Each chapter starts with a list of core areas and central themes in penology.
- *Key penologists* At the start of many chapters, important penologists are highlighted, each of whom has made a significant contribution to the central themes under discussion.
- *Summary boxes* These highlight and summarise key issues on a given topic.
- *Tips* and *common pitfalls* Tips boxes appear throughout the chapters and offer you key factors to remember, along with advice on what to do and how to best answer a question. Common pitfalls remind you of common mistakes and give you some indication of what not to do. These boxes will help you to question dominant assumptions and common-sense ideas on prisons and punishment.
- *Questions* Dispersed throughout the book, you are given example questions and indications of how these might be answered.
- *Taking it further* At the end of many of the chapters you are given details of recent debates, penal controversies or examples of in-depth readings on the topic area.

- *Bibliographies* These annotated bibliographies offer you a description of some of the best texts to read when developing your knowledge and undertaking background reading for an assignment.

The book is divided into four main parts.

**Part one**, chapter 1.1 provides you with a brief introduction to the discipline, followed by guidance on how you can learn to think like a penologist. Here, you are given advice on how to enter the mind-set of penal experts and you are introduced to the kind of terminology that they use. Chapter 1.2 assesses the strengths and weaknesses of the key sources of penal knowledge that you will come across as you try to make sense in your studies of prisons and punishment.

**Part two** begins with a discussion of the philosophical and sociological accounts of imprisonment and punishment. The book is largely focused on prisons and punishment in the UK, but chapter 2.2 examines international comparative studies of penology and their implications for thinking about penal sanctions closer to home. The next three chapters provide an account of the history, policy and organisational structures of penal systems in the UK, before moving on to consider some of the problems and controversies that are encountered in prison life and the current means by which penal systems are held accountable. Part two concludes with a discussion of probation and non-custodial forms of punishment and a review of three alternative visions of the future: penal expansionism; penal reductionism; and penal abolitionism.

**Part three** offers you further guidance with your studies. If you work your way carefully through part three, by its end you should be better equipped to profit from your lectures, benefit from your seminars, construct your essays efficiently, develop effective revision strategies and respond comprehensively to the pressures of exam situations. The chapters in this part present checklists and bullet points to help you focus your attention on key issues, and provide examples to demonstrate the use of such features as structure, headings and continuity.

**Part four** concludes the book with a glossary that contains brief definitions of a number of key penological terms and a bibliography listing the sources cited in the book.

# RUNNING THEMES IN PENOLOGY

No matter what area of penology you are writing about, it is probably not too difficult to predict that the subject in question will be marked out by similar 'running themes' that recur throughout the subject.

Always try to mention these themes and to think about how they make an impact upon the topic at hand:

> **Alternatives to prison** Non-custodial ways of dealing with wrongdoing. These can involve community penalties and other ways of dealing with harms and wrongs that do not adopt the punitive rationale.
>
> **Governmentality** A political term to denote new systems of ordering and governance in contemporary society. In penological terms, the term is used to describe new approaches to the control of crime and how these are shaped by changing economic, social and cultural imperatives.
>
> **Human rights** A normative principle that is based on the recognition of the innate dignity of a fellow human being. This can involve the recognition of legal entitlements and of the wrongdoer's shared humanity, and acknowledgement of all human suffering.
>
> **Labour market** The thesis that there are strong links between the form and nature of punishment, and the needs of the labour market.
>
> **Legitimacy** The moral and political validity of the exercise of penal power. The criteria defining what a legitimate response to wrongdoing entails are hotly contested, and there are a number of different approaches to thinking about penal legitimacy. These include theories from Emile Durkheim (on ritualism and the lack of legitimacy), Max Weber (on the belief in legitimacy and authority), David Beetham (on how institutions must conform to people's beliefs), and Gramscian and (neo-)abolitionist perspectives that call for philosophical and normative criteria for evaluating the rightfulness of punishments.
>
> **Less eligibility** The belief that conditions of imprisonment must not be higher than the living conditions of the poorest labourer. Adoption of this doctrine has major implications for the dehumanisation of wrongdoers.
>
> **Managerialism** A credo that claims that better forms of management, rooted in the principles of efficiency, effectiveness and economy, can solve the current penal crisis and provide services that are better value for money. It is an ethos that has dominated public services in the UK over the last twenty five years.
>
> **Pains of imprisonment** The inherent deprivations of prison life, as coined by Gresham Sykes (1958), who described the 'pains of imprisonment' for male prisoners as the deprivation of liberty, of heterosexual sex, of goods and services, of autonomy and of security.
>
> **Penal reform** The argument that the prison can be improved and made more humane or effective. Penal reformers are often humanitarians who believe that prisons can have good living conditions and constructive regimes, and can rehabilitate, if used for the appropriate people.

**Penological imagination** The application of creative, 'big' thinking to the study of prisons and punishment. Imaginative understandings of penal matters move beyond data-driven statistical analysis in order to explore relationships between penality and the human experience of it. The penological imagination is a quality of mind, a particular way of approaching, thinking about or interpreting complex issues and their possible resolution. Try to use your imagination to uncover wider social, political and economic factors that might influence who is punished and why.

**Power to punish** The definition and application of the penal rationale to discipline, exclude or control human behaviour. Penal critics have highlighted how the power to punish is disproportionately deployed against the poor and powerless.

**Public protection** The claim that prison and community penalties exist to contain dangerous offenders and those people who pose a considerable threat to ordinary members of society. Public protection is a major justification for increasing levels of prison security.

**Rehabilitation** A justification of punishment, which claims that prison can be used to restore an offender to his or her previous competency. The term is now often used interchangeably with other 're-words' such as 're-integration', 're-settlement', 're-entry', as well as 'reform'.

**Risk** A highly influential way of calculating and assessing the danger or harm that an offender may present in the future.

**Social divisions** Who loses and who gains in a given social context? To answer this question, penologists have paid particular attention to examining divisions centred on poverty, social exclusion, 'race', gender and age.

**Social justice** The equitable redistribution of products and resources, allowing individuals to meet their necessary needs. Alongside this, it requires a rebalancing of power, a reducing of vulnerabilities, and the fostering of trust, security and social inclusion. It also implies recognition and respect for the shared humanity of wrongdoers, whoever they may be.

## Remember!

*It is a good bet that, whatever you are writing about, most of these running themes can be squeezed into your essay or exam to give you a more critically rounded and wide-ranging answer. But bear in mind that the running themes listed above are nearly always interrelated.*

# 'FUGITIVE THOUGHT': A BRIEF INTRODUCTION TO PENOLOGY

We all have been punished and have probably perpetrated some form of punishment at some stage of our lives. Although the discipline of penology has been primarily concerned with punishments sanctioned and undertaken by the state, it is important to recognise that punishment does not begin there, but rather within wider society. Punishments can be physical or psychological, performed publicly or privately, and can be either informal or a formal and legal sanction. You may have experienced some form of sanction or punishment by a family member while as a child at home, or at school through informal interactions with friends or for breaking school rules. As an adult, such informal punishments may take place in relationships or in the workplace. You may feel that this form of punishment has served you well in your life, or you may have found it no use at all. From this experience, you may think that punishment is a 'necessary evil'—that is essential for the raising of children or for the regulation of adult human life—or it may have led you to think that such sanctioning is counterproductive, even harmful.

Punishments are invoked when someone is believed to have done something wrong. This means that they are believed to have breached the rules, whether those rules are legal, social, organisational or moral. Wrongdoing and rule breaking are probably inevitable in human societies, and so the pertinent question becomes 'how should we respond when wrongful acts and breaches of rules occur?' Should we aim to include or exclude offenders, to help them, to control them, or to harm them? Alongside this, we must also recognise that the manner in which rules are defined and understood may vary over time and space. Rule breaking and doing wrong reflect the different values, goals and interests of those in positions of power, and of those who define the rules in the first instance. Consequently, some wrongdoing is illegal and defined as a 'crime', while other forms of harm are not. Furthermore, whether a person is punished for a wrongdoing is not only a consequence of the act itself; it is just as important to think about who the offender is. You may often have heard the term 'don't do as I do, do as I say': an adult or teacher (people in positions of power in a given social context) who breaches family or school rules may be much less likely to face sanctions than a child or student (the powerless) who does the same.

The nature and extent of action that the government and its official servants take in response to human wrongdoing tells us a great deal about the kind of society in which we live. Many penologists and politicians have highlighted over the centuries that the way in which we deal with offenders is a major indication of the level of civilisation and commitment to human rights and civil liberties in our society. The study of punishment and penalties, then, is not only about those who are subjected to them, or even those who work in the criminal justice system, but is something that goes to the heart of our culture. We may only be bystanders in the punishment business, but it is in our names—and apparently our interests—that the harms of punishment are inflicted.

The study of punishment has a very long history. There are documents detailing penal philosophy in the times of the ancient Greek civilisation, and both Plato and Aristotle wrote on punishment. There is also evidence of penal theory in the Egyptian and Roman civilisations. You have probably heard the saying 'an eye for an eye, a tooth for a tooth'. This phrase is derived from the ancient Jewish tradition of *lex talionis* (the principle of balance). Although it is still widely used today, its real meaning of restoring balance is often misinterpreted. The great social thinkers, sociologists and philosophers—from Kant and Hegel, to Durkheim and Foucault—have all written about punishment, with the latter writing also on imprisonment. But the discipline of penology is often seen as emerging in the eighteenth century, with the philosophical insights of Enlightenment thinkers such as Cesare Beccaria and Jeremy Bentham, alongside the penal reforms inspired by evangelical Christians such as John Howard and George Onesiphourus Paul. What all of this indicates is that the history of 'fugitive thought' on wrongdoing and punishment is closely tied up with a number of different disciplines, and with the work of penal practitioners and reformers. You should be aware that this multidisciplinary approach and pragmatic application of knowledge continues to shape the discipline of penology today.

---

**What is penology?**

Penology is a multidisciplinary subject that aims to study and evaluate the application of penal sanctions to wrongdoers. It has broadly focused on the justifications, characteristics and effectiveness of penal institutions. Since the eighteenth century, many penologists have conceived of prison as a place with rehabilitative potential, emphasising

*(Continued)*

*(Continued)*

its role as a means of reducing reoffending or of instilling moral backbone into offenders. For much of its history, penology has concerned itself with the achievement of such progressive, practical and technical goals. More recently however, penologists have expanded their remit to examine the daily lives and culture of prisoners and staff, and some of the inherent dangers of confinement. This has highlighted the regressive consequences of prison. Since the 1960s, penologists who are very critical of the penal system have evaluated its practices and legitimacy, calling for society to end the use of imprisonment and to consider non-punitive responses to wrongdoing and rule breaking.

Penology attempts to understand the complex, difficult and emotive issues that are raised when we think about punishment:

- Penologists are interested in the responses to human wrongdoing and, specifically, in the practices, forms and evolution of the punishment and social controls that exist in contemporary society.
- Penologists focus on the criminal justice system/criminal process and develop arguments concerning its legitimacy.
- Although united in their focus of investigation, penologists come from a wide range of disciplines, including psychology, geography, history, philosophy, social policy, sociology and criminology.
- In general, penologists look to understand the deployment of penalties within their social, cultural, historical, economic and political contexts.
- When thinking about the criminal justice system/criminal process, penologists use their 'imagination' and do not take the practices, or even existence, of punishment at a straightforward or common-sense level.
- Unlike practitioners, who are concerned almost exclusively with the operational practices, laws and procedures shaping punishments and their apparent effectiveness, penologists also ask broader questions concerning who we punish, for what offence, when and why.
- Penologists are interested in the justifications of penalties and social sanctions, and develop a specific theoretical framework that informs, and shapes, their research and arguments.

You may have noticed we have not mentioned 'crime' here. It may be that you think the meaning of 'crime' is relatively straightforward. You know what it is, and you also have an idea about the kinds of people who commit it. But in reality 'crime' is not self-evident. It is constructed, defined and contested in different ways by different people. You may conclude that 'crime' causes 'harm', but who decides what counts as 'harm' and why? This is not to say there is no connection whatsoever between 'crime' and punishment, but the relationship is very complex and penologists have looked to other factors influencing punishments.

> Some penologists put the word 'crime' in inverted commas to indicate that the content and meanings of the term are contested. They may offer alternative words, such as 'troubles', 'problematic behaviours' or 'social harms' to describe rule breaking and wrongdoing.

# THINKING OUTSIDE THE BOX

The key to success in your course is to learn how to 'think like a penologist'—that is to say, to learn how to speak academic language, using the terms and phrases that mark out 'penologist speak' from that of everyday talk on 'crime', punishment and imprisonment. This book will give you hints and tips about when and how to use this language, and on the ways of thinking about the world that come with this language. It is important that you use the appropriate terms and phrases—but there are no easy shortcuts here: you must be able to unpack terms and use them. Academic language is a form of shorthand, and to get good marks you must be able to demonstrate that you fully understand the words you are using and their implications for the deployment of penalties in society.

To think like a penologist it is important that you think critically about prisons and punishment. This does not mean that you simply criticise everyone and everything, but rather that you are able to develop analytical skills that help you to evaluate and judge the issues that you are studying. 'Crime' and punishment are popular issues for debate, but discussions about them are often rooted in complete misunderstandings of key facts and issues. The kinds of stories that you read in newspapers or hear generally, in pub talk or on a radio phone-in, are pragmatic, individualistic and authoritarian. We assess the pitfalls of such 'everyday' sources of penal knowledge in the next chapter. You must allow yourself the opportunity to think beyond such penological illiteracy. You must be able to develop an analytical and critical framework when assessing the validity and appropriateness of current forms of punishment and imprisonment, and to engage with wider social theory, philosophy, social policy, history, psychology and, especially, sociology.

Thinking like a penologist involves challenging taken-for-granted and populist assumptions. It involves taking on what appears, at first, to be quite alien ideas. One of the most remarkable arguments made by penologists is that we should rethink the relationship between 'crime' and punishment. You have probably grown up and lived your life with the belief that the existence of punishments is intimately tied to the problem of 'crime', and that the extent of 'crime' is the most important factor in determining the level of punishment. But some of the most important and influential penologists, such as Emile Durkheim, Georg Rusche and Michel Foucault, argue that 'crime' is relatively insignificant, and that the form and extent of punishments in society must be understood through its relationship with other social, cultural, economic and political factors. This is why much penology draws on the 'classical' sociology of Emile Durkheim, Karl Marx and Max Weber. These Victorian scholars were concerned about the growing instability of social life during the period of nineteenth-century industrialisation. The world has changed dramatically since then but the crises of social order confronted by these thinkers and the ideas they developed from them continue to be of relevance today. A contemporary penological perspective is that public opinion has hardened over recent years in favour of more severe and increasingly vindictive forms of punishment. Economic uncertainty caused by rising unemployment and job insecurity has fuelled public enthusiasm for tougher 'crime' control measures. Governments seeking re-election have responded by instigating a new 'culture of control' (Garland, 2001) directed primarily at marginal and excluded groups held responsible for threatening the economic and social order (Feeley and Simon, 1992; O'Malley, 1999a). Thinking like a penologist means *thinking outside the box*.

Penology is a theoretical discipline and, when theorising about punishment and imprisonment, it is important that you are able to locate the issues and debates within the 'big picture'. One of the best ways to do this is to develop what has been described as your 'sociological, criminological or penal imagination' (Mills, 1959; Barton et al., 2006; Smith, 2008; Young, 2011). This is a quality of mind, a particular way of approaching, thinking about or interpreting complex, 'fugitive' social problems and their possible implications and resolution. Unlike 'pub talk', you look to uncover wider social, political and economic factors that might influence who is punished and why. Central to penological thought are concerns around power. This entails critical analysis of the form and nature of wider power relations in society, and of the exercise of the power to punish. You must constantly be aware of 'power' when thinking about punishment: who has the power to define and label; who are the powerless; who are the powerful; and how these power differentials shape crime controls.

To think like a penologist, you should attempt to understand punishments within their structural, social, historical and political contexts. You should try to form an understanding of the world in which individual choices, experiences and daily lives are located within a given historical moment and wider structural contexts, such as age, gender, sexuality, financial resources or perceived 'race'. You should consider how the wrongdoing and rule breaking of people at the lower end of the social hierarchy may be perceived and responded to differently from that of those at the top. You should also try to see things from different political ideologies and perspectives, including the world views of the prisoner and the powerless.

---

**Using your imagination**

It is perhaps stating the obvious to say that the only people who can tell us what the experience of imprisonment is really like are those who have actually been in prison. You can, however, study penological and sociological research on prison culture, and/or read prisoner autobiographies to gain some insight of what it would be like to be imprisoned. What is clear from these sources is that prison is a lonely, isolating, disempowering, brutalising and dehumanising experience.

Imagine being locked in your bathroom—put an inspection hole in the door; put bars on the windows; remove the bath and, in its place, put three beds. Then imagine what it might be like to spend 15–23 hours a day in this 'cell'. Imagine what it would be like if the two people you most dislike in the world were to be in the cell with you. You must eat, sleep and defecate in your cell in the company of others, and it is possible that all three activities may be going on in this small space at the same time. If you leave your 'bathroom/cell', you have only very limited choices, power or sense of personal responsibility: somebody else will open doors for you; somebody else will tell you what to do, where to go, when to eat, work, sleep and, perhaps, even when to speak.

*(Continued)*

> *(Continued)*
>
> This may be a worst-case scenario in relation to imprisonment in many Western nations, but it remains an all-too-common reality of prison life in the UK today. Using our imaginations in this way presents us with a frightening picture of the potential impact of imprisonment on the conception of the self, even before we start to talk about the minutiae of prison life: the (poor) quality of the food; the limited access to family, friends, and constructive activities; the negative attitudes and treatment of other prisoners or of the staff guarding you; and the day-to-day boredom. It is difficult to see how this environment can do anything to help the perpetrator acknowledge the harmfulness of their wrongful behaviour or meet the needs of victims, except perhaps to satisfy an understandable, although not necessarily healthy, desire for revenge. Yet prison persists.

When thinking like a penologist you can develop a new vocabulary for understanding the lived experiences of those you are studying. As Charles Wright Mills (1959) intended, using your sociological imagination can help you develop ways of understanding the social world that intimately connect individual meanings and experiences with wider collective or social realities. Moreover, it should help you understand why many penologists believe that prisons must be placed within wider social and structural contexts, rather than considered in isolation. For example, how the public meaning of punishment develops and changes over time according to cultural and political forces. To 'think like a penologist', then, entails using your imagination when contemplating punishments.

## "What factors do you think are important to consider when explaining the relationship between 'crime' and punishment?"

In framing your answer, you need to think past making a simple connection between the incidence of 'crime' and fluctuations in prison populations. This does not stand up to scrutiny. Consider the relationship more widely than this, taking into account how characteristics of penal systems are subject to social, cultural and economic change.

Identify specifically what these changes are, what they entail, and the impact they have on public and political responses to 'crime' and punishment.

## "How does thinking like a penologist differ from 'common sense'?"

First, reflect on how 'common-sense' understandings about punishment and prisons form. What has influenced you most, and how and why your own opinions and beliefs have changed over time. Consider personal experiences, as well as the experiences of others—family, friends or acquaintances at school. Think also about how 'crime' and punishment is presented on television programmes, in popular fiction, films and music lyrics; and by journalists, politicians and 'celebrities'. Acknowledge what has influenced you most. Your opinions and beliefs are important and you are entitled to express them. But be prepared to suspend and to challenge them. After all, the reason you have come to university is to learn new ideas and perspectives. Now compare the distinctive features of each of the 'common-sense' sources of your 'knowledge' and understanding with the definition of penology and the notion of the penological imagination presented above.

# BIBLIOGRAPHY

The following texts present key themes and ideas involved in punishment and the criminal justice process. Some of these are introductory text books while others are more critical analyses of 'crime', criminal justice and punishment. Each should help you understand what penology involves, the contribution it makes to critical and creative understandings of prisons and punishment, and what its distinguishing features are.

The 'classic' literature which has fundamentally altered the way we think about prisons and punishment includes:

- **DURKHEIM, E (1893; 1984)** *The Division of Labour in Society*, London: Macmillan.
- **FOUCAULT, M (1977)** *Discipline and Punish: The Birth of the Prison*, Harmondsworth: Penguin.

- **RUSCHE, G and KIRCHHEIMER, O (1939; 2003)** *Punishment and Social Structure*, London: Transaction.

A detailed critical analysis of the classic penological literature is:

- **GARLAND, D (1990)** *Punishment and Modern Society: A Study in Social Theory*, Oxford: Oxford University Press.

Historical accounts of prisons and punishment are:

- **GODFREY, B and LAWRENCE, P (2005)** *Crime and Justice 1750–1950*, Cullompton: Willan.
- **IGNATIEFF, M (1978)** *A Just Measure of Pain: The Penitentiary in the Industrial Revolution, 1750–1850*, Harmondsworth: Penguin.
- **MORRIS, N and ROTHMAN, D (1998)** *The Oxford History of the Prison*, Oxford: Oxford University Press.
- **RAWLINGS, P (1999)** *Crime and Power: A History of Criminal Justice 1688–1998*, Harlow: Longman.
- **SHARPE, J (1990)** *Judicial Punishment in England*, London: Faber and Faber.

Recent critical introductions to prisons and punishment include:

- **ASHWORTH, A and REDMAYNE, M (2010)** *The Criminal Process*, Oxford: Oxford University Press.
- **DAVIES, M, CROALL, H and TRYER, J (2010)** *Criminal Justice: An Introduction to the Criminal Justice System in England and Wales*, 4th edn, London: Pearson-Longman.
- **EASTON, S and PIPER, C (2008)** *Sentencing and Punishment: The Quest for Justice*, 2nd edn, Oxford: Oxford University Press.
- **ELLIS, T and SAVAGE, S (2011)** *Debates in Criminal Justice: Key Themes and Issues*, London: Routledge.
- **HUDSON, B (2003)** *Understanding Justice*, 2nd edn, Buckingham: Open University Press.
- **JEWKES, Y and BENNETT, J (2007)** *Dictionary of Prisons and Punishment*, Cullompton: Willan.
- **JOYCE, P (2006)** *Criminal Justice: An Introduction to Crime and the Criminal Justice System*, Cullompton: Willan.
- **SANDERS, A, YOUNG, R and BURTON, M (2010)** *Criminal Justice*, 4th edn, Oxford: Oxford University Press.
- **SMITH, P and NATALIER, K (2005)** *Understanding Criminal Justice*, London: Sage.

- **UGLOW, S (2009)** 'The Criminal Justice System' in C Hale, K Hayward, A Wahidin and E Wincup (eds), *Criminology*, Oxford: Oxford University Press.

Analysis of the concept of present day 'popular punitiveness' is found in:

- **BOTTOMS, A (1995)** 'The Philosophy and Politics of Punishment and Sentencing', in C Clarkson and R Morgan (eds), *The Politics of Sentencing Reform*, Oxford: Clarendon Press.
- **MATTHEWS, R (2005)** 'The Myth of Punitiveness', *Theoretical Criminology*, 9(2), pp. 175–201.
- **O'MALLEY, P (1999a)** 'Volatile and Contradictory Punishment', *Theoretical Criminology*, 3(2), pp. 175–96.
- **PRATT, J (2000)** 'Emotive and Ostentatious Punishment', *Punishment and Society*, 2(4), pp. 417–39.

And finally, when thinking about using your 'imagination', see:

- **MILLS, CW (1959)** *The Sociological Imagination*, Oxford: Oxford University Press.
- **BARTON, A, CORTEEN, K, SCOTT, D and WHYTE, D (eds) (2006)** *Expanding the Criminological Imagination*, Cullompton: Willan.
- **FRAULEY, J (ED) (2014)** *C. Wright Mills and the Criminological Imagination*, Aldershot: Ashgate.

# 1.2 SOURCES OF PENAL KNOWLEDGE

## TELLING SECRETS

A primary responsibility of penologists is to locate sources of information on prisons and punishment and evaluate its relevance and reliability. Prisons are closed and secretive worlds in which it is difficult to uncover the truth. As a student of penology, you need to understand how such state organisations work, what problems they encounter and whether they undertake their functions correctly. Yet you may find that, when researching state institutions, you uncover contradictory evidence, competing or even unsubstantiated knowledge claims, or are told that little or no data is available. This lack of 'visibility' presents major obstacles. Uncovering the truth and telling secrets about prison life requires that you ask the right questions, assess the value of different forms of knowledge and information, and access the most relevant and contemporary sources. For instance, you may wish to consider how much information about prison gets into the public arena, especially through the media. And related to this, whether the brutal realities of prison life and prisoner dehumanisation are becoming more visible to the general public as Fitzgerald and Sim (1982) have argued, or rather kept secret from them, held in a state of denial, as Cohen and Taylor (1978) and Cohen (2001) have argued. Thinking like a penologist entails asking such questions, exploring the meaning of prisons and punishment, critically unpicking myth from reality, and recognising stereotypes.

# THE ACADEMY: APPRECIATIVE OR CRITICAL RESEARCH VALUES

The most obvious and important source of penal knowledge, which you should prioritise in your studies, is that of academics. This is published in books and criminology journals, including electronic journals. Academic scholarship is considered 'trustworthy' because it has been judged through a rigorous process of 'peer review' in which scholars assess the work of other scholars. But, although academic presses and peer reviewed journals strive to be scholarly, objective, robust and reliable, very important to consider when turning to this source of knowledge are the research values of the penologist and the questions that are asked.

There are two broad approaches to undertaking academic penological research: appreciative inquiry (AI) and critical inquiry. Alison Liebling (2004) is a leading proponent of AI. She claims that AI modes of inquiry provide a faithful or truthful account of the respondent's positive achievements, survival strategies and success stories, alongside his or her negative experiences. Because the approach is future orientated rather than focused only on the present or the past, methodology and outcomes are intimately tied.

Questioning is appreciative in that it asks respondents to dwell on the *best* as well as the *worst* aspects of his or her prison experience. Interview questions focus on 'prison values' and are very specific. Respondents are asked to provide evidence of answers by way of an example, illustration or story drawn from his or her actual experiences. AI claims to provide a more sensitive, nuanced and instructive picture of the prison, and thus a more valuable approach than that of the traditional problem-orientated studies.

A number of criticisms have been made against AI:

- it does not uncover the truth and fails to highlight any real negative aspects of imprisonment;
- it is not really a research method;
- it is too closely tied to government agents, and the researcher can become a 'technician of the powerful' – i.e. his or her research can be manipulated to support the interests of the government.

By contrast, critical inquiry is independent and asks difficult questions that look to uncover the truth in a way that potentially challenges the interests of the powerful. Prison research should always aim to uncover real life, whatever this may look like. As Charles Wright Mills argues:

> Any style of empiricism involves a metaphysical choice—a choice as to what is most real ... One tries to get it straight, to make an adequate statement—if it's gloomy, too bad; if it leads to hope, fine.

> (1959, pp. 67, 78)

As a metaphysical choice, it seems more appropriate to allow the respondents to detail their stories, whether positive or negative, so that their construction of events and reality can be outlined and critically interrogated. In critical inquiry, there is no great aim to change the future prison *through the research process*, but rather the more modest aim of simply getting to the 'truth'. Such independent findings might not necessarily be good, or positive, but at least they are an account of actual experiences and illustrate their interpretive framework (Scott, 2014b).

*Always try to uncover the theoretical and research priorities of the authors of a given study. This will help you to understand the kind of questions they have asked and also to contextualise their findings.*

# LIES, DAMN LIES AND OFFICIAL PRISON STATISTICS

Another important source is official prison statistics. The government regularly produces statistical information on prisons and other forms of punishment in society. The Home Office, the Ministry of Justice (MoJ) and the National Offender Management Service (NOMS) all publish

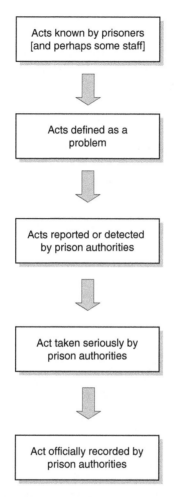

**Figure 1.1    The life of a prison statistic**

official data. Official prison statistics are an important source of information, but they are not designed, compiled or written in the interests of the general public; rather, they are written as records of the activities, budgets and workloads of state agencies.

Official prison statistics (see also Figure 1.1) provide data on:

- the 'crimes' of offenders sentenced to imprisonment;
- the demographic and social backgrounds of prisoners including age, gender and race;

- prison numbers and populations (annual receptions into custody, daily prison populations, population per 100,000 in England and Wales, prison population projections and international comparisons);
- size of the penal estate, costs and staffing;
- key performance indicators (such as data on overcrowding, educational attainments, escapes, health care, violence, drug treatments, suicides and self-harm, or time out of cell);
- offender management caseloads;
- recidivism, reconviction rates and known reoffending.

There are a number of reasons why using official prison data is important. Official data:

- provides a (limited) form of penal accountability and means of visibility;
- provides a useful means of measuring state activities;
- indicates why government develops certain priorities and policies, and deploys certain resources;
- indicates success or failure of policies.

## Common pitfall

*Over-reliance on official sources may lead to work that is uncritical. Statistics can be easily manipulated, and you must always look to alternative accounts to assess the relevance and accuracy of any statistics.*

Although they are a very useful source of knowledge, official prison statistics are, at best, only partial accounts of prison life. They are not objective and impartial accounts, but 'social constructions' of reality, reflecting the interests, goals and objectives of the gatekeepers of state institutions. There are many reasons why official data is limited. First, there are problems that are methodological (i.e. relating to how data is produced) and epistemological (i.e. relating to the limitations of quantitative data). Other concerns arise in terms of accuracy and the differences between reported data, recorded data, and what acts and events really occurred. Matthews (2009) informs us that such difficulties include:

- errors (data wrongly or falsely collated);
- 'dark figures' and omissions (no data or acts remain hidden);
- problems of 'categorisation';

- slippage (redefinition of what is measured);
- telescoping (over counting).

---

**'Not everything that can be counted counts, and not everything that counts can be counted' (Albert Einstein)**

Criticisms of official prison statistics frequently focus on the issue of managerialism, especially the tendency to prioritise what may be most easily counted and measured. Not only does this ignore the structural and social context of imprisonment, the methods used to collect official prison statistics can skew the conclusions reached. For example, in written evidence to the House of Commons Justice Committee on *Women Offenders: After the Corston Report* (2013) the campaigning group INQUEST questioned the official classification of 'non-self-inflicted' or 'natural' deaths in prison, arguing that insufficient notice is taken of prison conditions, in particular the quality of physical and mental health care for women and the treatment and management of drug problems.

---

# OFFICIAL REPORTS AND INQUIRIES

Official reports and inquiries are written and conducted by government departments and other official organisations, for example the National Audit Office. They consist of a number of different publications including:

- Command Papers (Green Papers, White Papers, reports of committees of inquiry);
- Parliamentary reports of Select and Standing Committees;
- Parliamentary Bills;
- Parliamentary debates (Hansard reports from the House of Commons and the House of Lords);
- and reports from other government departments including, in relation to prisons and punishment specifically, HM Inspectorate of Prisons, the Prisons and Probation Ombudsman, and HM Inspectorate of Probation.

Official reports are also often written by respected members of the establishment, such as senior police officers, members of the judiciary and the House of Lords or senior officers in the armed services, in response to penal crises or controversial events. Recent examples of such official inquiries include:

- the 1991 report of senior judge Lord Justice Woolf on the serious prison riots that occurred in England and Wales in April 1990;
- the 1991 report of Admiral Sir Raymond Lygo into the management of the Prison Service;
- the 1994 report of retired Chief Inspector of Constabulary Sir John Woodcock into the escape of six high security prisoners from Whitemoor prison, Cambridgeshire;
- the report by Admiral Sir John Learmont on prison security, published in 1995;
- the 2001 review of sentencing in England and Wales by senior civil servant John Halliday;
- the 2006 report by judge Justice Keith into the murder of Zahid Mubarek on the night before his release from prison;
- the 2007 report of Baroness Jean Corston into women with particular vulnerabilities in the criminal justice system;
- the 2009 report of Rt Hon Lord Bradley into people with mental health problems in the criminal justice system;
- and the 2010 report of Lord Patel of Bradford into reducing drug related crime and rehabilitating offenders in prison and on release.

Recent examples of other official government reports and command papers on criminal justice policy issues include:

- The 2009 report *The Future of the Parole Board*;
- the MoJ 2010 report *Breaking the Cycle: Effective Punishment, Rehabilitation and Sentencing of Offenders*;
- the 2012 report *Punishment and Reform: Effective Community Sentences*;
- the 2013 report *Transforming the Criminal Justice System*;

# CHECKLIST OF FACTS TO ASCERTAIN WHEN LOOKING AT AN OFFICIAL INQUIRY

- ✓ Circumstances in which the report was commissioned.
- ✓ Authors and advisers.
- ✓ Timescale, administrative support and legal powers.
- ✓ Terms of references and interpretation.
- ✓ Methodology.
- ✓ Range of people involved and those given greatest credibility.
- ✓ Recommendations and response of the government.

Official reports are normally presented as open and 'entirely independent of government' (Keith, 2006, p. 9), apparently providing a thorough, objective, comprehensive and impartial account of events. But official reports represent and promote a particular world view. This 'view from above' influences the definitions and scope of the problem investigated, and the possible means of its resolution. As a result, certain ways of approaching social problems are presented as legitimate, while others are de-legitimated and marginalised as 'irrational'.

> Some penologists have argued that the aim of official reports and other inquiries is simply to allay fears of a prison crisis by representing the problems they are investigating as temporary or relatively insignificant. The primary objective, it is argued, is to re-establish the credibility of the government. For such critics, official reports are not necessarily intended to discover the truth, but rather to re-legitimate the state and its agents.

## THE MEDIA: MORE BAD NEWS?

The term 'media' refers to mass communication systems with large audiences, such as the Internet, radio, television, film, newspapers and magazines. There are often very interesting websites, blogs, television and radio programmes, documentaries or debates about punishment such as *Panorama* and *Thinking Allowed*; and many newspapers, such as *The Guardian* and *The Times*, have dedicated prison correspondents who provide detailed discussions of prison life. To some extent, we are reliant on the media for keeping us informed of events that happen beyond the scope of the informal mechanisms that grant us access to knowledge or of own personal experiences.

The media are also an important source of penal knowledge because they:

- can visualise a hidden world;
- are an easy way of accessing knowledge;
- can be a means of shaming the government, providing forms of accountability and politicising controversial penal practices;
- can present data in a straightforward manner;
- can provide an up-to-date account.

## Common pitfall

*Remember that the news is competitive and commercial. The main intention is to appeal to a general audience and make money. The tension between providing information and the need to make stories entertaining can lead to attention being diverted away from certain serious issues to more superficial events or sensationalist takes on stories.*

Although the media is fractured, with each different media group in direct competition with the others, it is clear that certain stories and interpretations centred on 'crime' and punishment become dominant, and play a key role in the production and reproduction of current ways of thinking about social problems. In this sense, the media both reflect and perform a key role in shaping the construction of penal realities. In short, media stories are socially constructed around certain identifiable newsworthy criteria. Prison stories are patterned and must be immediate, dramatic and simple and, most of all, there must be a means of access to knowledge.

*The relationship between the media and prison authorities is institutionalised and access to official sources becomes structured, shaping, in effect, the remits of stories and the level of media critique.*

The media sets the agenda, prioritises contrasting accounts, selects the narrator of events, and privileges certain voices and forms of interpretation. Often, the accounts of prisoners are seen as neither credible nor reliable, and so it is penal authorities that exclusively shape the agenda, leading to the reinforcement of dominant values and common-sense assumptions on prison life.

*This dominant world view is sometimes referred to by penologists as **hegemony** or the **hegemonic vision**.*

A certain story may be reconstructed or repackaged into a given media formula that, although not quite fiction, is hardly a true reflection of events. Finally, the media do not provide context to their stories; rather, they present a specific narrative that underscores penal stories that isolate prisoner actions or protest. This narrative leads to constructions of prisoner resistance and dissent as illogical, pointing to the costs or damage caused, rather than as a rational response to a dehumanising lived reality. We know it is common to find stories particularly in the tabloid press which suggest prisoners lie around in bed all day enjoying 'holiday camp' jail perks (*Daily Mail*, 2012a). So pervasive has this stereotype become, the Howard League for Penal Reform has called on the Leveson inquiry into the culture, practice and ethics of the press (2011) to investigate the source of such stories. The power of the media to influence penal policy was also highlighted recently by the former Justice Secretary Ken Clarke who blamed the popular press for constantly urging an increase in prison numbers irrespective of the consequences. His proposal in 2010 to reduce prison populations by 3,000 was branded 'hugely controversial' by the *Daily Mail* (2012b) and 'soft' by the *Daily Express* (2011). In 2012 Ken Clarke was replaced as the Secretary of State for Justice by the more hard-line Chris Grayling.

> *Compare and contrast stories on prisons in different newspapers and written by different journalists. Look for the similarities and also the differences between the representations of a single prison story.*

# PENAL PRESSURE GROUPS AND THE UNIONS: ACCEPTABLE PENAL CRITICS?

Penal pressure groups provide an alternative to government agencies as a source of knowledge and expertise. There are four main groupings:

- the liberal penal lobby;
- the conservative penal lobby;
- the radical penal lobby;
- the staff unions.

## THE LIBERAL PENAL LOBBY

Although by no means homogenous, the liberal penal lobby traditionally have had the 'ear of the government'. In order to influence penal policy liberal reformers seek to have good relations with government officials, politicians and civil servants, but these personal connections have sometimes diluted their ability to be critical. The liberal penal lobby provides the core of the credible and acceptable humanitarian voice, selectively critiquing or supporting the Prison Service. As well as a number of left-of-centre 'think tanks' including the Institute for Public Policy Research, Demos and Compass, there are three main liberal pressure groups:

- **The Howard League for Penal Reform** The Howard League is the most established penal reform group in the UK. In 1866, The Howard Association took its name from the penal reformer John Howard. The aim of the Howard Association was the 'promotion of the most efficient means of penal treatment and crime prevention'. In 1907, the Penal Reform League was founded, merging with the Howard Association to become the Howard League for Penal Reform some fourteen years later in 1921. Until the late 1970s, the Howard League traditionally aimed to develop close relationships with government officials, rather than to present a radical critique of prisons. Its core beliefs are to work for a safe society in which fewer people are victims of crime and that offenders should make amends for what they have done. In recent decades, the Howard League has looked to adopt a more critical stance and has brought legal challenges under the Human Rights Act 1998, including the very significant case in which it applied the responsibilities of local authorities under the Children Act 1989 to child custody. The League has also campaigned vigorously against the imprisonment of women, suicides and self-injury, overcrowding and poor prison conditions. In 2007, the Howard League set up the independent Commission on English Prisons Today. Its report, *Do Better, Do Less* (Green, 2009) advocated for a significant reduction in the prison population, the replacement of short-term prison sentences with community based responses, and the dismantling of NOMS.
- **The Prison Reform Trust (PRT)** PRT is a relatively recent liberal penal pressure group, established only in the late 1980s. PRT aims to ensure that prisons in England and Wales are 'just, humane and effective'. PRT believes that prisons should be open and accountable institutions that are reserved for only the most serious offenders. It believes prison regimes should be constructive, safe and decent, and should prepare prisoners for resettlement in the community. Recent campaigns have looked to improve conditions, promote human rights and diversity, support prisoners' families, promote alternative community sanctions, reduce the number of children and young people in custody, improve mental health care in prison,

highlight the needs of older people in prison, and promote citizenship and successful community reintegration for prisoners after release.

• **Penal Reform International (PRI)** PRI is an international non-governmental organisation that looks to promote the development and implementation of international human rights instruments in relation to law enforcement and prison conditions, to reduce all forms of discrimination and to reduce prison numbers through the promotion of community alternatives. PRI works in partnership with, and is funded by, national governments and intergovernmental organisations such as the United Nations and the Council of Europe. It aims to provide global support, training and expertise for penal reformers. Recent campaigns have focused on prison privatisation, prison overcrowding, transnational justice, pre-trial detention and the abolition of the death penalty.

## THE CONSERVATIVE PENAL LOBBY

The conservative penal lobby is not as established as its liberal counterpart, although, in recent times, it has arguably been more influential. Although not strictly concerned with crime and criminal justice, rightwing think tanks such as the Adam Smith Institute, the Institute for Economic Affairs, Civitas, Reform and the Policy Exchange have each published politically significant work on prison privatisation, the aims and justifications of imprisonment, and the relationship between 'crime' and imprisonment rates. The privatisation of prison and probation services in recent years has also persuaded business organisations such as the Confederation of British Industry and even the manufacturer of photocopiers, HP, to publish reports on penal matters. Recent reports published by the conservative penal lobby include the Policy Exchange report *Future Prisons: A Radical Plan to Reform the Prison Estate* (Lockyer, 2013), the Reform report, *The Case for Private Prisons* (Tanner, 2013) and the Civitas report, *Acquisitive Crime: Imprisonment, Detection and Social Factors* (2012).

## THE RADICAL PENAL LOBBY

Much of the penal knowledge with which we are presented reflects the interests of the powerful. There are very few alternative sources of knowledge that are not, in some way or other, connected with, or reliant upon, those who promulgate the 'view from above'. The radical penal lobby provides an alternative voice and, although relatively few in number, and often starved of resources, in the past pressure groups such as Radical Alternatives to Prison (RAP), Preservation of the Rights of Prisoners (PROP) and No More Prison have contributed greatly to the penal reform movement. Groups which currently provide independent analysis of government penal policies and practices include:

- **INQUEST** INQUEST is a charitable organisation formed in 1981 by the families and friends of those who have died in custody. It works for 'truth, justice and accountability' and monitors issues surrounding deaths in custody (police, prison, immigration detention and deaths of detained patients) throughout the UK. INQUEST looks to campaign at Westminster for changes in inquest procedures and changes in the law, but perhaps most importantly it provides specialist, free, confidential and independent advice and support to those who have been bereaved.
- **Women In Prison (WIP)** WIP was formed by ex-prisoner Chris Tchaikovsky in October 1983 to campaign specifically around women's imprisonment. WIP points out that, because there are relatively fewer women than men in prison, the differential sentencing, experiences, pains and discrimination of women have been largely ignored or marginalised among mainstream penal pressure groups. Chris Tchaikovsky died in 2002, but WIP continues to struggle for justice for women in the courts, prison and after release.
- **Reclaim Justice Network (RJN)** RJN is a collaboration of individuals, groups, campaigners, activists, trade unionists, practitioners, researchers, and people most directly affected by the criminal justice process, who are working together to radically reduce the size and scope of the criminal justice system and build effective and socially just alternatives that provide genuine community safety. The RJN aims to promote this objective by organising a national movement across the UK that can engage with, and support, local activists and campaigners to challenge society's excessive reliance upon criminal law and the deepening of social inequalities around 'race', 'class', gender, age, ability and sexuality.

*Penal pressure groups are an indispensable source of information. They generally provide up-to-date commentaries on government policy and publish press releases, briefing papers, reports and books on current penal controversies. You are strongly advised, whatever level or focus of your study, to look regularly at their websites and publications (such as the* Howard Journal *and the* Bromley Briefings – prison factfile *published by PRT).*

## THE STAFF UNIONS

Prison officers, prison governors and probation officers also have specific pressure groups that promote their interests and lobby government. These are organised as trade unions:

- **The Prison Officers' Association (POA)** The POA has over 35,000 members and represents all prison officers and governor grades in public sector prisons in the UK. It also has a large number of members in private prisons. The POA aims to protect and promote the interests of its members, to improve working conditions and to provide free initial legal advice.
- **The Prison Governors Association (PGA)** The PGA has a much smaller membership than the POA and represents the most senior grades of governor. The PGA works in the interests of governors who have much better pay and conditions than those of prison officers.
- **The National Association of Probation Officers (NAPO)** NAPO represents more than 9,000 probation and family court staff. It formulates progressive probation policy and campaigns for positive change in the criminal justice system generally.

# NOVELS, BIOGRAPHIES AND FILMS: VIEWS FROM BELOW

Penologists who focus upon the 'view from below' privilege the knowledge of the powerless, and how they interpret and define their experiences. A long tradition of ethnographic and oral research has sought to understand the prison experience and its effects from the perspective of those who actually 'live it'. In this sense, the view from below can provide:

- an accurate and true account of offenders' everyday lived experiences;
- an insight into offender meanings and motivations;
- understanding of the prisoners' struggle to resist and maintain independence of thought;
- a platform for the voice of the disempowered (emancipating subjugated knowledge);
- initiation of an alternative source of legitimate knowledge;
- a way of lifting the lid on the secrecy of what goes on in prisons;
- a means of turning personal struggles into public issues.

There are a number of fictional accounts that help us understand penological themes. A good example is the Czech writer Franz Kafka. His *In the Penal Colony* (1919) depicts a barbaric system of criminal justice which demands blind conformity to laws which have no justification. And, in a similar vein, Kafka's *The Trial* (1925) tells the story of a man arrested and prosecuted by a remote and invisible criminal justice process. Also, Anthony Burgess's novella *A Clockwork Orange* (1962) is a study of state attempts to reform rebellious, violent youth. And the science fiction writer Phillip K. Dick's short story *The Minority Report* (1956) depicts a future 'carceral society' in which people are imprisoned for crimes it is predicted they would have committed had they not been incapacitated, while his novel *A Scanner Darkly* (1977) depicts a rehabilitative private prison for drug offenders which, in reality, is a farm on which drugs are grown.

There are also a number of biographical accounts of imprisonment which are based on the authors' own experience of penal servitude. Two of the most influential are by famous Russian novelists. Theodore Dostoevsky's *House of the Dead* (1860) and Alexander Solzhenitsyn's *One Day in the Life of Ivan Denisovich* (1963) provide highly descriptive and moving accounts of the pains of confinement. Many other prisoners have written about their experiences, and continue to do so. However, owing to their status as 'criminals', the personal accounts they provide are often rendered insignificant and worthless by the official and media powers that be. But while there is reason to assess carefully the value and credibility of prisoner testimonies, at their best they provide direct, unvarnished descriptions of the prison experience. A seminal prison autobiography is by the black American civil rights activist Eldridge Cleaver. His *Soul on Ice* (1968) is a controversial and brutally honest memoir and collection of essays written in Fulsom State prison where he was imprisoned for sexual assault with intent to murder. Other good examples from the UK include: John McVicar's *McVicar By Himself* (1974), Jimmy Boyle's *A Sense of Freedom* (1977), Mark Leech's *A Product of the System: My Life In and Out of Prison* (1993), Johnny Steele's *The Bird That Never Flew: The Uncompromised Autobiography of One of the Most Punished Prisoners in the History of the British Penal System* (2002), Ruth Wyner's *From The Inside* (2003) and Noel 'Razor' Smith's *A Few Kind Words and a Loaded Gun: The Autobiography of a Career Criminal* (2005). Such books may be some of the most graphic and interesting titles that you will read on your degree programme.

Some of the above titles have been turned into films. And indeed, there are many other films that have looked to uncover the prisoners' world view. Some of the best of the genre are: *Scum* (1979); *Brubaker* (1980); *Ghosts of the Civil Dead* (1988); *In the Name of the Father* (1993); *The Shawshank Redemption* (1994); *Das Experiment* (2001); *Carandiru* (2003); *Hunger* (2008); *A Prophet* (2009); *R* (2010); and *Caesar Must Die* (2012).

---

You may wish to look up an official report on the Prison Service and see how far it goes to present the 'truth' about prison life; although on some issues you may find considerable difficulty accessing relevant information to make such a judgement. Reference was made above to the paucity of evidence presented in relation to deaths in custody. Deaths in custody are officially investigated by a number of different bodies including the Prisons and Probation Ombudsman, Local Primary Care Trusts, Local Safeguarding Children Boards, Coroners (a doctor or a lawyer) and Inquest Juries. Despite a wealth of material being collected and analysed, including interviews with staff and prisoners, to establish the circumstances in which each death in prison occurs, a recent report by Prison Reform Trust/INQUEST (2012) found that not all reports are published and available for public examination. Although an amendment made in 2008 to Rule 43 of the Coroners Rules (ibid.) specifies that reports of deaths in custody must be responded to within 56 days by the custody agencies involved, the summaries of reports and responses published by the MoJ are 'filtered, scant in detail and not a comprehensive overview of the reports. There is no publicly-accessible database or website which allows access to these key reports: for coroners, prisons, healthcare bodies, local authorities or central government' (2012, p. 9).

TAKING IT FURTHER

---

## "By what criteria should you seek to evaluate the relevance and worth of penological source material?"

Think about the content of different kinds of penological material, and its depth and detail. Ask yourself the following questions: Is it fact or opinion? How objective is it? Why was it written? Are there any vested political or commercial interests you should be aware of? Who funded the research and why? Are the research methods used valid and robust? Is the subject matter generalisable? Or does it present just one point of view?

# BIBLIOGRAPHY

Detailed and critical studies of prisons and punishment include:

- **DRAKE, D (2011**) *Prisons, Punishment and the Pursuit of Security*, London: Palgrave.
- **MORGAN, R and LIEBLING, A (2007)** 'Imprisonment: An Expanding Scene' in M Maguire (ed), *The Oxford Handbook of Criminology*, 4th edn, Oxford: Oxford University Press.
- **SPARKS, R (2001)** 'Prisons, Punishment and Penality' in E McLaughlin and J Muncie (eds), *Controlling Crime*, London: Sage.
- **SCOTT, D (ed.) (2013)** *Why Prison?* Cambridge: Cambridge University Press.
- **SIM, J (2009)** *Punishment and Prisons: Power and the Carceral State*, London: Sage.

The following texts investigate the 'truth' of imprisonment, its lasting effects and everyday realities:

- **MATTHEWS, R (2009)** *Doing Time*, 2nd edn, London: Palgrave.
- **SCRATON, P, SIM, J and SKIDMORE, P (1991)** *Prisons Under Protest*, Milton Keynes: Open University Press.
- **SIM, J. (1994)** 'Reforming the penal wasteland? A critical review of the Wolf Report', in E Player and M Jenkins (eds), *Prisons After Woolf: Reform Through Riot*, London: Routledge, pp. 31–45.
- **SPARKS, R, BOTTOMS, AE and HAY, W (1996)** *Prisons and the Problem of Order*, Oxford: Clarendon Press.

Two introductory overviews of prisons and punishment, which in some key respects compliment this volume, are:

- **FLYNN, N (1998)** *Introduction to Prisons and Imprisonment*, Winchester: Waterside Press.
- **SCOTT, D and CODD, H (2010)** *Controversial Issues in Prisons*, Buckingham: Open University Press.

A useful book on media representations of crime and punishment is:

- **JEWKES, Y (2007)** *Media and Crime*, London: Sage.

Texts which describe research and researching 'crime' and criminal justice include:

- **FINCH, E and FAFINSKI, S (2012)** *Criminology Skills*, Oxford: Oxford University Press.
- **SAPSFORD, R (ed.) (1996)** *Researching Crime and Criminal Justice*, Milton Keynes: The Open University.
- **SCOTT, D (2014)** 'Critical Research Values and the Sociological Imagination', in J Frauley (ed), *C. Wright Mills and the Criminological Imagination*, Aldershot: Ashgate.
- **WESTMARLAND, L (2011)** *Researching Crime and Justice: Tales from the Field*, London: Routledge.

Key academic journals which cover penological themes and issues include:

- *American Journal of Criminal Justice*, Springer
- *British Journal of Criminology*, Oxford
- *Criminal justice Studies*, Routledge
- *Criminology and Criminal Justice*, Sage
- *Criminology and Public Policy*, Wiley
- *Howard Journal of Criminal Justice*, Wiley
- *Punishment and Society*, Sage
- *Theoretical Criminology*, Sage

And finally two blogs written by academic criminologists you might find useful are:

- www.bunker8.pwp.blueyonder.co.uk (written by the British criminologist John Lea)
- http://governingthroughcrime.blogspot.com (written by the American criminologist Jonathan Simon)

# PART II
# CORE AREAS OF THE CURRICULUM

# 2.1 JUSTIFICATIONS OF PUNISHMENT

## Key penologists

**Cesare Beccaria (1738–94)** Considered by many scholars to be the most influential Enlightenment thinker on penal reform in Europe, Beccaria was born to Milanese nobility and studied law at the University of Pavia, Italy. Under the guidance of his friends Pietro and Alessandro Verri, Beccaria became involved in a movement called 'the academy of fists' which sought to reform Italian society, including its criminal justice system. Denouncing the arbitrary, discretionary power of judges and extreme inconsistency in sentencing, Beccaria published his most significant treatise, *Essays on Crimes and Punishment* in 1764. This has become one of the foundational texts in penology and was hugely influential in terms of both the theories of punishment and the development of modern criminal justice systems in Europe and beyond. Beccaria promoted the ideas prevalent today that punishment should be justified through deterrence, and that sanctions must be public, speedy, necessary, the minimum possible in the given circumstances, proportionate to crime, and determined by the law.

**Jeremy Bentham (1748–1832)** An Enlightenment philosopher and lawyer who had a massive influence on theories of punishment and the design of the penitentiary, Jeremy Bentham was awarded a law degree from Oxford, but moved away from legal reforms towards advocating the wider philosophical credo of utilitarianism. In promoting the 'greatest happiness of the greatest number', utilitarianism, he believed, would transform the rational, moral and legislative basis of society. In particular, Bentham argued in favour of the reforming potential of prison, which he called 'a mill for grinding rogues honest'. He is famous for his 'panopticon' prison design, a circular structure comprising cells distributed around a central surveillance tower, which, although never built, influenced Victorian prison architecture in the UK and prisons in the US, such as Stateville. He constantly petitioned the British government to run a panopticon prison for profit, but he never succeeded in this goal. Being profoundly irreligious and having a keen interest in embalming, when he died, Bentham had his body stuffed and it still can be seen today on display at University College London.

**Thomas Mathiesen (b. 1933)** A highly influential contemporary Norwegian penologist, Thomas Mathiesen is Professor of Sociology of Law at the University of Oslo. Mathiesen co-founded the Norwegian prisoner union KROM in 1968, and his Marxist studies and penal activism led him to advocate penal abolitionism. His key books include *The Politics of Abolition* (1974 – new 40th anniversary edition in 2014), which has had a massive influence on the radical prison lobby in the UK, and *Prison On Trial*, originally published in 1990, which argues persuasively that prisons persist despite being generally recognised as 'a fiasco'.

# THE FIVE RULES OF PUNISHMENT

Penologists have asked important philosophical questions about all forms of punishment, regulation and control. We are to consider the following three:

- What is state punishment?
- Are state punishments necessary and justifiable?
- Do we need to punish at all?

Let us start by thinking about the first question: 'What is state punishment?' Broadly speaking, a 'punishment' is an act that intentionally inflicts pain, harm and suffering on another person, perhaps in response to an illegal act. It also implies that somebody has the right or the legitimate power to create human suffering. An influential definition of punishment has been provided by Professor Andrew Flew (1954), who argued that, for an act to be defined as a punishment, it must conform to five basic rules.

---

**The five rules of punishment**

The penal sanction must:

1 create human suffering;
2 arise as a direct result of the perpetration of an offence;

---

3   only be directed at the person who undertook the offence, i.e. the offender;
4   be the intentional creation of other humans in response to that offence;
5   be inflicted by an authorised body representing the embodiment of the rules or laws of the society in which the offence was committed.

For a given penal sanction to be understood as a *state punishment*, it must arise through a person's illegal wrongdoing, it must be painful to the offender and it must be imposed only by state officials who have been given the power to punish in that given society. This is a feature of 'the social contract', the political basis on which citizens agree to uphold certain rights and obligations including the law of the land. Following this reasoning, any suffering that is meted out in response to a 'crime' by non-authorised personnel (i.e. vigilantes) must be condemned as illegitimate.

But the very idea of organised practices that are rooted in the deliberate infliction of human pain and suffering necessarily raises key moral and political questions of 'legitimacy'. This leads us to our second question: 'Are state punishments necessary and justifiable?'

Justifications of punishment can be divided into three main approaches: philosophies that look to justify punishment in terms of preventing future offending; philosophies that focus on responding to the actual offence; and philosophies that maintain that punishment can be neither morally nor politically justified.

**Main philosophical approaches to the justification of punishment**

**Future crimes**

- Reform and rehabilitation
- Individual and general deterrence
- Prevention, protection and incapacitation

**Past crimes**

- Retribution, denunciation and just deserts

*(Continued)*

*(Continued)*

**Beyond punishment**

- Redress
- Reparation, restitution and restorative justice

# PUNISHING FUTURE CRIMES

The idea of reforming, deterring and preventing offenders from committing future crimes is very much rooted in the classical thinking of Cesare Beccaria and Jeremy Bentham. Although there were significant philosophical differences between them, both Beccaria and Bentham argued that punishment, rather than being arbitrary and cruel, should be regular, predictable and determined by law. Centred on the Enlightenment notion of the free-willed, rational actor, the overall purpose of exacting pain through punishment should be to change the mind-set of the reasoning criminal.

## REFORM AND REHABILITATION

The terms 'reform' and 'rehabilitation', although often used interchangeably, in fact mean very different things. Reform ultimately means the changing of the offender. The aim of reformative punishment is to alter the individual by attempting to re-educate, teach, train or instil a new morality. The transformation of the offender would have been necessary even if he or she had not committed the particular act for which he or she is currently incarcerated, because the offender's immorality, irresponsibility or lack of respectability is rooted in either cultural deprivation or individual weakness. The offender is in need of moral education, in the form of work, religion, schooling or vocational training.

Rehabilitation, by contrast, does not attempt to change the offender, but rather to restore the individual to that state in which he or she was before the crime was committed. There are two types of rehabilitation: a social or welfare model which seeks to address 'criminogenic' background factors thought to contribute to offending such as a lack of education, training and work; and a medical or treatment model which assumes that offenders have, in some way, been changed through the 'crime' they have committed, or that the 'crime' occurred because of the offender's mental, physical or moral degradation. The 'treatment and training ideology' provided the orientating focus of the prison service in the UK in the mid-twentieth century. It suggests that, as with medicine, if problems are correctly diagnosed, we should be able to cure the offender and ultimately society of problematic behaviour. This idea is linked to the work of forensic psychology, psychiatry and medical experts.

## Common pitfall

*Be careful, when an essay or exam question asks about 'reform', not to confuse the philosophical justification about individual change with ideas about changes in the criminal justice system, such as improving prison environments, or the introduction of new laws and penal sanctions.*

In practice, rehabilitation and reform have been applied together. Underscoring both are the beliefs that:

- offenders are different to 'normal' people and that this difference is directly linked to their offending behaviour;
- we can positively alter or 'normalise' people through social engineering and that we have the right to do so;
- punishment generally, and imprisonment specifically, can act as a catalyst for the restoration or alteration of the offender.

According to Philip Bean (1981), the key strengths to the rehabilitation argument are that it:

- treats people as individuals and attempts to deal with the actual person and context of the crime;
- promotes individual responsibilities;
- places emphasis on the personal lives of the offenders, focusing on offender motivations and possible processes that can be invoked to challenge offending or to help someone to cope with life;
- allows for flexibility and new ways of responding to offending behaviour, such as developing constructive sentences. In this sense, something good comes from the 'evil of punishment'.

But reform and rehabilitation have been heavily criticised:

- 'Crime' is not an illness or disease, but a social construct. It may be a perfectly understandable response to a specific set of circumstances. Offenders may not necessarily be different from other people, and their behaviour may reflect the labelling process that is imposed by those with the power to define.
- We are moral beings who must be allowed to make choices. Humans should not be treated like animals, to be conditioned or trained.
- Many alleged cures do not actually work and treatments can effect more harm than that of the initial wrong.
- Sentences imposed for reasons of rehabilitation are open-ended, thus undermining due process. The offender must complete the proposed transformation, or be cured, before release.

## DO PRISONS REHABILITATE OR DEHABILITATE OFFENDERS?

After nearly two hundred years of the prison experiment, it seems that a sentence of imprisonment is more likely to increase, rather than decrease, future offending:

- The prison environment is dehumanising and dehabilitating. The inherent pains of imprisonment are likely to be counterproductive. The act of imprisonment may lead to the embedding of a psychology that promotes the rejection of rejecters, therefore building barriers to positive learning.
- The prison is a 'school for scoundrels', a 'university of crime' in which prisoners learn new skills from their peers.
- Can we learn how to be law abiding while we are in captivity? People act differently in prison to how they do on the outside. Incarceration may lead to people losing skills that are essential for coping on the outside. The harms of imprisonment are also likely to exacerbate any social or psycho-logical problems that the prisoner may have had before coming to prison.

## Common pitfall

*Ensure that, when looking at a question on punishment, you are clear on whether you are being asked to evaluate the philosophical justifications or how effective they have been when used in prison. It is possible that the question will be asking you to assess both the philosophy and its practical application.*

# INDIVIDUAL AND GENERAL DETERRENCE

The philosophical justifications concerning deterrence are rooted in utilitarianism, a moral and political philosophy that emphasises the importance of developing social policies that maximise the good and minimise the bad. Utilitarians believe we are able to devise an equation between pain and pleasure. In relation to punishment, this relates specifically to the pains of punishment as a utility in reducing the pains inflicted upon victims. Utilitarians argue we can work out a system of punishment that can discourage and deter offending behaviour. The system must be certain and 'crimes' must be punished.

There are two central issues concerning deterrence: 'individual' and 'general'. Individual deterrence involves punishments having a direct impact on the offender who has committed the offence. This is clearly a psychological approach. General deterrence is applied to the whole community, i.e. as a method of social control.

## INDIVIDUAL DETERRENCE

For Bean (1981), individual deterrence is directly linked to the following:

- **Physical freedoms** To break the law in wider society, we must be empowered in various ways. Individual deterrence is rooted in the power of an institution to prevent the offender physically from committing an offence in public spaces.
- **Conditioning** The punishment is intended to remove the desire to offend from the offender by bringing about psychological change in that offender.
- **Individual fear calculus** The desire to offend is kept in check by the fear of the consequences should the person be caught. The rationality of the offender is emphasised in this approach, with the offender deciding that the pleasure of crime cannot outweigh the pain of imprisonment.

## GENERAL DETERRENCE

General deterrence involves social control, and central to this is the 'social fear calculus'. It works in a similar way to the 'individual fear calculus', but the individual is not subjected to the pain him- or herself. Rather, the individual sees the pain of others and is deterred from the activity that led to it, because he or she does not want to be subjected to such suffering. It relates to wider social relations and, although directed against an individual, is intended to have implications beyond the person who is actually punished.

## DETERRING WHO? THE LIMITATIONS OF DETERRENCE

There are a number of problems with the deterrent approach:

1 Is it possible to quantify the individual human experiences of pain and pleasure, and to devise a calculus that can produce an equation of equivalence? Can we actually compare the pain of being a victim of crime to that of a punishment?

2 Can we scientifically measure the deterrent effect? On both the social and individual levels, we do not know if deterrence actually works. Today it is common for 'recidivism' to measure the reconviction of offenders within one year of release. Recidivism rates in the UK are high: 73 per cent of children between 10 and 17 years old, 58 per cent of young adults between 18 and 20, and 47 per cent of adult offenders are reconvicted within a year of release from custody (MoJ, 2013a). And yet this will always be an underestimate, because the figures do not include those who reoffend and are not caught.

3 How can we be certain that others will react to these deterrents in the same way in which you or I would? What may deter me may not deter you, and vice versa.

4 Do we all sit down and calculate the consequences of our every action? What about impulsive and opportunistic 'crime', or 'crime' commuted under the influence of strong emotions or drugs? Much wrongdoing, including serious harms, does not necessarily rely upon rational choice.

5 There is no good evidence that harsh sentences work. There is evidence of a correlation between harsh punishments and a decrease in recorded drink-driving. What has not been proved, however, is whether this is a causal relationship. Given the influence of other factors—demographic change, the impact of moral education or improvements in policing for example—it is difficult to conclude that there is a particularly strong relationship between deterrence and crime reduction.

6 Is it moral to punish a person so that it will deter others? Can we justify the infliction of pain onto one person in an attempt to deter others?

7 And if the aim of punishment is to deter the wider public, is it right that it does not actually matter who is punished? The punished may be either guilty or innocent, but if it serves a wider utility and deters other people, the punishment is deemed to have been justified.

> A **correlation** is when two phenomena occur at the same time, but are not necessarily linked. For example, a recorded increase in the consumption of carrot juice may coincide with a decline in recorded 'crime'. Both have happened at the same time, but are not linked with the other. The discovery of a **causal relationship** is the golden fleece of penology. A causal relationship is much more difficult to prove and arises only when one phenomenon has a direct relationship with another—in short, when there is a cause and effect.

## PREVENTION, PROTECTION AND INCAPACITATION

'Incapacitation' means the reduction of the physical capacity of the offender to commit crimes in order to protect the public. Its simple 'common-sense' appeal has led some right-wing penologists and politicians to call for the incapacitation of all criminals and there are many who consider arguments around selective incapacitation plausible. This justification has been attractive because it:

- can lead to the removal of persistent and dangerous offenders;
- is thought to reduce crime rates and state expenditure on crime control;
- has been a politically popular option.

## THE LIMITATIONS OF INCAPACITATION

- **'Crime'** is cyclical and generational, and, for incapacitation to work, we would have to constantly incarcerate large sections of each generation at great cost. The removal of persistent offenders only has an impact for a small number of years, after which their place is taken by a new, younger group of offenders. It has been estimated that in order to reduce crime rates in the UK by just one per cent, prison populations would have to rise by 25 per cent (Tarling, 1993).

- **Incapacitation** is grounded in positivism, prediction and risk assessments. If we are to protect society, we must first be able to assess who is a risk to society. West and Farrington (1973) undertook to assess which of a group of 7-year-olds would be convicted of an offence by the age of 14 and which would still be offending at the age of 21. Despite taking into account the normal indicators, they only got half of their assessments right. Such failure in prediction leads to false negatives or false positives.

---

### False negatives and false positives

- **False negatives** Offenders—on parole, for example—who have been regarded as unlikely to reoffend when released from prison. Predictions of low risk have been made, but the ex-offender has consequently reoffended.
- **False positives** Those who are wrongly predicted as being likely to reoffend. They are more difficult to discover, because they have been imprisoned. These people would not have offended had they been freed.

Thomas Mathiesen (2006) asks us two very important questions in relation to false negatives and false positives:

Should we lock people up who have done nothing wrong?
If we make mistakes, should we lock people up who are not going to offend in order to protect ourselves from those who may reoffend in the future?

---

*Despite the obvious limitations of positivism and prediction, there have been many studies following in the tradition of West and Farrington (1973). Individual, family, peer, school, community and socio-economic risk factors are used as standard to assess the likelihood of future involvement in offending. For example, a Common Assessment Framework is used to risk assess young offenders, and an Offender Assessment System (OASys) to assess adult offenders. You will be able to access information on these risk assessment instruments through the Home Office and Ministry of Justice websites.*

# PUNISHING PAST CRIMES

## RETRIBUTION, DENUNCIATION AND JUST DESERTS

Talk of retribution is often linked with talk of 'justice'. The argument is that we get what we deserve. Retribution, in its various forms, is rooted in the principle that, if we harm another human being, we ourselves deserve to be harmed. The retributive approach to punishment has the advantage of focusing on an offender's guilt and thus equating the punishment to a wrong that has been done. It is based on the principle that it is wrong to punish offenders more than their crimes deserve in order to rehabilitate, deter or incapacitate them. It is a fundamental human right that all people, including offenders, should not be subject to threats, coercion or used as a means to an end for reasons of general deterrence. Instead, punishment should fit the crime. The German Enlightenment philosopher Emmanuel Kant has argued:

> punishment ... can never be inflicted merely as a means to promote some other good for the criminal himself or for civil society. It must always be inflicted upon him only because he has committed a crime. For a man can never be treated merely as a means to the purposes of another.

> (1796–97, p. 140)

Retributivism therefore argues for equivalence and proportionality, in that lesser crimes should be punished in a lesser way and greater crimes more harshly. Retributive punishments are a public statement that the behaviour punished is wrong and should not be engaged in. It shows that society disapproves of such behaviours. Offenders have gained an unfair advantage over those of us who abide by the rules. In punishing past crimes we are demonstrating that the behaviour is wrong by denouncing them.

In recent times, retribution has been popularised through the arguments of 'just deserts'. This perspective has been championed in the work of Andrew von Hirsch. In *Doing Justice* (1976), von Hirsch argued that punishment should be proportionate to the seriousness of the offence. Just deserts, however, should not be seen as an all-encompassing justification for punishment; rather, it is linked to sentencing and is called a 'distributive justification'. This means that it is involved in justifying the distribution or the meting out of punishments. There are two primary ways of deciding on proportionality:

- **Cardinal proportionality** An overall anchoring point—for example, relatively low levels of incarceration which limits retributivism.
- **Ordinal proportionality** The ranking of individual offences according to seriousness and imposing punishments relative to these.

It might be assumed that retributivist and utilitarian justifications for punishment are mutually exclusive, but penal policies today draw on both simultaneously. The long-term incapacitation of dangerous offenders for public protection, alongside the proportional use of lesser sentences for lower-risk offenders, is known as 'bifurcation'.

A difficulty the idea of just deserts has encountered centres on the measuring of the seriousness of a 'crime' and whether we should focus on the offender's *intentions* or the *consequences* of his or her wrongdoing. It is necessary to consider issues of power and to ask who decides on seriousness and what is proportional, and according to what criteria? Should it be left to the judicial discretion of judges and magistrates; should it be subject to structuring principles, guidelines and tariffs; and should it reflect public opinion and political directives?

Another difficulty centres on whether or not it is justified to increase the severity of punishment for persistent offenders. As offenders have already been punished should they be punished again for the same offence? For von Hirsch (1986), while it is justifiable for first-time offenders to receive a first offender discount, continually increasing punishments for persistent offenders leads to disproportionate punishment. Mandatory minimum sentences of imprisonment for persistent petty offenders, and 'three strikes and you're out' laws in the US, whereby repeat offenders are jailed for life irrespective of the seriousness of their third offence, have been criticised on this basis. For others however (see Halliday, 2001), while it appears reasonable to consider a first offence as a mitigating factor and to impose a ceiling on sentence severity, it is misguided for sentencers to completely ignore previous convictions as aggravating factors.

Two wrongs? A critique of retribution:

1 We live in an unequal society, in which the enforcement of the criminal law is focused upon working-class property offenders.

2 Thomas Mathiesen (2006) reminds us that the people we punish are generally poor, in terms both of finances and of life chances.

3 Braithwaite and Pettit (1990) point out that we only punish a small number of offenders. Is it right to continue with the punishment of the

few, when the great majority of offenders never receive any formal punishment at all? Should we scapegoat the small minority or should we look to decrease our emphasis on punishment?

4 Is it healthy to want somebody else to experience pain and suffering? Does punishment further dehumanise offenders, leading to a greater likelihood of offending, and dehumanise those who call for such human degradations?

5 Two wrongs cannot make a right: how can the infliction of more pain repair or redress the harm and pain created by the misdemeanour?

6 Perhaps the most significant philosophical flaw in the retribution argument is that it fails to establish a case as to why someone should be punished in the first instance. We often hear the argument of an 'eye for an eye' or a 'life for a life', yet such principles were developed as a means of ensuring that, if a conflict existed between two Jewish tribes and lives were lost, the *lex talionis* was invoked to ensure that one tribe would not be destroyed. Contrary to current understandings, this did not mean that a life was taken for a life lost, but rather that a life was given from one tribe to another to ensure parity. The principle is not one of harm escalation or retribution, but one of the restoration of balance.

## Common pitfall

*Ensure that you fully explore the meaning of all of the concepts that you use. Many terms have different meanings at different times to different people. Two obvious examples are 'justice' and 'lex talionis'.*

Ultimately, then, we are left with a number of serious problems and contradictions—and these concerns lead us to our third question: 'Do we need to punish at all?'

## THINKING BEYOND PUNISHMENT

Some penologists have challenged the legitimacy of punishment, and have looked beyond strategies of penalisation as means of responding to personal troubles, harms, social problems and illegalities. Imprisonment is understood in wider sociological and symbolic terms, and not simply as a utilitarian or retributivist response to 'crime'. This stance has been adopted by the abolitionist penologist Thomas Mathiesen (1974, 2006) who has argued that no rationale of imprisonment—be it reform, rehabilitation, individual or general deterrence, prevention or incapacitation—justifies the continuing use of imprisonment. Instead, imprisonment must be understood according to functions that go beyond punishment or crime control, each of which falsely imbues the prison with a positive role within society. This includes its:

- **'expurgatory function'** to isolate and control 'unproductive' members of society: the poor, homeless, unemployed, mentally ill;
- **'symbolic function'** to stigmatise and label 'unproductive' people in prison in comparison to 'productive' people outside of prison;
- **'power-draining function'** to limit the responsibility and contribution of 'unproductive' people rendering them powerless;
- **'diverting function'** to focus attention on those without power, thereby diverting attention away from the 'crimes' of the powerful;
- **'action function'** to signal high-profile government intent that serious and effective action is being taken to combat harm.

Abolitionists have therefore generally argued that we need to understand 'crime' and punishment within three distinct contexts:

1 The daily lived experiences of prisoners and the harms created by the prison and direct penal interventions in the community.

2 The failure to sufficiently morally justify the current excessive use of the penal rationale—punishment—and its deployment in the criminal process.

3 The structured inequalities of society and the implications of the use of the prison and the penal rationale in maintaining such social divisions.

This triple-layered approach to punishment and the criminal process distinguish penal abolitionists from liberal penal reformers. They are also differentiated by their call for radical alternatives to penal excess and social inequalities alongside direct and pragmatic interventions in response to social problems and individual troubles. The abolitionist

thinker Willem de Haan (1990) argues that we should think beyond punishment and offers the concept of 'redress' in its place. This is a concept with ancient origins and involves the consideration of historical and anthropological forms of dispute settlement and conflict resolution.
Redress means:

> to put right or in good order again, to remedy or remove trouble of any kind, to set right, to repair, rectify something suffered or complained of like a wrong to correct, amend, reform or do away with a bad or faulty state of things, to repair an action or misdeed or offence, to save or deliver from misery, to restore or bring back a person to a proper state, to happiness or prosperity, to the right course.
>
> (*Concise Oxford Dictionary*, cited in de Haan, 1990, p. 158)

Similar principles are implied in the other 'R's of community responses: restoration, reparation, restitution, repayment, reconciliation and reintegration. Stan Cohen (1985) reminds us that these are visions of inclusionary, rather than exclusionary, social control that are rooted in social integration and community. Restorative or relational justice has received considerable support in recent years. Using a much wider array of criminal justice responses than traditional utilitarian or retributivist punishment, for some restorative justice establishes a 'humanitarian' response to 'crime' which replaces punishment altogether (Zehr, 1991). But a danger is that informal means of control can lead to a further extension of state powers, a widening of the punishment net and to new modes of discipline, surveillance and regulation. Both Cohen (1985) and Mathiesen (1980) remind us that community responses to 'crime' can blur boundaries. They may intensify state controls that are directed at serious offenders but also extend control measures to whole groups and categories of people. Further, Scull (1977) has argued that the move towards 'decarceration' and community based control is motivated more by economic than humanitarian considerations.

## "Consider the moral and political arguments for and against incapacitation."

Define and outline the main arguments for incapacitation. Then highlight the moral concerns: notably, that we do not have the ability to predict future behaviour and, consequently, that many are punished even though they may not have reoffended. Move on to overview the political realities, pointing to the disproportionate imprisonment and control of people from poor and working-class backgrounds.

## "Are the arguments for retributivist justice plausible in a society with 'race', 'class' and 'gender' structural fault lines?"

First, explain the main principles of retributivist justice, and then highlight how it does not recognise that punishments are defined and shaped through wider social divisions. Consider how retributivism leaves wider structural inequalities and injustices unchanged. Finally, consider whether the inability to challenge power effectively leaves retributivism vulnerable to be co-opted by the powerful.

You have encountered a number of arguments that appear to indicate that it is actually very difficult to justify punishments for all people, at all times and in all different social circumstances. This goes against our common-sense assumptions that punishments continue to be used because, somehow, they work. Think critically about the following questions:

- Does punishment, overall, reduce or increase human pain?
- Does punishment repair the harm done in the wrongdoing?
- Does punishment reduce the recurrence of problematic incidents?
- Is the use of punishment morally justifiable?
- Why do we continue to punish people when it does not appear to work for human good?

### Sentencing and the London riots of August 2011

In recent years governments in the UK have often justified the increased use of imprisonment as a way of demonstrating 'toughness' on matters of law and order. A recent example was the remanding and sentencing to imprisonment of large numbers of people for petty shoplifting and handling offences committed during the London riots of August 2011. Examples of sentences include:

*(Continued)*

*(Continued)*

Nicolas Robinson, 23, of Borough, south-east London jailed for six months for stealing a £3.50 case of water from Lidl.

Mother-of-two Ursula Nevin, from Manchester, was jailed for five months for receiving a pair of shorts given to her after they had been looted from a city centre store.

Jordan Blackshaw, 21, of Marston, and Perry Sutcliffe-Keenan, 22, of Warrington were jailed for four years for using Facebook to incite disorder, although none actually resulted.

Anderson Fernandes, 22, was warned by a judge at Manchester Magistrates' Court that he may face jail after he admitted stealing two scoops of ice cream.

David Beswick, 31, Stephen Carter, 26, both from Salford, and Michael Gillespie-Doyle, 18, from Tameside were jailed for up to two years in relation to the disorder in Manchester.

As a consequence of such harsh and disproportionate sentences, on 2 December 2011 the prison population reached a current record high of 88,179. The response by the courts to the rioting has been criticised for being disproportionate and inconsistent with sentences imposed for similar offences at other times and in other circumstances, and subsequent appeals have resulted in sentences being revoked or reduced (Piper, 2011). In the light of this, think critically about the following questions:

- Is the principle of exemplary sentencing ever compatible with the principle of proportionality?
- Is justice served by imposing disparate sentences for similar offences?
- Should aggravating and mitigating circumstances justify increases or decreases in sentencing severity?
- Is it legitimate for politicised messages and statements to influence sentencing severity?

# BIBLIOGRAPHY

Books which critically discuss the different justifications for punishment include:

- **BEAN, P (1981)** *Punishment: A Philosophical and Criminological Inquiry*, Oxford: Martin Robertson.
- **CAVADINO, M, DIGNAN, J and MAIR, G (2013)** *The Penal System: An Introduction*, 5th edn, London: Sage.

- **DAVIES, M, CROALL, H and TRYER, J (2010)** *Criminal Justice: An Introduction to the Criminal Justice System in England and Wales*, 4th edn, London: Pearson-Longman.
- **ELLIS, T and SAVAGE, S (2011)** *Debates in Criminal Justice: Key Themes and Issues*, London: Routledge.
- **HONDERICH, T (2006)** *Punishment: The Supposed Justifications Revisited*, London: Pluto Press.
- **HUDSON, BA (2003)** *Understanding Justice*, 2nd edn, Milton Keynes: Open University Press.
- **JOYCE, P (2006)** *Criminal Justice: An Introduction to Crime and the Criminal Justice System*, Cullompton: Willan.
- **McCONVILLE, S (ed.) (2008)** *The Use of Punishment*, Cullompton: Willan.
- **TONRY, M (ed.) (2012)** *Retributivism Has a Past: Has it a Future?* Oxford: Oxford University Press.
- **VON HIRSCH, A (1976)** *Doing Justice: The Choice of Punishments*, New York: Hill and Wang.
- **VON HIRSCH, A (1993)** *Censure and Sanctions*, Oxford: Clarendon Press.

Books on sentencing principles and policies are:

- **ASHWORTH, A (2010)** *Sentencing and Criminal Justice*, 5th edn, Cambridge: Cambridge University Press.
- **ASHWORTH, A and ROBERTS, J (2012)** 'Sentencing Theory, Principle and Practice', in M Maguire, R Morgan and R Reiner (eds), *The Oxford Handbook of Criminology*, 5th edn, Oxford: Oxford University Press.
- **EASTON, S and PIPER, C (2008)** *Sentencing and Punishment: The Quest for Justice*, 2nd edn, Oxford: Oxford University Press.

Books on penal abolitionism include:

- **DE HAAN, W (1990)** *The Politics of Redress: Crime, Abolition and Penal Abolition*, London: Sage.
- **MATHIESEN, T (2006)** *Prison on Trial*, 3rd edn, Winchester: Waterside Press.
- **ROLSTON, B, TOMLINSON, M, MOORE, JM and SCOTT, D (eds) (2014)** *Beyond Criminal Justice*, Bristol: EGSDSC.

# 2.2 THEORISING ABOUT PRISONS AND PUNISHMENT

## Key penologists

**Emile Durkheim (1858–1917)** One of the founding fathers of sociology, Emile Durkheim is one of the most significant writers on the sociology of punishment. A French scholar who worked for many years at the Sorbonne in Paris, his main writings include his PhD thesis *Division of Labour in Society* (1893) and magnum opus *The Elementary Forms of Religious Life* (1912). Durkheim is often wrongly caricatured as a dry, conservative functionalist thinker, but he was, in fact, deeply radical for his time, making important contributions to moral philosophy. He was always a reformist socialist, rather than a revolutionary—but he was an idealist. He did not simply describe the functions of society, but rather wanted to identify what society needed to do to resolve its conflicts and to develop a moral consensus. Durkheim's thought is an attempt to offer advice on how society could, or should, operate, rather than an assessment of how it currently is. Durkheim died, allegedly of a broken heart, not long after hearing that his son had been killed during the Great War.

**Georg Rusche (1900–50)** Rusche was a key Marxist thinker at the Frankfurt School, Germany, and co-wrote a foundational text of modern penology, *Punishment and Social Structure* (1939). His life was dogged with controversy, condemnation (because of his homosexuality), bouts of depression and financial precariousness. Although he had written a large part of the text of *Punishment and Social Structure*, prior to its publication the manuscript was revised by Otto Kirchheimer. The changes were made when the Frankfurt School relocated to the US after the rise of the Nazi party in Germany. The US had been traditionally hostile to Marxism and it was felt the manuscript needed to be toned down for its new audience. Rusche died alone, in poverty, after poisoning himself with domestic coal gas in October 1950.

**Michel Foucault (1926–84)** Perhaps the most influential thinker in penology over the last thirty years, Michel Foucault lived a notorious personal life, but wrote some brilliant—although very complicated—work on penology. His main book on penology is *Discipline and Punish: The Birth of the Prison* (1977), which continues to be one of the leading works in the field. An inspiration to a whole generation of thinkers, his influence can be divided into two traditions: those who look at disciplinary power, and those who focus on his later work on governmentality. Foucault was a radical penal activist and a staunch critic of the establishment in France, and his work opened up new ways of thinking about penal power. He died of an AIDS-related illness in 1984.

# PROGRESS, MODERNITY AND CIVILISATION

Theories of punishment and prisons are often linked with ideas of 'civilisation', 'morality' and 'social progress'. In these theories, punishment is seen as evolutionary and is often tied to the notion of 'modernity'.

*Modernity is a period in human history that was shaped by the privileging of rationality and reason above emotions. It is tied to the rise of the Enlightenment in the seventeenth century, which privileged secular human knowledge and scientific, neutral and objective analysis above religion and folklore. It is tied productively to mass technological change begun during the Industrial Revolution which, owing to constant reproduction in the age of mass consumerism, is always in a state of becoming **(post)modern**.*

## ADMINISTRATIVE PENOLOGY

Administrative penology is the official version of prison life. Changes in punishments since the eighteenth century are perceived to have been progressive and underscored by humanitarian reforms. These reforms are considered to have been motivated by benevolence, altruism and efforts to make the penal system more efficient through the application of scientific principles.

> In this 'quintessentially optimistic' world view, the prison is perceived as a sign of progress in both penal administration and the sensibilities of the nation. The emergence of administrative knowledge and practices provided the platform for the birth of the discipline of penology itself.

But there is a far bleaker vision of this essentially rational and legislative process. It is that the move from feudal punishments based on torture, mutilation and death to modern forms of punishment based on imprisonment is 'not so much progress in humanitarianism as progress in bureaucratized rationalism, necessary to meet the social control needs and legitimacy conditions of modern societies' (Hudson, 2003, p. 91). For the sociologist Max Weber (1864–1920), Enlightenment rationality, while it led to scientific and technological progress, erected an 'iron cage' of mundane, routine efficiency which stifled freedom of expression and human creativity. A consequence of bureaucratised, administrative sophistication is a lack of meaning, impersonality and moral blindness. David Garland has written that

> because penal violence is generally sanitized, situational, and of low visibility, the conflict between our civilized sensibilities and the often brutal regimes of punishment is minimized and made tolerable. Modern penality is thus institutionally ordered and discursively presented in ways which deny the violence which continues to inhere in its practices.
>
> (1990, p. 243)

Administrative penologies provide excellent descriptions and are often well researched. Good examples are: *English Prisons under Local Government* (Webb and Webb, 1922) and *History of the Criminal Law* (Radzinowicz and Hood, 1986). You should read such accounts, but bear in mind that administrative penologists accept implicitly the claims of those they are investigating.

TAKING IT FURTHER

## EMILE DURKHEIM

Durkheim believed that society is a moral entity with a reality all of its own. Common beliefs and shared moral sentiments shape what he called the 'conscience collective'. Immersion into the moral boundaries of the conscience collective guides interactions and determines human behaviour. Durkheim was interested in how the social system is protected from those who challenge these wider shared beliefs and values. He argued that some acts that are against the law ('crimes'), and other behaviours that go against the norms of a society ('deviance'), can be signs of progress and a healthy society. This marks him off as a functionalist thinker. Irrespective of whether punishment deters or reforms people, it functions as a source of social stability and cohesion. Indeed, a society without 'crime' and punishment is inconceivable. In such a society the constraints of the conscience collective would be so rigid that no one would oppose them, and that would be unhealthy.

And yet there are 'crimes' that should be denounced, condemned and punished because they are such an outrage to humanity they inflict damage to the conscience collective. The whole of society is the victim of these 'crimes' and all 'healthy' members of society are repulsed and offended by them. For Durkheim, 'crime' highlighted the fragility, insecurities and weakness of society. The barbarity of the response shows how deeply the moral emotions are offended. The weaker the moral order and social integration, the stronger the threat to the social order, and, consequently, the stronger and more extreme the punishment invoked.

> *Durkheim argued that punishment reinforces the wider constructions of morality and social cohesion. While punishments cannot create consensus, they can express condemnation, and reinforce the morality and consensus that already exists.*

The form of punishment is linked to the progress society has made. For Durkheim, feudal, primitive, 'mechanical' societies were characterised by repressive laws. They constituted a small number of individuals for whom social solidarity was based on similarity and who had an extremely punitive psychological disposition. Punishments were extremely severe and offenders were executed in the most awful ways imaginable: stoned; crucified; hanged; hung, drawn and quartered, with parts of their bodies sent throughout the kingdom; hurled from cliffs; crushed beneath the feet of animals. In contrast, advanced, industrial, 'organic' societies are heterogeneous, featuring a specialisation of tasks and recognition of diversity and mutual interdependence. In a more secure society, punishments become less severe and restitutive laws replace those that are repressive.

> *For Durkheim, a strong, morally legitimate social order requires very little punishment to reinforce social solidarity.*

Durkheim's theoretical analysis has been commended for providing an account of the evolution of punishment which throws light on its changing cultural meaning and symbolic importance (Smith, 2008). However, Hudson (2003) points to a number of criticisms that can be made of Durkheim's thesis. Durkheim is vague about the historical process in which mechanical societies change into organic societies. There is no intermediary society that features elements of both of these forms of punishment. There is evidence to suggest a contrary historical movement: that we have seen a shift from restitution to repressive forms of punishment in advanced capitalist societies. Durkheim is also wholly positive about punishment. He does not consider punishment as a source of conflict and repression in society, or fully engage with power and inequality, and the manner in which consent is organised is not explained. Punishment in a 'law and order society' is used to create consensus, rather than to reinforce existing morality, and the conception of hegemony may provide a more plausible explanation.

## NORBERT ELIAS

In his magnum opus, *The Civilising Process*, first published in 1939, Norbert Elias outlines how Western sensibilities have changed since medieval times. Through close readings of etiquette manuals, fictional works, fine art and various other documents of instruction or description, Elias charts, in fascinating detail, changes in table manners, dress, aesthetic appreciation, attitudes towards bodily functions, sexual behaviour, habits of washing and cleanliness, and the proper way of addressing strangers.

> For Elias, the civilising process involves a tightening of the controls that are imposed by society upon individuals and an increased level of psychological inhibition. Elias argues that humans gradually internalise fears, anxieties and inhibitions that are imposed upon them by their parents and their social environment, developing a 'superego' that inhibits the expression of instinctual drives in accordance with the demands of cultural life. This transformation of the human psyche implies that the more civilised a society is, the more its inhabitants are repressed.

Today, a whole range of possible punishments—tortures, maimings, stonings, public whippings—are simply ruled out as unthinkable because they strike us as impossibly cruel and barbaric. According to Garland, 'as with other signs of brutishness, the sight of violence, pain, or physical suffering [became] highly disturbing and distasteful to modern sensibilities' (1990, p. 223). In keeping with the demands of a civilised society, the experience of pain is kept private, ushered behind the prison walls.

Following Elias, Dutch penologist Pieter Spierenburg (1984) concentrates on changing sensitivities to suffering that, in a crucial sense, mediated the link between the emergence of nation states and common nationalities and less conspicuous and more restrained modes of repression. Similarly, the historian VAC Gattrell (1994) argues that a growing revulsion to violence ended public executions in England and Wales and led eventually to the concealing of punishment from public view.

> Many critics have questioned whether there really has been any progress around penal sensibilities, while other critics have taken exception to the argument that civilisation and penal reforms can only be achieved through the psychical repression of a naturally evil human nature.

Elias is vulnerable to criticism in relation to his pessimistic vision of the social order and his notion that the perceived civilisation of moral acts is merely an example of psychological conditioning and the 'rationalisation' of human conduct. As Pratt (2002) has observed with reference to the re-emergence of visible displays of humiliation such as chain gangs in the southern states of the US, the form and severity of punishment is strongly influenced by cultural belief and economic and political history.

# ZYGMUNT BAUMAN

If society is subject to a civilising process, how might we explain relatively recent events such as the Holocaust? In one of the most acclaimed books of recent times, *Modernity and the Holocaust* (1989), Bauman argues that the systematic extermination of 20 million people in the Nazi Holocaust was not an aberration, but rather a problem that is central to the functioning of modern civilisations. Bauman points out that modernity facilitates a 'gardening state' with big visions aimed at the creation of a new and better society. Alongside great progress, modernity can lead to scientifically and rationally conceived genocide—i.e. genocide with the purpose of creating a better and more civilised society.

> For Bauman, the Holocaust would not have been possible without a civilised, rational, bureaucratic modern society weakening the moral basis of human interaction.

Bauman argues that, in this instance, obedience to bureaucratic orders and the dehumanisation of 'the other' neutralised any sense of responsibility, leading to the social production of moral indifference. Most 'normal' bureaucrats involved in the Nazi killing machine were doing administrative duties as part of a rationally and bureaucratically ordered chain. They did not see the end results, and relationships were characterised by distance. This distance was both physical, through the division of labour, and psychological, through the depersonalising and devaluing of certain categories of human being. The only escape is to prioritise our moral and unreciprocated responsibilities for others and to create a sense of psychic proximity with all fellow humans.

The implications for penology of this analysis are immense. The rational, bureaucratic and managerial are privileged above the ethical, and one of the main groups of people most easily defined as 'vermin' or 'weeds' are those we imprison. Christie (1993, 2000) has made this connection as has Bauman himself with reference to economically marginalised populations rendered superfluous and 'criminalised' within neo-liberal market society (Bauman, 2004). For Christie a key problem is privatisation. 'Crime' is exploited by commercial interests that, supported by politicians and the media, promote authoritarian penal strategies and are 'seen as cleaning up, removing unwanted elements from the social system' (1993, p. 111).

The work of Bauman has been hugely influential. It has been criticised, however, because it is difficult to relate his analysis to other, less technocratic, genocides in the twentieth century, and on the basis that his challenge to modern progress may be politically conservative, because it denies the possibility of a better, all-inclusionary alternative. Further, his analysis critiques modernity itself and so is inconsistent with modernist theorists.

**Common pitfall**

*When considering the work of Bauman, Elias and Durkheim, ensure that you are aware of their very different views on human nature.*

# SOCIAL DIVISIONS, POWER AND THE DISTRIBUTION OF PUNISHMENTS

Penologists have also looked at the way in which punishments have been unequally distributed in modern societies among the social divisions of class, 'race' and gender. Problematising the link between 'crime' and the continued existence of the prison, penologists have attempted to uncover the real functions of imprisonment through analysis of political economy, power, patriarchies and the demands of the labour market. These theorists reflect contemporary political traditions such as liberalism, Marxism and feminism.

## LIBERALISM

Liberalism takes the humanitarian visions of penal reformers at face value, but recognises that they had disastrous consequences. This approach is described by Stanley Cohen (1985) as the 'we blew it thesis'. In a prime example of this tradition, American penologist David J Rothman's *The Discovery of the Asylum* (1971) identified the importance of religion, humanitarianism and benevolence in the development of the asylum in the US. Rothman argued that the reformers believed that people could be changed through incarceration, yet, in practice, confinement in total institutions was creating greater harm to, rather than helping, inmates.

> *In essence, the liberal penological approach provides us with a pessimistic warning from history that benevolence itself should not be trusted.*

Critics have claimed that liberalism has failed to learn from past mistakes, holding firm to the belief that penal reforms can work, if only the great humanitarian principles could be correctly implemented on the ground.

## MARXISM

Karl Marx (1818–83) wrote little about 'crime' or punishment, but his central idea that the character of social institutions reflects the means of economic production has influenced penologists to assess criminal justice in these terms. Traditional Marxist penology analyses the political economy of punishment. It contends that within capitalism one class (the ruling) exploits the other (the ruled). 'Crime' therefore is a product of capitalism's contradictions and inequalities, and its privileging of self-interest and competition. Acts are defined as 'criminal' because it is in the interests of the ruling class to so define them. Furthermore, the legal system is used to protect those self-same interests. Perhaps the most important contribution to Marxist penology is *Punishment and Social Structure* (Rusche and Kirchheimer, 1939; 2003). The book is firmly located within a material economic framework and aimed to uncover 'why certain methods of punishment are adopted or rejected in a given social situation' (p. 3). Moving beyond the idea that criminal justice is used simply to dominate and repress the lower classes, Rusche and Kirchheimer argued that punishment is an independent social phenomenon that has a complex relationship with 'crime'. Most importantly, it is linked to changes in the value of labour.

> *Punishments are historically specific and correspond to the given mode of economic production. In conjunction with non-penal institutions of the state, punishments perform a hidden role in the regulation of poverty. Shifts in the organisation of the economy, then, have implications for the form that punishments will take (Rusche, 1933).*

Rusche and Kirchheimer identified three historical epochs:

- *Feudalism in the Middle Ages (13th–15th centuries)* Small parochial societies within which the fine was the main punishment.
- *Mercantilist capitalism (16th–18th centuries)* A society featuring a shortage of labour and the adoption of new reclaiming punishments that were based on hard labour.
- *Industrialisation (18th–20th centuries)* Societies experiencing massive population growth, urbanisation, pauperism and the creation of a 'relative surplus population'.

Rusche and Kirchheimer identified three functions of imprisonment in the industrialised historical epoch:

1 *Controlling the poor* Under capitalism, human value is intimately tied to labour market value (i.e. employability). When labour is abundant and paid work is scarce, imprisonment is based upon control of the relative surplus population (i.e. the unemployed).

2 *Disciplining the poor* In times during which labour demand is high and the offender is seen as a valuable human resource, the prison becomes a mechanism for disciplining labour reserves so that they will submit to the demands of the labour market.

3 *Deterring the poor* The morality of the poor is perceived by the ruling classes as susceptible to vice. Imprisonment must act as a deterrent to the poor. Criminals must be symbolically excluded as 'less eligible' or less deserving of help than the working poor.

A number of criticisms have been raised against this thesis. It is considered to be historically unreliable. Economic imperatives do not always explain penal practice. Prison populations are not determined necessarily by changes in the demand for labour and not all capitalist economies develop in the same way. Prisons are expensive and therefore not a rational response to labour market economic demands. The analysis also ignores ideological constructions of imprisonment and, in particular, is accused of being gender-blind, because there is no consideration of the different forms that the social control, regulation and punishment of women can take. Nevertheless, ideas centred on the political economy of punishment remain hugely influential, most prominently in relation to the impact over the past two decades of neo-liberal economic policies on rising rates of poverty, social marginalisation, 'crime' and imprisonment (Di Georgi, 2006; Melossi, 2008; Simon, 2007; Wacquant, 2001, 2009).

## ANTI-SLAVERY

J Thorsten Sellin's *Slavery and the Penal System* (1976) follows in the tradition of Rusche and Kirchheimer (1939) and German legal theorist Gustav Radbruch, in his claim that current legal punishments are derived from slavery.

> *Both imprisonment and slavery entail the loss of citizenship, dehumanisation and 'othering', the deprivation of liberty and being forced to undertake manual labour.*

Sellin argues that legal punishments were originally the private domestic punishments of slaves, but that over the centuries they have been made applicable to all offenders. In ancient civilisations such as the Roman Empire, slavery was legitimated and freemen were exempt from punishments. Hard labour in the imperial metal and salt mines (*ad metalla*) or in the chain gangs repairing roads, cleaning sewers and public baths (*opus publicum*) became the primary punishment of the poor.

The incorporation of slave punishments into state punishments was also evident in the Middle Ages in Europe. Slavery was firmly established among the Germanic peoples and manual labour was considered beneath the dignity of freemen. Offences by freemen against persons of property were settled by payment of financial indemnities, often without official intervention. But as property relations developed, the dehumanising labour-orientated slave punishments were thought to be appropriate to impoverished freemen unable to purchase immunity.

> *Sellin highlights how only the nobles, the titled and the rich retained their exemptions from physical punishments. Socio-economic and political changes gradually placed a greater premium on labour, and public authorities started to punish offenders through public work for the profit of the state.*

*Opus publicum* (forced public labour) was revived, and was performed both indoors and outdoors in irons. Sellin argues that, by the late sixteenth century, penal slavery was deeply embedded in legal punishments across Europe and its colonies, such as in North America. He places a premium on highlighting how imprisonment is connected to a wider, dehumanised slave condition.

Sellin has been criticised on similar grounds to the Marxist penologists and, specifically, on the basis that his analysis of penal servitude is too broad and geographically disparate.

## NEO-MARXISM

Steven Box, in his book *Recession, Crime and Punishment* (1987) and in a number of articles co-written with Chris Hale in the early 1980s, provides one of the most impressive neo-Marxist analyses of imprisonment. Box and Hale (1982) challenge the orthodox account of the relationship between unemployment, 'crime' and imprisonment. They argue that official crime rates are not necessarily influenced by unemployment and economic hardship, but that the *belief* that unemployment and 'crime' are intimately connected has significant consequences for who is imprisoned.

> 'Neo' means 'new', so **neo-Marxism** simply means 'New Marxism'. For an excellent example of neo-Marxist criminology, see Hall et al. (1978).

For Box and Hale, in times of recession, the sentence of imprisonment is 'an ideologically motivated response to the perceived threat of crime posed by the swelling population of economically marginalised persons' (1982, p. 363). Judges believe that unemployment will lead to an increase in 'crime' among certain sub-populations of the relative surplus population and consider it to be important to punish the 'sub-proletariat' to send a deterrent message to society. Looking at ideology can help to explain why prison is used when it is clearly not the most rational or cost-effective solution to social problems.

Neo-Marxist approaches are critiqued for being functionalist.

## MODERNIST FEMINISM

Penology has been criticised for being written by men, for men and about men. Male knowledge has been presented as 'the' knowledge.

> *Until the 1980s, penological studies largely ignored how the punishment of women differed from that of men. In recent years, feminist penologists have highlighted this theoretical blind spot, detailing the ways in which women are regulated differently from men through informal means of social control and how women experience state punishments very differently from men.*

Francis Heidensohn (1985) outlined how women offenders are seen as *doubly* deviant, having broken both legal and gender rules of conduct. Their punishment might be determined by how well they are able to conform to gender expectations and middle-class respectability. Pat Carlen (1983) interviewed women prisoners at Scotland's Cornton Vale prison and outlined how the pains of imprisonment for women were harsher than those of men. This was due to:

- isolation and being a long distance from home;
- the creation of dependency through imprisonment;
- being treated like children;
- the use of heavy discipline by staff;
- the expectation of excellence in domestic duties;
- denial of their status as either real criminals or real women.

Modernist feminists have argued for a 'woman-wise' penology.

## MICHEL FOUCAULT

Michael Foucault's *Discipline and Punish: The Birth of the Prison* (1977) is one of the most influential books in modern penology. Taking as his backcloth the 'great transformation' from capital punishment to the timetabled regimes of the penitentiaries and the 'technologies of power' deployed within them, Foucault rejected the liberal argument that the prison was a form of humanitarian progress, claiming instead that prisons developed 'not to punish less; [but] to punish better, to insert the power to punish more deeply into the social body' (p. 82).

Although he did not reject the 'top-down' Marxist approach of penologists such as Rusche and Kirchheimer, Foucault used a different analytical framework in order to understand how power operates 'bottom up' as a property of systems. He was interested in how disciplinary power impacted on the human soul (the psyche) at the micro level.

> For Foucault, power is productive, dispersed throughout society and intimately related to the construction of knowledge. Foucault wished to understand how the '*power/knowledge*' axis could be deployed not to punish individual crimes so much as to observe and render human beings obedient.

Taking Bentham's panopticon design and inspection principle as his cue, Foucault argued that the wider application of such 'technologies of power' had created a modern 'carceral society' of disciplinary control. Hunt and Wickham (1994) explain how, for Foucault, disciplinary power operates on three levels:

1. **Hierarchical observation** Differentiated positions of power that are rooted in surveillance, categorisation and classification.

2. **Normalising judgements** Dominant definitions, rules, norms and expected behaviour.

3. **Micro penalties and rewards** Means of regulation to ensure conformity and obedience.

The prison was not the only means through which disciplinary power operated—other places included the family, the school, the barracks, the workplace and the hospital—but it was at the pinnacle of a 'carceral' continuum.

> It is not important that imprisonment is a failure in terms of recidivism. To justify wider disciplinary controls, Foucault argues, the prison deliberately invents delinquents. In this sense, a state of permanent conflict exists to meet the needs of a crime control industry and to legitimate wider disciplinary controls. Certain illegalities are isolated and made manageable, while offenders are retrained and turned into disciplined, docile and productive human beings.

Foucault has been criticised for overgeneralising disciplinary punishments used against juveniles to those used against adults and for providing only a partial analysis of punishments that requires synthesis with one or more of the earlier modernist 'total theories'. His theory that punishment operates through norms and techniques of rationality negates any consideration of wider cultural meanings, judgements and understandings punishment has for people. He has also been criticised on the bases that, like the Marxists, his analysis is functionalist and masculinist, and his conception of power simply a restatement of the basic sociological concept of socialisation.

## GOVERNMENTALITY

In recent years, some penologists have looked to develop the later writings of Foucault on penal governance. These are often referred to as 'governmentality' theorists, of which Malcolm Feeley and Jonathon Simon (1994) are good examples. An important theme of this work is that within (post)modernity, macro economic and social transformations (e.g. global competition for scarce raw materials, the demise of full employment and the withdrawal of welfare protection) have caused society to become increasingly preoccupied with fear and uncertainty. Risk today is incalculable, unpredictable and irreversible: 'a systematic way of dealing with hazards and insecurities induced and introduced by modernization itself' (Beck, 1992, p. 21). Science does not solve social problems, it causes new ones: pollution, war, global warming, famine, disease. The result is a mistrust of 'experts'. The name of the game simply is to avoid catastrophe.

'Crime' today has become a normal fact of life, an inevitable outcome of social inequality inherent in the neoliberal economic system. No longer justified as a means of 'disciplining' or 'normalising' people, prisons are used to manage the effects of social insecurity, precarious wage labour and unruly populations (Feeley and Simon, 1992). Non-legal factors, 'race', unemployment and homelessness are the primary 'risks' (Hudson, 2003). The key aim is to punish the poor (Wacquant, 2009).

The 'new penology' thesis (Feeley and Simon, 1992) has been criticised for overplaying the level of insecurity in (post)modern society. Life has always been a risky business. Furthermore, throughout history prison has been used to hold disproportionate numbers of poor and marginalised people. And efforts to transform offenders have not withered and died. Punishment and welfare have always coexisted, and reducing reoffending remains a key purpose of prisons and punishment.

'Critical Race Theory' (CRT) explores power disparities within legal and criminal justice systems which in effect are discriminatory. For example, Angela Y Davis (2003, p. 29) has traced the historical antecedents of the over-representation of poor African American people in US jails today to new systems of incarceration implemented after the abolition of slavery, and the use of black prison labour as a source of profit by private entrepreneurs to the convict lease system and debt peonage introduced after the American Civil War. CRT seeks to challenge the perceived neutrality of such practices by advocating new arrest, prosecution, jury and sentencing procedures (Delgado and Stefancic, 2001).

## "Durkheim attempts to make clear the symbolic importance of punishment. What is the justification for this view?"

Weigh up the different theoretical perspectives on punishment. Is punishment strictly rational as Foucault contends, or is it invested with wider social and cultural meaning as Durkheim argues? If so, what are these meanings, and to what extent are they given expression in the way punishment is justified and delivered today?

## "What has been the contribution of feminist studies to our understanding of the role of imprisonment?"

When answering this question, it is important that you identify the main feminist writers on imprisonment, Pat Carlen in particular. Highlight how they locate the historical and contemporary punishment of women within wider forms of social control and regulation, and how the needs and pains of women offenders and prisoners have been neglected. Demonstrate knowledge of alternative masculinist penologies, but do not lose your focus on feminist epistemology (i.e. knowledge).

The theories discussed above continue to be relevant to penologists writing today. Table 2.1 lists a number of recent books and their connections to the penological traditions discussed above:

**Table 2.1   Recent publications relating to penological traditions**

| Contemporary penologists | Theoretical tradition |
| --- | --- |
| Centre for Social Justice (2009) *Locked Up Potential* | Administrative penology |
| Philip Smith (2008) *Punishment and Culture* | Durkheimian |
| John Pratt (2002) *Punishment and Civilisation* | Eliasian |
| Nils Christie (2000) *Crime Control as Industry* | Baumanian |
| David Ramsbotham (2003) *Prisongate* | Liberalism |
| Jeffrey Reiman (2007) *The Rich Get Richer and the Poor Get Prison* | Marxist |
| Loic Wacquant (2009) *Punishing the Poor* | Anti-slavery/anti-racism |
| Christian Parenti (1999) *Lockdown America* | Neo-Marxist |
| Kelly Hannah-Moffat (2001) *Punishment in Disguise* | Feminist |
| Joe Sim (1990) *Medical Power in Prisons* | Foucauldian/neo-Marxist |
| Jonathan Simon (2007) *Governing through Crime* | Foucault/governmentality |

# BIBLIOGRAPHY

It is always worth reading the foundational texts, but for critical reviews of the work of Durkheim, Weber, Elias, Foucault and Rusche and Kirchheimer see:

- **CAVADINO, M, DIGNAN, J and MAIR, G (2013)** *The Penal System: An Introduction*, 5th edn, London: Sage.
- **GARLAND, D (1990)** *Punishment and Modern Society: A Study in Social Theory*, Oxford: Oxford University Press.
- **GARLAND, D and YOUNG, P (eds) (1983)** *The Power to Punish: Contemporary Penality and Social Analysis*, Oxford: Heinemann Education.
- **HUDSON, BA (2003)** *Understanding Justice*, 2nd edn, Milton Keynes: Open University Press.
- **MELOSSI, D (ed.) (1999)** *The Sociology of Punishment*, Aldershot: Ashgate.
- **SMITH, P (2008)** *Punishment and Culture*, Chicago, IL: University of Chicago Press.
- **WACQUANT, L (2009)** *Punishing the Poor: The Neoliberal Government of Social Insecurity*, Durham: Duke University Press.

For developmental perspectives on Foucault's 'discipline' thesis in particular see:

- **COHEN, S (1985)** *Visions of Social Control: Crime Punishment and Classification*, Cambridge: Polity Press.
- **MELOSSI, D and PAVARIANI, M (1981)** *The Prison and the Factory: Origins of the Penitentiary System*, London: MacMillan.

A concise presentation of Bauman's own perspective on punishment and prisons can be found in:

- **BAUMAN, Z (2000)** 'Social issues of Law and Order', in D Garland and R Sparks (eds), *Criminology and Social Theory*, Oxford: Oxford University Press.

Feminist perspectives on 'crime', criminal justice and imprisonment are:

- **CARLEN, P (1983)** *Women's Imprisonment: A Study in Social Control*, London: Routledge.
- **CARLEN, P and WORRALL, A (2004)** *Analysing Women's Imprisonment*, Cullompton: Willan.
- **HEIDENSOHN, F (ed.) (2006)** *Gender and Justice*, Cullompton: Willan.

Key works on governmentality are:

- **FEELEY, M and SIMON, J (1992)** 'The New Penology: Notes on the Emerging Strategy of Corrections and its Implications', *Criminology*, 30, pp. 449–74.
- **GARLAND, D (2001)** *The Culture of Control: Crime and Social Order in Contemporary Society*, Oxford: Oxford University Press.
- **O'MALLEY, P (1999)** 'Governmentality and the Risk Society', *Economy and Society*, 28: 138–48.

Recent works which synthesise insights around 'race', class, gender include:

- **DAVIS, AY (2003)** *Are Prisons Obsolete?* New York: Seven Stories Press.
- **DAVIS, AY (2005)** *Abolition Democracy,* New York: Seven Stories Press.
- **DAVIS, AY (2012)** *The Meaning of Freedom and Other Difficult Dialogues,* San Francisco, CA: City Light Books.
- **OPARAH, J (2013)** 'Why No Prisons?', in D Scott (ed.), *Why Prison?* Cambridge: Cambridge University Press.

# 2.3 COMPARATIVE PENOLOGIES

## Core areas

investigating prison populations: international and comparative studies
the importance of comparative analysis
the analytical framework of comparative analysis
case studies
learning the lessons?

## Running themes

- Human rights
- Labour market
- Less eligibility
- Managerialism
- Pains of imprisonment
- Power to punish
- Social divisions

Throughout this book reference is made mostly to penal theories and practices as they pertain to the UK and the US. For obvious reasons your studies will focus on penal matters which are proximate to you. But social and political contexts differ significantly throughout the world, and concerns popularly expressed about punishment tend to resonate between countries with similar political climates. For example, while penal policy in the UK and the US has become dominated by exclusionary measures in recent years, Nordic social democracies have adopted a more inclusionary approach based on decarceration and welfare support. A look at Table 2.3 reveals significant differences in prison populations throughout the world.

**Table 2.3   Prison populations in 21 countries**

| Country | Prison population total (number in penal institutions, including pre-trial detainees) | Prison population (per 100,000 national population) | Percentage occupancy level (based on official capacity) |
|---|---|---|---|
| Australia | 29,383 | 130 | 105.9 |
| Brazil | 548,003 | 274 | 171.9 |
| Chad | 4,831 | 41 | 229.6 |
| China | 1,640,000 | 121 | Unknown* |
| Colombia | 117,015 | 243 | 154.5 |
| Cuba | 57,337 | 510 | Unknown |
| Finland | 3,214 | 60 | 100.0 |
| France | 66,995 | 101 | 117.7 |
| Germany | 65,889 | 80 | 84.9 |
| India | 372,296 | 30 | 112.1 |
| Italy | 65,917 | 108 | 140.1 |
| Japan | 68,788 | 54 | 83.3 |
| Netherlands | 13,749 | 82 | 83.4 |
| New Zealand | 8,623 | 194 | 83.7 |
| Norway | 3,575 | 71 | 92.1 |
| Russia | 693,400 | 484 | 83.6 |
| South Africa | 153,000 | 289 | 131.7 |
| Sweden | 6,364 | 67 | 90.3 |
| UK (England and Wales) | 83,897 | 148 | 107.7 |
| US | 2,239,751 | 716 | 106.0 |
| Venezuela | 50,000 | 169 | 270.1 |

*Sentenced prisoners only

*Source:* International Centre for Prison Studies, 11 June 2013

# INVESTIGATING PRISON POPULATIONS: INTERNATIONAL AND COMPARATIVE STUDIES

A number of non-government organisations (NGOs) investigate prison conditions and prisoners' experiences around the world. These include Amnesty International, Penal Reform International and Human Rights Watch. The reports of NGOs highlight torture, prison overcrowding and appalling prison conditions as a means of shaming a given government or of raising consciousness among other nations and their governments.

COMPARATIVE PENOLOGIES 77

## Common pitfall

*Remember that, although NGO reports have been very effective in achieving many of their aims, they are largely descriptive rather than analytical. Students are not their intended audience. For essays, always complement the information from such organisations with academic work.*

There is great interest in comparing the numbers of people sent to prison. The International Centre for Prison Studies (Walmsley, 2011) presents details of prison population rates per 100,000 of the national population in 223 countries. In May 2011, there were more than 10.1 million people held in penal institutions throughout the world. Almost half were held in three countries: the US (2.29 million), China (1.65 million plus pre-trial detainees and those in 'administrative detention') and Russia (0.81 million). Today, the US has the world's highest prison population rate at 716 per 100,000 of the general population (see Table 2.3), while the England and Wales prison population is the highest in Western Europe.

As revealing as these figures are, statistical comparative studies are limited in terms of their measurement and compilation. Specifically, there are concerns that:

- not all forms of administrative detention are included in official records, so in many countries the figures are underestimates;
- in some countries, such as those in Eastern Europe, there may not be sufficient statistical information available;
- there are differences in the way 'data' are counted, 'offenders' are categorised, and between legal systems;
- data is often collated in different countries at different times or years;
- national populations may be inaccurate and may therefore distort the claimed prison population per 100,000;
- the data looks only at daily populations, and therefore neglects the equally significant annual input and throughput of prisoners.

## THE IMPORTANCE OF COMPARATIVE ANALYSIS

The study of comparative penal systems is very important. Cavadino and Dignan (2006) remind us that it helps us to avoid reductionist, deterministic and ethnocentric social analysis. It allows us to understand the similarities, differences and broad trends in the way imprisonment has been deployed historically around the globe. It can also help us to understand why changes occur in our country, both through examining the policies of similar countries and through analysing the influence that other penal initiatives have had on our own country. This is particularly useful when thinking about the growth in prison populations and the decline of the welfare state in many Western countries. Comparative analysis can also be used to examine the complex relationship between 'crime' and punishment, the correlations between official crime and prison rates, and similarities and differences in the social backgrounds of prisoners and the offences they have committed. Comparative analysis can either demonstrate the validity of a given theory or illustrate its parochial nature and even its inaccuracy.

---

### Prison populations compared to rates of crime (2005–9)

Comparative analysis undertaken recently by the National Audit Office (2012) found no consistent correlations between prison numbers and levels of crime. Changes in prison populations compared to rates of crime during the period 2005–9 showed:

- countries where crime had decreased as the prison population increased (England and Wales, Scotland, Northern Ireland, the US, Australia, Canada, France);
- countries where crime had increased as the prison population increased (Republic of Ireland, New Zealand);
- the Netherlands, where crime decreased as the prison population decreased;
- Finland, where crime increased as the prison population decreased.

---

On a more instrumental basis, comparative analysis can also provide governments and penal administrations with valuable new policy insights and examples of good practice. Penologists have employed comparative analysis to investigate:

- the social contexts of imprisonment in different countries and to attempt to uncover possible commonalities in social structures, cultures, ideologies or political economies;
- a particular region of the world—e.g. nations in the European Union—and to attempt to uncover commonalities, harmonisation and/or differences between penal policies and practices;

- continuities and discontinuities between two or three specific countries;
- the policies of a given country—e.g. the US—to see if similar policies might be adopted by other governments elsewhere;
- the nature and extent of one specific issue—such as deaths in custody, prison labour, drugs, HIV, prison overcrowding and conditions or the legal rights of prisoners—in a number of different countries;
- historical factors and colonial contexts shaping the development of the prison around the world.

> *When reading a comparative study, ensure that you are aware of what the analysis is trying to achieve. Look at the questions it is asking and at which countries are involved.*

# THE ANALYTICAL FRAMEWORK OF COMPARATIVE ANALYSIS

Comparative analysis has a number of strands. It provides rich and detailed descriptions of a given nation, and is able to draw out the main configurations that shape the form, nature and extent of punishment in that country at any given moment. In so doing, it aims to:

- compare like with like;
- identify continuities and forms of penal convergence alongside differences;
- examine whether similar societies have similar patterns of punishment;
- assess the influence of specific countries (such as the US) on penal policy and practice elsewhere.

Comparative analysis entails consideration of most of the following factors:

- **Socio-economic**: political economy; labour market demands; commitments to welfare; and fiscal pressures.
- **Governmental**: law; criminalisation and age of criminal responsibility; social and penal policies; patterns of punishment; managerialism; aims of imprisonment and penal administration; attitudes of policymakers, politicians, civil servants and penal professionals; and the role of the judiciary and sentencing.
- **Control**: the balance between informal social controls, such as family, school, work and community, and formal social controls; and gendered and/or racialised differences in social control.

- *Cultural*: specific historical and geographical legacies; societal and penal norms, values and sensibilities; public opinion, the media, and law and order ideology; individualism or collective orientations; and perceived levels of social insecurity and anxiety.
- *Extraterritorial*: migration; globalisation; accelerating international information exchange; and foreign national prisoners.

## Common pitfall

*The above list of criteria is useful for thinking about prisons and punishment even when exclusively looking at England and Wales. This is sometimes referred to as **penality**.*

Some very good examples of comparative penologies that adopt these criteria include Ruggiero et al.'s *Western European Penal Systems: A Critical Anatomy* (1996) and Cavadino and Dignan's *Penal Systems: A Comparative Approach* (2006).

# CASE STUDIES

Weiss and South (1998, p. 2) argue that there have been five great developments shaping imprisonment in recent times:

1 The rise of neoconservative governance and neoliberal political economy in the West, alongside economic decline, class polarisation and fiscal crisis.

2 The introduction of the market economy in China.

3 The collapse of the Soviet Union and associated Communist regimes.

4 The return to civilian rule in most of Latin America, as well as a renewed push towards privatisation and other neoliberal economic prescriptions.

5 The fall of apartheid in South Africa.

To this list, we might add the following two major developments of the last ten years.

6   The consequences of the US-led war on terrorism and the subsequent increase in global insecurities.

7   The re-emergence of (the visibility of) slavery and human trafficking.

# AUSTRALIA

Australia is a federal state and a former British colony. It was the destination of over 162,000 British felons between 1787 and 1869, and the contemporary distribution of punishments must be understood within this colonial context. Australia is a country with rising prison populations.

In 1986, there were 70 prisoners per 100,000 of the population. By 1996, the rate had risen to 119, with an average daily population (ADP) of 16,399 adult prisoners. In 2006, this had increased to a rate of 126 and an ADP of 25,353 prisoners. In 2011 this increased to a rate of 130 and an ADP of 29,383 prisoners. The most recent figures (2012–13) reveal that the ADP of full-time adult prisoners has increased once again by 1,097 to 30,323 (4 per cent). (International Centre for Prison Studies, 2013)

> In Australia, there is no federal penal system and very few federal prisoners (911 in March 2013). Punishments are delivered by different states. Two issues are central to understanding contemporary imprisonment in Australia: the massive difference in rates of incarceration between states and the over-representation of Aboriginal people in prison. (A similar situation is to be found in New Zealand, where the Maori population is significantly over-represented in the prison system.)

Whereas some states—such as the Australian Capital Territory and Tasmania—have comparatively low rates of 85 and 115 per 100,000 of the adult population respectively, others—such as the Northern Territory (889), followed by Western Australia (263) and New South Wales (175)—are significantly higher. People of Aboriginal descent make up about 2 per cent of the overall Australian population, but over 28 per cent of the prison population. The number of Aboriginal prisoners is increasing. In 2013, the average daily number of full-time Aboriginal and Torres Strait Islander adult prisoners in Australia was 8,462; an imprisonment rate of 4,356 for Aboriginal men and 412 for women. This represented an increase during the period 2012–13 of 7 per cent for men and 12 per cent for women. Three states account for approximately 73 per cent of the total Aboriginal and Torres Strait Islander prison population: New South Wales (2,299), Western Australia (1,995) and Queensland (1,849). In general, Australian states with high Aboriginal populations tend to have higher rates of imprisonment. (Prison rates presented here are sourced from the Australian Bureau of Statistics (2013) and are calculated according to the adult rather than the national population.)

## BRAZIL

Brazil is a federal republic with 26 states. Around 26 per cent of the Brazilian population live below the poverty line, with 11.5 million people living on less than US $45 a month. Many of the poor live in slums (*favelas*). In 1834, Brazil became the first Latin American nation to build a penitentiary, adopting the idea from the southern states of the US. It is difficult to access accurate data on Brazilian prisons and prison conditions. In 2001, it was reported there were 147 military prisons, 100 penitentiaries, 66 public jails and 33 agricultural penal colonies in Brazil. There is also no general information about human rights violations.

Over the last 10 years, the Brazilian prison population increased by 100 per cent. In 1995, there were 95 prisoners per 100,000 of the population and an ADP of 148,760 prisoners. In 1997, this had increased to 109 prisoners per 100,000 and an ADP of 170,602. By 2006, the rate had rocketed to 191 prisoners per 100,000, an ADP of 361,402. Today there are nearly 550,000 prisoners, a rate of 274 prisoners per 100,000. (International Centre for Prison Studies, 2013)

> *Brazilian prisons are filled with the relative surplus population and their practices are rooted in the doctrine of less eligibility. Ninety-six per cent of Brazilian prisoners are men, and they are largely unemployed and sentenced for robbery, theft or drug trafficking. Prisons are acutely overcrowded, with poor hygiene, living conditions and health care.*

In recent years, an increasing number of human rights violations in Brazilian prisons have been submitted to the Inter-American Court of

Human Rights. Reports show that that a profound dehumanisation of prison life has led to an epidemic of sexual violence, mutiny, rebellion and violent escapes, and to deadly clampdowns by the Brazilian military on prisoners and their families. (The 2003 film *Carandiru* is based on the true story of a massacre that occurred in 1992 at Carandiru Penitentiary in São Paulo, in which 111 prisoners died, 102 shot by the police and 9 killed by other prisoners.) A growing problem is violent prison gangs. Brazil's most powerful gang, the Primeiro Comando da Capital, was founded at Taubaté gaol in São Paulo and is now reported to run most gaols in the area. In 2012, the Minister of Justice, José Eduardo Cardozo, stated: 'we have a medieval prison system, which not only violates human rights, it does not allow for the most important element of a penal sanction, which is social reintegration. From the bottom of my heart, if I were given many years in some of our prisons, I would rather die' (*Rio Times*, 2012).

## CHINA

China is a People's Republic and has a population of 1,344 billion. The Communist Party dominates and has a poor reputation for upholding the human rights of its citizens. In China, strong government is good government. Keeping face is culturally very important, and requires both individuals and the state to appear dignified and in control. Opponents of the regime may be imprisoned without a trial as was made evident recently with the detention of the Chinese dissident writers Chen Xi and Chen Wei and the artist Ai Weiwei. In 1978, China 'modernised' and introduced major economic reforms. This not only led to massive economic growth, but also had significant social consequences. There is high labour mobility and massive internal migration of transient populations, with around 50–60 million people per day 'on the road'. This migration is coupled with rising unemployment, inflation, crime rates and recidivism.

Incarceration in China is divided between the detention sector and the prison sector. Detentions are organised by the Ministry of Public Security and we do not know exactly how many people are incarcerated. Penal philosophy is linked to 'thought reform' and the transformational role of penal labour, which has roots in the Confucian tradition under which physical labour is understood as a form of enslavement. This tradition was reinforced by the importation of Western penal philosophy in the nineteenth century and by the influence of the Soviet Gulags in the twentieth century. Until recently, prisoners were leased out to local employers, who were obliged to offer them work after release. To counter claims of slavery, in December 1994, the Chinese renamed 'reform through labour' as imprisonment.

> *The economic reforms that China introduced in the 1970s have undermined both informal means of social control and the effectiveness of rehabilitative pro-grammes. The rise of unemployment, crime and recidivism has led the Chinese government to lose its socialist face, but its restoration can only be achieved if it is prepared to lose further face by reversing its free market reforms.*

## FINLAND

Finland is a secular and highly bureaucratic social democratic country. Like other Nordic countries (Sweden, Norway, Denmark and Iceland), Finland is heavily influenced by its neighbours. It is a small and relatively wealthy country with a population of 5.4 million concentrated mainly in the south. The country spends heavily on education, training and research, and enjoys a high quality of life.

Finland's prison rate dropped from the very high rate of 190 per 100,000 in 1950 to 118 by 1976. From this time, Finland witnessed an unbroken 23-year reduction in imprisonment rates. The rate stood at 55 in 1995 and fell as low as 46 per 100,000 in 1999. In recent years, however, the prison population has fluctuated, standing at 75 per 100,000 in 2006, but decreasing to 58 per 100,000 in 2013 (International Centre for Prison Studies, 2013). Changes in the imprisonment rate in Finland have had little impact on recorded 'crime', and Finnish governments have, so far, been successful in keeping penal policy away from populist political rhetoric (Cavadino and Dignan, 2006).

## JAPAN

Japan is an 'oriental liberal corporatist' capitalist state (Cavadino and Dignan, 2006) which, in recent times, has had a very low imprisonment rate compared to other developed countries. Japan is a group-orientated society and citizenship is closely tied to the collective identity of the nation. There is close social integration into families, and both the education system and workplace foster mutual bonds. The Japanese culturally favour informal mechanisms of social control as opposed to penal harshness, and honour, shame, apology and reciprocal obligations to others have special significance in everyday life. The vast majority of Japanese offenders confess and repent, and those offenders who can show a capacity for resocialisation are likely to receive suspended sentences or probation. Japan has very harsh and authoritarian laws, but these are mitigated by the discretionary lenience of practitioners. In this sense, the criminal justice system provides an ideological function that can promote the impression of majesty, justice and mercy.

In 1935, Japan had an ADP of 55,000 prisoners (56 per 100,000). It then reached the very high level of 198 per 100,000 in 1950, before declining to 64 in 1970 and reaching a low of 36 per 100,000 in 1992. In 1999, the prison rate stood at 42 per 100,000 and by 2002 Japan had an imprisonment rate of 52 per 100,000. In 2006, this had edged up to 62 per 100,000 of the national population, which is nearly double the rate of 14 years earlier. In 2013, it had declined again to 51 per 100,000. (International Centre for Prison Studies, 2013)

Prison life is highly regimented and very orderly. Punishments are intended to foster social inclusion and reintegration. The movement of a prisoner, even in his or her cell, is heavily controlled. Prisoners are banned from talking except during periods of association and work is compulsory. In 1990, there were only three escapes from Japanese prisons. Prisoners who have tried to escape, or who are perceived as a discipline problem, are made to wear leather or metal restraints that immobilise the movement of their hands.

> *Japanese life and culture operates through highly restrictive, repressive and disciplinarian authoritarian communitarian principles that permeate the whole of society and which Western people can find intolerably oppressive. The Japanese prison system has been criticized for violating human rights and falling far short of international standards. In particular, its adherence to strict rules of conduct and widespread use of solitary confinement has been condemned for affecting the mental health of prisoners.*

# RUSSIA

Since the collapse of the Union of Soviet Socialist Republics (USSR) in 1991, Russia has been a federal, semi-presidential republic comprising 83 regions. Spanning nine different time zones and incorporating over 160 different ethnic groups and indigenous peoples, Russia is the largest and ninth most populous country in the world. Under the communist regime, the USSR was a police state, an authoritarian society, and 'crimes' were designated actions committed directly and deliberately against the Soviet way of life. The prison and punishment system sought to change 'deviants' and 'dissenters' into loyal and obedient citizens. Until the late 1950s 'political correction' took place in what were known as 'Gulags', a giant industrial complex of prison labour camps. It is not known how many people were held and killed during this period but it is generally thought to be between 10–20 million.

During the 1980s, with the advent of President Gorbachev's policy of *glasnost* (openness), a process of ideological upheaval and political change began which had a profound effect on the penal system. The number of people imprisoned dropped and the full extent of the massive overcrowding, brutality and torture, disease and malnutrition was exposed. Since the dissolution of the Soviet Union, Russian prison populations have fallen but remained high. In 2001, the imprisonment rate was 670 per 100,000 of the population, in 2007 it had dropped to 613 per 100,000, and in 2013 it had fallen further to 475 per 100,000. (International Centre for Prison Studies, 2013)

> *Russia has instigated a national programme of penal reform. But the legacy of the Gulag era is a penal system comprising detention centres, prisons and 'correctional colonies' which is under resourced and poorly maintained. In many regions (oblasts) prisoners must work to survive as budgets from the central prison authority for basic necessities such as food and clothing are low and unreliable. The Russian Federation ratified the European Convention on Human Rights in 1998, but human rights violations in Russian prisons are regularly reported by Council of Europe inspectors. And although there has been reform to the rule of law, authoritarian political power has re-emerged, the arrest and imprisonment in 2012 of three members of the feminist punk rock group* Pussy Riot *for protesting against the policies of President Vladimir Putin being the best known example.*

Penal atrocities and human rights violations have been acknowledged by Russian prison authorities but strict militarised regimes based on discipline and 're-education' remain firmly in place.

## SOUTH AFRICA

South Africa is a country that is in transition from an authoritarian apartheid society to one that is rooted in the principles of democracy.

*Despite recent changes, South Africa's 47 million inhabitants remain pro-foundly divided in terms of race, class and power. The political system was transformed when the African National Congress (ANC) gained power in 1994, but post-apartheid South Africa's great divides in wealth and power have not yet been adequately addressed.*

In 1980, South Africa had a prison rate of 423 per 100,000—at that time, the highest in the world. In 1995, the official imprisonment rate declined to 273 per 100,000 of the general population. Although many members of the now-ruling party, the ANC, have experienced imprisonment at first hand, this has not led to a concerted effort to reduce imprisonment for the largely poor Black property offenders who are incarcerated. By 2006, the rates had crept back up to 335 per 100,000 and an ADP of 157,402 prisoners. However by 2013, the imprisonment rate had decreased to 294 per 100,000. (International Centre for Prison Studies, 2013)

## THE US

The US is the most advanced capitalist society and the richest nation on earth; it also has the largest prison population. It is an economic and cultural leader, and this 'imperialism' can also be seen in terms of penal policy. In the late 1960s, President Richard Nixon adopted a tough 'law and order' ideology that has led to an increase in prison populations since the mid-1970s that is unprecedented in a democratic society. Over the past thirty years there has been a 500 per cent increase in prisoner numbers. This expansionism was further fuelled by the 'war on drugs' initiated by President Ronald Reagan during the 1980s.

In 1980, 19 people out of every 1,000 people arrested for drug offences were sent to prison. By 1992, this had increased to 104. The US's ADP stood at 744,208 in 1986. By 1998, it had reached 1,725,842 prisoners. In February 2000, the ADP broke the 2 million mark and, by 2006, it had continued to rise to 2,186,230. Since then the imprisonment rate has fluctuated, reaching 755 per 100,000 of the population in 2008, but then falling to 731 per 100,000 in 2010 and slightly again to 716 per 100,000 in 2013. The number of people under correctional supervision (i.e. in prison, on probation or on parole) at the end of 2011 was 6.98 million—just under 3 per cent of the population. Louisiana had the highest incarceration rate in 2013 (1,138) and Maine the lowest (273). Factors that explain variances in state imprisonment rates include the implementation of minimum mandatory sentencing policies and the maintenance of strict drug enforcement laws. About one in three African Americans are sent to prison during their lifetime, although they constitute only 13 per cent of the general population. (Mauer, 1999)

> Black American men are eight times more likely to be imprisoned than White Americans and more than 60 per cent of the people in prison are racial and ethnic minorities. About one in ten Black American men aged in their 30s is in prison on any given day.

## VENEZUELA

Venezuela has one of the worst reputations for the treatment of prisoners. Throughout the 1990s, like many Latin American nations, it held a large number of pre-trial detainees, with prisoners awaiting trial for an average of three years. The armed forces ran the penal system, and prisons were filled with prisoners accused of drug-related offences, terrorism and offences 'against public security'. In 1992, an ADP of at least 29,000 were held in prisons with a capacity for just over 15,000. In this period, Venezuelan prisons had the greatest known number of prisoners killed daily in the world. Not even Venezuela's Director of Prisons knew how many people were in prison. Prison conditions were very poor and violence endemic.

Over the last decade, there have been major political changes in Venezuela and attempts have been made to reform the penal system. A consequence of this was that between 1993 and 2005 the rate of imprisonment fell from 109 to 73 per 100,000 of the population. Since then, however, the prison population has increased dramatically, reaching 85 per 100,000 in 2008 and a massive 161 per 100,000 in 2013. In 2011, after a major uprising in a prison outside Caracas, President Hugo Chavez created a prison ministry to reform the penal system, but the situation has worsened. Prisons built to accommodate 12,000 prisoners now hold four times that many and brutality, violence and corruption are rife. In many prisons control has been surrendered to armed gangs who exchange drugs and guns openly. In January 2013 at Uribana prison in the Western state of Lara, following a fierce gun battle between prisoners and the National Guard, 61 people were killed and 120 wounded. (*Huffington Post*, 2013)

# LEARNING THE LESSONS?

Comparative analysis can lead us to a greater understanding of the forms that punishment is currently taking throughout the world and what factors may underscore current trends. This can lead us to certain conclusions about the justifications, use, nature and extent of imprisonment:

1   'Crime' has been politicised by all mainstream parties, especially right and centre-left politicians.

2   There is a worldwide increase in the use of imprisonment as a solution to social problems.

3   Imprisonment rates are relatively independent of 'crime' rates.

4   Imprisonment is increasingly being used as a means of stigmatising and controlling non-productive labourers and migrant workers.

5   Punishments are directed against the poorest people in the world.

6   Penal labour and prison work/profitability are central to penal debates.

7   Less eligibility continues to feature in moral discourses on state responsibilities for the incarcerated.

8   There has been a cheapening of human value and a denial of human rights.

9   Sentences have the greatest impact on prison numbers.

10   There has been bifurcation of penal policies and a rise of selective incapacitation.

11   An increase in anxiety, insecurity and fear has been seen in wider society, along with increases in forms of security when dealing with prisoners. The perception that in some countries today the general

public is increasingly desirous of more severe punishments is known in the academic literature as 'popular punitiveness'.

12 There has been a hardening of penal philosophy, a decline in liberalism and growing intolerance of the poor and non-productive labour.

13 Public sentiments and penal cultures may form a key link between political economy and penal expansionism.

14 There has been a growth of managerialism.

15 Greater penal privatisation has been the norm.

16 The use of repression and the rolling back of the welfare state has been favoured over redistribution, while more authoritarian forms of control have become more deeply embedded. Dealing with the poor in this way is known in the academic literature as 'penal welfarism'.

17 There is evidence of a link between penality and different types of political economy: the harsher the social exclusion under political economy, the harsher the punishment.

18 There is evidence that the penal solution is, in fact, both irrational and counterproductive.

## "Have we seen a greater harmonisation and intensification of penal sanctions in Western European nations?"

When answering, ensure that you identify the key countries in Western Europe, and then examine their similarities and differences in penal policies, imprisonment rates and forms of social control. Look wider than this as well. Examine different political economies and cultural attitudes towards marginalised populations to assess their likely impact on prison policies. Highlight both continuities and discontinuities. The work of Ruggiero et al. (1996) is indispensable, but look also at more recent data and debates available in journals and from organisations such as Statewatch, as well as conducting a detailed Internet search on the different countries involved.

In looking at different forms of punishment, you may want to compare countries with relatively high rates of imprisonment (e.g. the UK and the US) to countries with low-imprisonment rates (e.g. Scandinavia). Pratt (2008) has looked at Finland, Norway and Sweden to assess the reasons for low rates of imprisonment and high-quality prison conditions in these countries. His research tells us the roots of penal moderation in Scandinavian countries are both political and cultural. Egalitarian social policies founded on a strong interventionist state and democratic self-government provide for a penal system which aims to normalise prisoners through good-quality health care and welfare support. Prison conditions reflect strongly held values of social solidarity compared to the rigid class divisions which pertain in hierarchical societies, for example the UK where a powerful land-owning aristocracy strongly influences the social and economic orthodoxy. What do you think this tells us about the differential influence of political opportunism, the media, public opinion, market forces and privatisation on imprisonment rates and prison conditions in countries around the world?

# BIBLIOGRAPHY

The following texts compare US, European and other penal systems throughout the world:

- **ALLEN, R (2012)** *Reducing the Use of Imprisonment: What Can We Learn From Europe?* Report for the Criminal Justice Alliance.
- **CAVADINO, M and DIGNAN, J (2006)** *Penal Systems: A Comparative Approach*, London: Sage.
- **NELKEN, D (2010)** *Comparative Criminal Justice: Making Sense of Difference*, London: Sage.
- **PAKES, F (2010)** *Comparative Criminal Justice*, 2nd edn, Cullompton: Willan.
- **PRATT, J (2008)** 'Scandinavian Exceptionalism in an Era of Penal Excess, Part 1: The Nature and Roots of Scandinavian Exceptionalism', *British Journal of Criminology*, 48(2), pp. 119–37.
- **PRATT, J (2011)** 'Penal Excess and Penal Exceptionalism: Welfare and Imprisonment in Anglophone and Scandinavian Societies', in A Crawford (ed.), *International and Comparative Criminal Justice and Urban Governance*, Cambridge: Cambridge University Press.
- **PRATT, J and ERIKSSON, A (2012)** *Contrasts in Punishment: An Explanation of Anglophone Excess and Nordic Exceptionalism*, London: Routledge.
- **RUGGIERO, V and RYAN, M (eds) (2013)** *Punishment in Europe*, London: Palgrave

- **RUGGIERO, V, RYAN, M and SIM, J (eds) (1996)** *Western European Penal Systems: A Critical Anatomy*, London: Sage.
- **SCOTT, D (ed.) (2013)** *Why Prison?* Cambridge: Cambridge University Press.
- **STERN, V (1997)** *A Sin Against the Future*, Harmondsworth: Penguin.
- **SUDBURY, J (ed.) (2005)** *Global Lockdown: Race, Gender, and the Prison-Industrial Complex*, New York: Routledge.
- **TONRY, M (ed.) (2007)** *Crime, Punishment and Politics in Comparative Perspective*, London: University of Chicago Press.
- **VAN SWAANINGEN, R (1997)** *Critical Criminology: Visions From Europe*, London: Sage.
- **VAN ZYL SMIT, D and DUNKEL, F (eds) (2001)** *Imprisonment Today and Tomorrow: International Perspectives on Prisoners' Rights and Prison Conditions*, 2nd edn, London: Kluwer Law International.
- **WEISS, R and SOUTH, N (eds) (1998)** *Comparing Prison Systems: Toward a Comparative and International Penology*, Amsterdam: Overseas Publishers Association.

There are few English language publications which describe penal matters in non-Anglophone countries, but a vivid account of the Russian prison system is:

- **PIACENTINI, L (2004)** *Surviving Russian Prisons*, Cullompton: Willan.

For further details of critical researchers on prisons and punishment across the globe see the international forum Global Prisons Network at: https://sites.google.com/site/gprnnetwork.

The *European Group for the Study of Deviance and Social Control* also have a 'working group for prison, detention and punishment'. For further details see the European Group website [www.europeangroup.org] and for details of the 2013 working group manifesto see the anthology:

- **GILMORE, J, MOORE, JM and SCOTT, D (eds) (2013)** *Critique and Dissent*, Ottawa: Red Quill Books.

Statistical data on world prison populations is available at:

- **WALMSLEY, R (2011)** *World Prison Populations List*, London: International Centre for Prison Studies.

World Prison Brief is available at: http://www.prisonstudies.org/info/worldbrief/.

# 2.4 A HISTORY OF IMPRISONMENT IN THE UK: UNTIL 1997

## Core areas

the Bloody Code
the age of reform
the 'great experiment'
the aims of imprisonment in the twentieth century
the history and aims of imprisonment in Northern Ireland and Scotland

## Running themes

- Human rights
- Less eligibility
- Managerialism
- Penal reform
- Rehabilitation

## Key penologists

**John Howard (1726–90)** A wealthy aristocrat with profound religious conviction, John Howard became Sheriff of Bedfordshire in 1773. He undertook detailed inspections of jails under his jurisdiction and, later, of a further hundred prisons across the country, as well as prisons throughout Europe. In his exhaustive study, *The State of the Prisons in England and Wales* (1777), Howard revealed that more people died as a result of appalling prison conditions than were being publicly executed. Howard was influential in shaping the Penitentiary Act 1779. He argued that regular, steady discipline in a penitentiary had the power to turn the 'unhappy wretches' who broke the law into useful members of society. Howard died of typhus while investigating prison and hospital conditions in the Ukraine in 1790.

**Edmund du Cane (1830–1903)** Born in Colchester, Sir Edmund du Cane made his reputation organising convict labour in Australia in the 1850s, while still serving in the Royal

Engineers. In the 1860s, he became chairman of the board of directors of convict prisons and, from 1877, headed the prison system throughout England and Wales. The architect of Wormwood Scrubs, du Cane was a harsh disciplinarian and presided over brutal penal regimes that were rooted in separate confinement; penal servitude labouring at stone breaking; picking oakum (separating strands of rope); the tread wheel and crank; and long periods of silence. Famous for promising the Victorian public that 'criminals' would get 'hard labour, hard fare and hard board', owing to mounting public criticism, his controversial reign of terror came to an abrupt end in 1894.

**Lord Justice Woolf (b. 1933)** Born in Newcastle upon Tyne, Harry Woolf is the son of a builder and architect. One of England's most senior judges, he was appointed to the High Court in 1979 and was Lord Chief Justice from 2000 until 2005. He has been a major figure in promoting liberal penal reform since he conducted a major inquiry into the riot at Manchester 'Strangeways' prison and other prison disturbances in April 1990. In the subsequent report and in later speeches, Woolf has criticised inhumane prison conditions and overcrowding. His promotion of a balance between 'security, control and justice' continues to influence liberal penologists.

# THE BLOODY CODE

> The historian assembles data and is even more aware than the physical scientist how inadequate his [sic] data are. Much of the evidence on which we could base our knowledge of the past has either been destroyed or was never recorded. We guess from the few remaining fragments much as geologists reconstruct a prehistoric monster from a single bone.
>
> (Taylor, 1968, p. 11)

In England in 1166, King Henry II issued the Assize of Clarendon, which ordered his sheriffs to build a jail in each county. Jails held debtors and felons awaiting trial. In 1556, the first 'house of correction' was established at Bridewell and, in 1609, to control the poor and vagrant and provide work for the idle, James I made such houses of correction (popularly referred to as 'Bridewells') obligatory in every English county. These facilities held people who were sent to prison for very short sentences.

Alongside various forms of corporal punishment such as the stocks and ducking stool, the workhouse enshrined the principle of less eligibility and was intimately linked to the birth of the prison. The control of women rule-breakers was different to that of men. Women were controlled largely through informal patriarchal social controls, but, in terms of the development of penal institutions, the nunnery was a crucial instrument in disciplining deviant, rebellious and sexually promiscuous women.

---

**The scolds bridle**

The 'scolds bridle' was used when a woman publicly challenged or insulted her husband. The woman was forced to wear a bridle, which involved a metal cage that was placed around the woman's head. A small pallet with a spike in it was inserted under the woman's tongue. If she attempted to speak her tongue would become impaled on the spike. The woman could then be publicly humiliated, placed in stocks and pelted with rotten vegetables.

---

In 1750, England was a small parochial society and its population stood at 6.5 million. Seventy-five per cent of the population lived in the countryside and three-quarters worked in agriculture. Local landowners were often the local magistrates, and these enforced the law. There was little public debate on punishment and no legal safeguards against wrongful conviction. During this time, there were over 200 separate Acts, most of them property offences that commanded the penalty of death by public hanging, often involving a theatrical last confession, in which criminals were expected to atone for their 'sins' in the presence of others. This system of laws and punishments has become known as the 'Bloody Code'.

Despite its apparent barbarity, only about 10 per cent of people sentenced to death were actually executed. For historian Douglas Hay (1975), the Bloody Code was really an ideological system of social control combining:

- *majesty*: the power and authority of the law;
- *justice*: everybody could be prosecuted under the rule of law;
- *mercy*: local elites gained pardons through petitions to the monarch.

Alongside public hangings, the Transportation Act 1718 introduced the transportation of offenders. A first experiment in the privatisation of criminal justice, from 1718 to 1775, merchant shippers made large profits transporting over 30,000 people to the US. The American War of Independence ended the practice, but 12 years later, in 1787, transportation was reintroduced. From 1787 to 1869, 162,000 people were transported to Australia.

*Remember that there are different historical perspectives. When reading a history book, try to locate the theoretical perspective from which the author is writing.*

# THE AGE OF REFORM

In the eighteenth century, there were a number of significant changes that undermined the Bloody Code. Industrialisation, urbanisation and massive population growth transformed the agricultural and parochial system. The old 'moral economy' gave way to a new 'political economy' of wealth creation founded on trade, the 'enclosure' of land and privatisation of property. By 1800, the population stood at 15 million and an anonymous and diverse society was being formed that was not beholden to the local gentry.

Stan Cohen (1985, p. 13) argues that, during this period, new master patterns of social control developed. These comprised:

- increasing involvement of a centralised state;
- increasing classification of deviants by experts;
- increased incarceration of deviants into 'asylums'—penitentiaries, prisons, mental hospitals and reformatories;
- the mind replaced the body as the object of penal repression.

The context to the development of these patterns of control included:

- structural changes in society and the political economy;
- a perceived rise in 'crime' and the threat to order;
- fear of the so-called 'criminal' or 'dangerous classes';
- a belief that immorality was the cause of 'crime';
- ideological commitment that prison could reform offenders.

There was a change in emphasis from elimination to reclamation and a rise in the belief that new 'reformed prisons' could act as a 'technology of salvation'.

*Two diametrically opposed philosophies developed. On the one hand, Christian reformers believed in the concepts of original sin and the universality of guilt. Immorality was to be rectified by manipulating the shameful offender, using isolation in a prison cell as a condition under which he or she might reflect on, and repent of, his or her unrighteousness. Utilitarian philosophers, on the other hand, pleaded for the universality of reason. 'Crime' is a free choice, a rational appraisal of potential costs and benefits and therefore reformation could only take place through the socialisation of the offender's proclivity for pleasure. This would be achieved by constant inspection.*

# THE 'GREAT EXPERIMENT'

The publication in 1777 of John Howard's detailed investigations of prison conditions in the UK and throughout Europe aroused considerable public interest and soon led to calls for institutional change. Feted by royalty and aristocrats, Howard lobbied for improvements to prisoner health and hygiene as well as independent systems of inspection. The Hulk Act 1776 was the first move towards a convict prison and the principles of reformation. These decommissioned navy ships, 'floating hells', were rife with disease and many prisoners lost their lives in these miserable wooden coffins. Although parliament sanctioned their use for two years only, a steady rise in the prison population demanded they remain in use for over 80 years. Nevertheless, the penal system remained a major cause for concern and two years after the Hulk Act, William Eden, William Blackstone and John Howard introduced the reformist Penitentiary Act 1779.

---

**The Penitentiary Act 1779**

William Blackstone sums up the principles of this legislation:

In framing the plan of these penitentiary houses, the principle objects were sobriety, cleanliness and medical assistance by a regular series of labour, by solitary confinement during the intervals of work, and some religious instruction to preserve and amend the health of the unhappy offenders and to enure them to the habits of industry, to guard them from pernicious company, to accustom them to serious reflection and to teach them both the principle and practices of every Christian and moral duty.

(1779, cited in Ignatieff, 1978, p. 94)

---

Jeremy Bentham, while sharing the desire of religious reformers to improve the penal system, took a strictly rational approach to prison reform, devising the Panopticon prison on scientific architectural principles. Constant surveillance and hard work would replace the brutal arbitrariness of the old penal system. These reforming ideas had been presented to parliament in response to the end of transportation to the US, but when transportation to Australia started in 1787 the reform movement lost some momentum. The Panopticon was never built. In

1794, however, an attempt to reform prisoners through a strict regime of solitary confinement and silence was trialled at Coldbath Fields House of Correction in London and in 1810, the legal reformer Samuel Romily argued that the Penitentiary Act should be resurrected. The government responded by appointing the Holford Committee (1810), which recommended that a convict prison should be built at Millbank, on the River Thames in London, where the Tate Britain art gallery stands today (McConville, 1995).

---

### The General Penitentiary at Millbank

Opened in 1821, the General Penitentiary cost £0.5 million and was designed to hold 1,000 prisoners. Abandoning Betham's Panopticon design, it consisted of six pentagons radiating from a central circular chapel. Beset with structural and regime problems from the outset, this huge 'monument of ugliness' became a 'maniac-making machine' (Webb and Webb, 1922, p. 48). In the 1830s, Reverend Daniel Nihil was appointed chaplain governor, and solitary confinement and religious indoctrination became central to the prison regime. The penitentiary proved an unmitigated disaster and was eventually pulled down in 1893.

---

Nevertheless, the centrally administered convict prison was born, although it had clearly been a hard labour. The 1823 Gaol Act required local justices to carry out prison inspections and in 1835 Inspectors of Prisons were officially appointed by Parliament. In 1842, Pentonville prison was opened. It held 520 prisoners in separate cells and became the new model prison of the Victorian era. Its regime was based on:

- solitude;
- hard labour;
- religious indoctrination;
- surveillance.

In 1865, the Prison Act finally ended the official difference between 'jails' and 'houses of correction', renaming them 'local prisons' and, in 1877, the Prison Act gave the Home Office control of the prison system which increasingly was modelled on solitary confinement and hard labour. Following this period the modern prison was to become the ultimate sanction of the state, although throughout the nineteenth century dissatisfaction with prison regimes and high rates of reoffending continued to exercise the minds of penal administrators and reformers.

> *It is very important that you have a solid grasp of penal history. You will be able to understand the present use of imprisonment and the disputes and challenges it faces much better if you are able to understand its past, so spend some time reading about the development of the prison.*

## THE AIMS OF IMPRISONMENT IN THE TWENTIETH CENTURY

As legislated for in the 1857 Penal Servitude Act, the 1865 Prisons Act, and under the guidance of Sir Edmund du Cane, Assistant Director of prisons from 1863 and Chairman of the Prison Commission between 1877 and 1895, the 'Silent System' of imprisonment was harsh, brutal and rooted in the doctrine of deterrence and less eligibility. Prisoners were required to work the crank or tread wheel and flogged if they did not conform. Food was monotonous, and clothing, haircuts and standards of personal hygiene deliberately demeaning.

> **Less eligibility** *is predicated on the assumption that there exists a universal free, rational and calculating subject who is infused with an individual sense of responsibility. Criminal activity is understood as a free choice that is based upon weighing up the potential benefits and costs of such behaviour. Harsh and punitive regimes will instil moral fibre, discipline and backbone into the criminal, thus eradicating the individual deficiencies that were major factors for his or her offence. The application of the doctrine of less eligibility therefore ensures that the upper margin of prison conditions are guaranteed not to rise above the worst material conditions in society as a whole and so, in times of social hardship, the rigours of penal discipline become more severe to prevent weakening its deterrent effect.*

However, it was only a matter of time before the secret, repressive world of Victorian imprisonment came to public attention. Du Cane's disciplinary, deterrent practices were eventually challenged in 1895 when the Gladstone Committee was commissioned. The press had already begun to expose the deleterious and debilitating effects of hard labour and the silent system, most famously on the Irish writer Oscar Wilde, imprisoned for homosexual acts between 1895 and 1897. Suicide and insanity were all too common and recidivism the norm. In response, Gladstone advocated that the primary and concurrent objects of imprisonment should be deterrence and reformation. For Gladstone,

> prison discipline and treatment should be more effectually designed to maintain, stimulate, or awaken the higher susceptibilities of prisoners, to develop their moral instincts to train them in orderly and industrial habits, and whenever possible to turn them out of prison better men and women, both physically and morally, than when they came in.
>
> (1895, cited in Radzinowicz and Hood, 1986, pp. 577–8)

Du Cane resigned his post as Chairman of the Prison Commissioners, and in 1898 the Prisons Act abolished separate confinement and hard labour. However, Gladstone did not so much break with the past and the philosophical underpinnings of less eligibility as introduce a new *manifest* task of prison treatment. As legislated for in the Prevention of Crime Act 1908 and Mental Deficiency Act 1913, by the 1920s a new treatment and training ideology gained ascendancy. Criminal justice came to be founded on positivist criminology and a new therapeutic model of imprisonment. Rather than freedom of choice and rational calculation, increasingly 'crime' was ascribed to mental deficiency or environmental circumstance. It was believed that criminal behaviour could be diagnosed and cured through psychiatric and psychological interventions, or transformed by the provision of social welfare (Garland, 1990). Punishment was individualised and proportionality of sentence rejected in favour of indeterminacy.

While containment persisted, treatment and training focused upon rehabilitation through work, education, physical training and the nurturing of positive staff relationships. Under the stewardship of Sir Evelyn Ruggles-Brise, Prison Commissioner from 1895 to 1921, a separate system of imprisonment was introduced for offenders between the ages of 16 and 21. Intended to keep young offenders away from the corrosive influence of adults, 'borstal detention' combined strict discipline, hard physical work, moral instruction and educational and industrial training. After the First World War, educational and work facilities were extended throughout the prison system and, under the watch of another influential prison commissioner, Alexander Paterson, the first open prison was established in 1933 at Lowdham Grange, Nottinghamshire. Nevertheless, prison conditions remained harsh and impersonal.

Periods of enforced separate confinement were not abolished until 1930 and penal servitude, hard labour and flogging until 1948.

Throughout the century, as prisons became less brutal, the impetus to reform prisoners gathered momentum. Imbued with a strong sense of optimism that reoffending could be reduced, if not eliminated, by applying scientific principles of individualisation, throughout the 1950s and 1960s, 'penal experts'—criminologists, psychologists, psychiatrists and social workers—developed new models of offender rehabilitation. But faith in the reforming potential of prisons was not to last. During the 1960s and 1970s, new security, overcrowding and resource priorities retarded the further development of prisoner treatment and welfare, and a number of important official reports reshaped the aims of imprisonment. Most notably, the Mountbatten Report (1966), written after a number of high-profile escapes, including the spy George Blake from Wormwood Scrubs, focused attention on increasing prison security. Mountbatten proposed that all male prisoners should be classified into four categories: A, B, C and D, A being the most and D the least secure.

*Mountbatten advocated what is known as a '**concentration policy**', which would have placed all high-risk prisoners together in a new maximum security facility on the Isle of Wight, allowing much lower security across the rest of the penal estate.*

However, the subsequent Radzinowicz Report (1968) rejected the concentration policy in favour of what is known as the 'dispersal policy'. Under this policy, category A prisoners were to be dispersed with category B prisoners in specially designed high-security training prisons. Together with the growing problem of prison overcrowding, prisoner disturbances and increasingly high recidivism rates, throughout the 1970s the adoption of the dispersal policy led to a heightened focus on risk and security and the downplaying of the training and treatment role of prisons. In this context, another important official report of the period was that of the May Committee (Home Office, 1979), chaired by the Honourable Judge Mr Justice May. As a replacement for Rule 1 of the Prison Service, that prisoners should be encouraged to lead 'good and useful lives', the committee advocated the notion of 'positive custody' which emphasised the simple occupying role of work and education. This proposal was met with official silence and faced criticism from influential penological commentators who branded it 'wooly'. It has now been quietly forgotten (Scott, 2007).

## Common pitfall

*The recommendations of official reports do not have to be accepted by the govern-ment. Some recommendations will become policies, but others are discarded.*

With the election of Margaret Thatcher's Conservative Government in 1979, an attempt was made to stem prison overcrowding by implementing a bifurcated policy strategy consisting of long sentences for violent offend-ers, community sentences for less serious offenders and 'short sharp shock' detention for young offenders. At the same time, a new penal realist con-sensus developed rooted in the principles of 'humane containment'. Rather than reform offenders, humane containment had the much more modest aim of simply holding them in safe, humane and publicly acceptable living conditions. Penal realism may, unfortunately, accurately sum up about all that is achievable through imprisonment, but such an agenda could hardly provide inspiration for those administering punishments. The 'starkness' of humane containment led one influential liberal commentator to consider this aim to be 'ontologically insufficient' (Bottoms, 1990, p. 9).

The attempt to stem prison overcrowding proved unsuccessful. Through-out the 1980s, the prison population continued to rise, 'short sharp shock' detention centres were abolished in 1988 owing to high reoffending rates, and the liberal penological consensus reached its high tide with the publi-cation of the Woolf Report on the 25 February 1991. Lord Justice Woolf had been commissioned to investigate the riot that occurred at HMP Manchester from 1 April to 25 April 1990 and disturbances at five further institutions: Glen Parva, Dartmoor, Cardiff, Bristol and Pucklechurch. The Woolf Report (1991) is widely regarded as the most significant official report on prisons in England and Wales since the Gladstone Report.

### The Woolf Report (1991)

The Woolf report:

- tapped into the logic of the penological consensus and justified imprisonment through the aims of humane containment;
- called for the creation of 'community prisons' for prisoners to be held as close to their homes as possible;

- argued that the Prison Service should balance the key principles of 'security, control and justice';
- ended the practice of 'slopping out' and introduced in-prison sanitation;
- advocated a cap on prison overcrowding;
- believed that prisons should encourage offenders to take personal responsibility through facilitating greater opportunities for prisoners to make meaningful choices;
- premised, through advocating prisoner compacts, the fulfilment of responsibilities as a perquisite for just, humane containment;
- placed great emphasis on incentives, privileges and legitimate expectations;
- defined prisoners as consumers;
- introduced an independent system of prisoner complaints adjudication.

The Woolf Report highlighted the sense of injustice prisoners felt at being held in decrepit and overcrowded prisons as the primary cause of the disturbances, but its agenda has been criticised by Joe Sim (1994a) because it:

- worked within the axioms of state-defined penal truth;
- aimed to re-legitimate the prison;
- ignored the experiences of women prisoners;
- ignored wider processes of disciplinary control in society;
- depoliticised prisons by adopting consumerist language.

The government White Paper, *Custody, Care and Justice: The Way Ahead for the Prison Service in England and Wales* (1991) accepted all of Woolf's recommendations bar the cap on prison overcrowding. Undoubtedly, in key respects prison conditions improved as a result. But in committing no extra resources to prison, the implementation by the government of the most costly recommendations, in particular the creation of multi-functional community prisons, in practice were suspended.

In subsequent years, prisoner disturbances and serious breaches of security continued to have a significant impact on the role of prisons. In September 1994, six high-risk prisoners, including five IRA terrorists, escaped from the Special Security Unit at Whitemoor Prison in Cambridgeshire. The escapees had rope, bullets, two guns, over £400 in cash and a torch. One officer was shot during the escape. Shortly after the prisoners were recaptured, semtex explosive was found in the Unit. Recommendation 62 of the resulting Woodcock Report (1994) emphasised the 'central importance of security in all aspects of activity' and that all new policies 'should be tested against whether they add to or detract from security standards'. The government ordered a new inquiry to review security procedures across the prison estate, but its terms of reference were altered by a further politically embarrassing escape: this time of three life-sentence prisoners from Parkhurst Prison on the Isle of Wight on 3 January 1995. On this occasion, the escapees had tools, a ladder, a toy gun and a key. The resultant Learmont Report (1995) advocated the joint priorities of 'custody, care and control'. Prisons should protect the public and deter potential offenders by keeping those sent to them by the courts in 'custody'. Prisons should 'care' for prisoners by providing opportunities for them to make redress, learn from their mistakes and re-establish family ties. And prisons should 'control' prisoners though inducements, based on both incentives and sanctions, and on the better training of prison officers. Most importantly, there was a renewed emphasis on security for prisoners assessed as constituting an escape risk, including enforced segregation, regular strip searches and closed visits. The overall approach was heavily critiqued by liberal commentators as amounting to the creation of new highly repressive and dehumanising iron coffins, the former Chief Inspector of Prisons Judge Stephen Tumim describing it as 'the road to the concentration camp'.

As the prison population increased substantially throughout the 1990s, the growing costs of imprisonment led to concern about the economy of punishment. New managerialist approaches, including the privatisation of prisons, came to the fore which, in focusing on cost efficiency, impacted significantly on prison conditions and rehabilitation ideologies and practices. Its *Corporate Plan 1993–6* (HM Prison Service, 1993) provided details of the Prison Service's new managerial vision, goals and values. Remarkably, in the space of only a few years, the Prison Service had shifted from a sense of realism, under which any progressive aims of imprisonment seemed beyond its reach, to the delivery of a plethora of indicators, purposes, visions, goals and values that appeared to have little in common with the aims that had been promoted during the previous decade (Scott, 2007). Since the election of the 'New Labour' Government in 1997, the role of imprisonment in the UK has continued to be strongly influenced by political imperatives. The embracing of neo-liberal market economics by Conservative and Labour governments alike has tended to prioritise penal exclusion over penal welfare (Lacey, 2008), notwithstanding the Labour Government's attempt to chart a 'third way' between them.

# A HISTORY AND AIMS OF IMPRISONMENT IN NORTHERN IRELAND AND SCOTLAND

## NORTHERN IRELAND

Tomlinson (1996) points out that Northern Irish (NI) prisons cannot be understood without consideration of:

- its colonial context;
- the penal system in the whole of Ireland until the 1920s;
- the use of imprisonment during 'the Troubles' from the late 1960s.

Ireland was incorporated into the UK under the Act of Union in 1800, although it had been subject to British control for a number of centuries before that. The first prison in Ireland opened in Dublin at Richmond in 1818. After nationalist uprisings, the Anglo-Irish Treaty of 1920 left only Northern Ireland under British rule, but partition did not end the republican struggle. The struggle became increasingly intense in the late 1960s, with the denial of civil rights for Catholic citizens and the murder of unarmed protestors on what became known as 'Bloody Sunday'.

The history of imprisonment in NI is linked to 'the Troubles' and the political and security situation. Since 1969, some 29 staff have been murdered and many others have been injured. During the Troubles, a number of people were interned (held without trial). In the 1970s–90s, the NI Prison Service (NIPS) was heavily criticised for its treatment of political prisoners. In 1975, the Gardiner Committee ended the special status of political prisoners and such prisoners were housed in rapidly built 'H-blocks' at Long Kesh, near Belfast, and Magilligan, near Derry. In response, political prisoners refused to wear prison clothes and to wash, and covered their cell walls in their own excrement. Out of desperation, republican prisoners embarked on a sustained hunger strike, leading to the deaths of ten prisoners in 1981, including Bobby Sands who had been elected as an MP during these protests. A number of notorious prisons, such as the Maze, have been closed since the peace settlement in the 1990s. The Good Friday Agreement— signed in April 1998—had a major impact on the NIPS and, from September 1998, led to the release of many paramilitary prisoners.

## SCOTLAND

Prisons and houses of correction were not as entrenched in Scotland as they were in England and Wales, being fewer in number and housing relatively small numbers of people. Although Bridewells did exist in places such as Glasgow, a correctional system did not develop in Scotland until the 1830s. In 1839, the (Scottish) Prison Act introduced a General Board that undertook the daily administration of prisons and, in 1842, a new 'general prison' was opened at Perth. Later, developments under the Prisons (Scotland) Administration Act 1860 and Prisons (Scotland) Act 1877 created a centralised system with one penitentiary and 56 county prisons. Remarkably, one of the first steps in the new centralised system was to reduce the number of prisons to 15 by the 1890s. In 1939, the administration of prisons was given to the Secretary of State for Scotland and, until recently, prisons were run by the Scottish Office and Health Department. Today, the Scottish Prison Service is an agency of the Scottish Executive.

## "Why did penal reforms continue in the mid-nineteenth century in the face of such obvious humanitarian failure at Millbank and Pentonville prisons?"

You should first establish that the early prison reforms were abject failures. Then, consider the arguments for further expansion. Identify how prisons are intimately linked with a number of other disciplinary institutions such as the factory, school, army barracks, the reformed workhouse and the hospital. Also highlight social anxieties and a society that increasingly came to see 'crime' as the result of laziness and degeneracy, and of a dangerous and contagious criminal class that needed to be controlled. Finally, consider how prison reform throughout history has been driven by a strong faith in science and progress.

TAKING IT FURTHER

Historiographies of prisons and punishment differ. The study of penal history inevitably has repercussions for the way in which data is interpreted. History is commonly understood in relation to periods of significant economic and social upheaval. Criminal justice historians such as Rusche and Kirchheimer (1939; 2003) have assessed the influence of economic developments on the changing role of punishment over time. Foucault's (1977) conception of punishment as having developed within a wider disciplinary apparatus of power/knowledge is somewhat different. Eschewing economic evolutionism, Foucault's analysis encompasses a range of hierarchical and conflicting social discourses, not just those which function as mechanisms of political progress. More recent historical accounts based on revisionist feminist perspectives and Critical Race Theory have analysed penal change in relation to specific cultural forces including gender differences, racial discrimination and patriarchal relations (Bosworth, 2010). In writing this book we have attempted to be as objective and impartial as possible. However, as with all historical analysis, our views are influenced by our research interests and preferences and the ethical stance we adopt towards prisons and punishment. In reading penal historiographies it is important you keep this in mind.

# BIBLIOGRAPHY

There are numerous books, and chapters in books, on the history of prisons and punishment. A few key ones include:

- **BOSWORTH, M (2010)** *Explaining US Imprisonment*, London: Sage.
- **CAVADINO, M, DIGNAN, J and MAIR, G (2013)** *The Penal System: An Introduction*, 5th edn, London: Sage.
- **COHEN, S and SCULL, A (eds) (1983)** *Social Control and the State*, Oxford: Blackwell.
- **EMSLEY, C (1996)** *Crime and Society in England 1750–1900*, London: Longman.
- **EMSLEY, C and KNAFLA, LA (eds) (1996)** *Crime History and Histories of Crime: Studies in the Historiography of Crime and Criminal Justice in Modern History*, London: Greenwood Press.
- **FOUCAULT, M (1977)** *Discipline and Punish: The Birth of the Prison*, Harmondsworth: Penguin.
- **GELTNER, G (2008)** *The Medieval Prison: A Social History*, Princeton, NJ: Princeton University Press.
- **IGNATIEFF, M (1978)** *A Just Measure of Pain: The Penitentiary in the Industrial Revolution 1750–1850*, London: Macmillan.
- **McLENNAN, RM (2008)** *The Crisis of Imprisonment: Protest, Politics, and the making of the American Penal Estate, 1776–1941*, Cambridge: Cambridge University Press.
- **MORRIS, N and ROTHMAN, D (1998)** *The Oxford History of the Prison*, Oxford: Oxford University Press
- **RAWLINGS, P (1999)** *Crime and Power*, London: Longman.

- **ROTHMAN, DJ (1971)** *The Discovery of the Asylum*, Boston and Toronto: Little Brown.
- **RUSCHE, G and KIRCHHEIMER, O (1939; 2003)** *Punishment and Social Structure*, London: Transaction.
- **SCOTT, D (2007)** 'The Changing Face of the English Prison: A Critical Review of the Aims of Imprisonment', in Y Jewkes (ed.), *Handbook on Prisons*, Cullompton: Willan.
- **SHARPE, J (1990)** *Judicial Punishment in England*, London: Faber and Faber.
- **SMITH, P (2008)** *Punishment and Culture*, Chicago, IL: University of Chicago Press.
- **WIENER, MJ (1990)** *Reconstructing the Criminal: Culture, Law and Policy in England 1830–1914*, Cambridge: Cambridge University Press.

# 2.5 PENAL POLICY: UNTIL 2013

**Core areas**

managerialism: performance and privatisation
decency, moral performance and human rights
'making punishment work': nothing works, 'What Works', resettlement
pathways out of crime, a 'rehabilitation revolution'

**Running themes**

- Human rights
- Labour market
- Legitimacy
- Less eligibility
- Managerialism
- Rehabilitation
- Risk

Penal policies are influenced by political imperatives, practical cost and efficiency considerations, and also shaped by public opinion. But penal policy is not simply about public administration and management. Who we punish, how we punish, and how much we punish; why certain acts are criminalised and not others, and why it is we tend to punish the wrongdoing of some people but leave others alone, entails close consideration of the 'fairness' and 'justice' of punishment.

## MANAGERIALISM: PERFORMANCE AND PRIVATISATION

In 1993, the Prison Service became a 'next steps' agency of government and the role and aims of imprisonment were revised to be in tune with a now politically dominant 'managerialist' ethos.

> *Managerialism* promises autonomy, entrepreneurship and innovation, prioritising cost-effectiveness, service efficiency and value for money, while at the same time apparently guaranteeing quality services and products. Promising new flexible and responsive services that can better address the needs of service users, managerialism privileged new rational purposes, goals, mission statements and visions for the prison, and the promotion of new methods to enhance its performance. Under the guise of new public managerialism, the Prison Service developed strategic business plans and targets for monitoring achievement, and commissioned reviews and reports to measure progress and provide evidence of 'value for money'. Importantly, managerialism is framed through a preoccupation with organisational design that is pragmatic and orientated towards action and change: i.e. means rather than ends. Underscoring the logic of managerialism is the privileging of the consumer: the free, rational, empowered and self-disciplined, self-governing subject is morally responsible for the good or bad choices that he or she makes, and thus for minimising or maximising potential risks. When bad things happen, blame falls squarely on the 'flawed consumer's' shoulders. Further, consumers have only a certain set of entitlements and expectations that are detailed in compacts or contracts, as opposed to the rights and responsibilities of citizens.

## PERFORMANCE

A 'performance culture' was first introduced into the Prison Service in England and Wales in 1984. From 1993 onwards, managerial buzzwords and performance monitoring through key performance indicators (KPIs) and targets, managerial standards and internal audits have had a massive impact on Prison Service policies and practices, and have opened the door to market testing. Under the principles of 'new public managerialism' (NPM), the capitalist state is transformed from a provider of public services to a 'facilitator', 'purchaser' or 'commissioner' of services. Competition in the marketplace and privatisation are perceived as the spurs to innovation, cost effectiveness and value for (taxpayers') money. Through embracing a competitive ethos and new management techniques centring on 'ownership', 'visions' and 'mission statements', existing public sector services are expected to improve their performance significantly. This performance culture and its associated standards are rooted in the requirement of the government to be able to measure, monitor and audit public service outputs. If performance is poor, a private sector competitor can replace the current public service provider.

> *Criteria for successful performance revolve around 'the three e's':* economy, efficiency *and* effectiveness. *'Economy' refers to prioritising those methods that are most suited to obtaining the best possible results for the resources utilised. The 'holy grail' of 'efficiency' entails securing the maximum output of the organisation for the minimum resources expended. 'Effectiveness' refers to the compliance between organisational goals and actual outputs.*

NPM has been criticised on the following grounds:

- It simply measures outputs, rather than meets social objectives, outcomes or human needs.
- It is rooted in neoliberal political economy, which privileges privatisation and competition. Rather than inspire an increase in service levels, such an emphasis may, in fact, be divisive and reduce the quality of services.
- It provides the capitalist state with a new cloak of legitimacy, because blame for failure is now attributed to the service provider and not to the functioning of the state itself.

On coming to power in 1997, the 'New Labour' Government ensured that the *Prison Service Strategic Framework* (HM Prison Service, 1998) provided further elaboration of the role of the Prison Service—this time detailed through primary aims, objectives and principles.

---

### Benchmarking: measuring and improving performance

Since 2004, punishment has been administered in prisons and the community by the National Offender Management Service (NOMS), an executive agency of the Ministry of Justice (MoJ) which bridges the gap between the public and private sector by commissioning services from public and private sector organisations and partnerships. In line with an ideological shift in governance which has seen the rolling back of the state in public affairs in recent years, the corporate plan of the Prison Service has today been re-written to reaffirm the need to manage resources cost efficiently and effectively, including the commissioning of rehabilitation services to reduce reoffending from new private and voluntary sector partners. The purpose of the Prison Service is to serve 'the public by keeping in custody those committed by the courts. Our duty is to look after them with humanity and help them lead law-abiding and useful lives in custody and after release.'

NOMS' strategic direction, as set out in a MoJ Corporate Vision document (2011–15), is 'to deliver a transformed justice system and a transformed department more efficient, more effective, less costly and more accountable and responsive to the public' (MoJ, 2012b, p. 4).

---

### NOMS Operational Performance Measures (2011–12)

1 The percentage of orders and licences successfully completed.
2 The percentage of prisoners held in overcrowded accommodation across the prison system.
3 The rate of self-inflicted deaths per 100,000 prisoners.
4 The rate of drug misuse in prisons as reflected by those testing positive in mandatory drug tests.
5 The number of category A escapes.
6 The number of escapes from prison and prison escorts.
7 The rate of escapes from prison and prison escorts as a proportion of the average prison population.
8 The number of escapes from contractor escorts.
9 The rate of escapes from contractor escorts as a proportion of the throughput of prisoners.
10 The percentage of offenders in employment at the end of their sentence, order or licence.
11 The percentage of offenders in settled or suitable accommodation at the end of their sentence, order or licence.
12 The average number of working days lost through sickness absence in public prisons and probation trusts.
13 The proportion of black and minority ethnic staff in NOMS Agency.

(MoJ, 2012c)

---

Similar performance targets have been set for the Northern Ireland and Scottish Prison Services. Acknowledging recent criticisms of organisational weakness, including the release of prisoners in error, the Northern Ireland Prison Service has been the subject of over 20 external reviews and inspection reports and is currently undergoing a four-year period of reform. The vision of the Strategic Efficiency and Effectiveness (SEE) programme is that by 2015 the Northern Ireland Prison Service will:

- be well led and competently managed;
- have a fit, flexible, motivated, well trained, well rewarded staff;
- be compact and cost-effective;
- have the offender at the centre of its focus;

- reduce the risk of offenders reoffending on release;
- be respected and valued by the community we serve.

The *Scottish Prison Service Corporate Plan 2012–15* highlights that its operation objectives for the period will include:

- maintaining performance in relation to security and good order;
- maintaining safe and caring prisons;
- reducing access and use of drugs and alcohol;
- improving public protection through risk assessment and management;
- maximising benefits of the new partnership with the NHS;
- investing in the prison estate;
- maximising interventions, in particular for first time in custody offenders, young people in custody, women offenders, low-tariff persistent offenders;
- building on the lessons learned from the first fully community facing prison, HMP Grampian, when it opens in 2014;
- implementing standards for the management of sex offenders.

---

Every year NOMS publishes on its website an Annual Report and Accounts with data on penal performance against operational delivery and transformation priorities. This can be a source of more up-to-date information for your essays than that which is cited in textbooks. You can download the current aims, values and objectives of the prison services in England and Wales, Scotland and Northern Ireland or read their most recent annual reports and accounts at their websites:

- www.hmprisonservice.gov.uk
- www.niprisonservice.gov.uk
- www.sps.gov.uk

**TAKING IT FURTHER**

---

# PRIVATISATION

Privatisation occurs when government functions are systematically transferred to the private sector. There are three main ways in which privatisation has impacted on prisons:

- the delivery of services (escorts, catering, education and employment);
- the management of existing prisons;
- the design, construction, financing and management (DCFM) of new prisons.

Privatisation of criminal justice has a long history. The transportation system in which convicts were sold as indentured slaves to plantation owners in the Americas was the standard form of punishment for over 150 years; and from the Middle Ages until 1877, when prisons were nationalised, it was common for 'gaol keepers' to charge their captives for necessities such as fuel and clothing, and sometimes receive payment as 'bribes' for releasing them. The idea that the labour of prisoners would pay the costs of the prison system was also a core proposal of Bentham's Panopticon prison. For most of the twentieth century, however, prison privatisation received little political or commercial interest. That was to change in the 1990s. The privatisation of criminal justice services was reintroduced because of the:

- ideological commitment of the New Right to denationalisation;
- belief that privatisation and better management might solve the prisons' crises, particularly of overcrowding.

Initially, the proposal to privatise prisons met with strong ideological objection. In opposition, the former Labour Party Home Secretary, Jack Straw, stated that 'it is not appropriate for people to profit from incarceration. This is surely one area where a free market certainly does not exist' (*The Times*, 1995). However, after Labour gained power such ideological objections were quickly dispelled and, in practice at least, prison privatisation is now firmly established as a primary means of driving down costs and quickly building new prisons. The most prominent advocates of prison privatisation have been right and centre-right think tanks, e.g. The Adam Smith Institute and Reform. In a number of influential papers they have argued that private companies are able to provide services more cost efficiently, and are more innovative in design, delivery and management than the public sector.

Private prisons were established by the Conservative Party under the 1991 Criminal Justice Act and the Private Finance Initiative, which requires all public expenditure to be agreed only after the potential for private finance has been considered. The first prison to be privately managed in recent times, Wolds Remand Centre in Yorkshire, opened in April 1992. This paved the way for private security companies such as Group 4 and Securicor to play an increasing role in the running of prisons. Contracts have been awarded on the basis of 'market testing', which involves private companies competing with the Prison Service for existing prisons, and also the building and management of new prisons run by consortiums comprised of security and construction companies. The first newly constructed prisons—Altcourse prison in Liverpool, built by Tarmac and managed by Group 4, and HM Prison Parc in Bridgend, South Wales, built by Costain and managed by Securicor—opened in 1997. Since 1992, the return of some prisons to the Prison Service as well as commercial mergers and acquisitions have altered the governance of prison management. At the end of February 2013, there were 14 private prisons in England and Wales holding 13,076 prisoners (approximately 16 per cent of the prison population). In addition, there are four privately run Secure Training Centres holding juveniles up to the age of 17. Today, the prison market is dominated by three main 'penal entrepreneurs': G4S Justice Services, which runs six prisons; Serco Custodial Services, which runs five prisons; and Sodexo Justice Services, which runs three prisons.

A theme that has developed alongside the privatisation of criminal justice is that it is the *victim* who is the real customer of the correctional services (Home Office, 2004c). The New Labour Government intended to bring about a cultural change to improve customer services and reduce offending in the interests of victims. According to the then Prime Minister, Tony Blair:

> Sentencing will ensure the public is protected from the most dangerous and hardened criminals but will offer the rest the chance of rehabilitation ... This whole programme amounts to a modernising and rebalancing of the entire criminal justice system in favour of victims and the community.
>
> (2004, Foreword)

Very much supporting this, the present Coalition Government has recently published a new draft Code of Practice for Victims of Crime aimed at victims, agencies in the criminal justice system and all who work with victims of 'crime'. According to Helen Grant, Minister for Victims and the Courts, the new Code

> is designed to provide clarity for victims about their entitlements at each stage of their journey through the Criminal Justice System. It also clarifies the obligations upon Criminal Justice agencies to ensure people do get the entitlements they need.
>
> (MoJ, 2013b)

**Penal privatisation has, and continues to be, heavily criticised on both moral and political grounds**

1 It is immoral to make profits out of the pain of others.
2 Labour in private (and public) prisons is a form of penal slavery.
3 With the increased focus on efficiency, human needs are erased.
4 It is a smoke screen. It diverts attention away from the fundamental crisis of prison overcrowding.
5 It creates tensions and conflict between public and private sectors.
6 Market testing increases staff insecurity leading to poor morale.
7 Private prisons are less accountable than those in the public sector. More removed from democratic control, ultimately private companies are accountable to their share holders, not to government.
8 Profits can only be made by having either fewer, and poorly trained, staff or by providing inferior services.
9 Inferior conditions of employment in private prisons result in high levels of staff turnover, which can lead to poor quality services. A low staff-to-prisoner ratio also raises serious security and safety concerns.
10 Research undertaken to assess the relative strength of private compared to public prisons is inconclusive. Comparing like for like is difficult as publicly run prisons tend to be considerably older and suffer higher levels of overcrowding than new private prisons. Moreover, on grounds of 'commercial confidentiality', private companies frequently withhold important financial information necessary to make valid comparisons.
11 The profit motive results in greater pressure for penal expansion. Private companies have a vested interest in seeing prison populations rise and keeping people in prison for longer.
12 The probity of some of the companies involved has been questioned. In 1999, a previous player in the market, Wackenhut UK Ltd, was criticised for accounting malpractice and, as this is being written, G4S and Serco are being investigated by the Serious Fraud Office for overcharging, and Serco by the City of London police for alleged fraud. The private sector companies Serco and G4S are alleged to have charged the justice ministry millions of pounds for the tagging of offenders when tags had never been fitted or had been removed. This crisis reached a new pinnacle on 22 November 2013 when the Minister of Justice, **Chris Grayling**, was forced to cancel the **privatisation** of three South Yorkshire prisons (Hatfield, Moorland and Lindholme) because of the Serious Fraud Office investigation into **Serco**, who were the leading bidder to run the three jails.

*(Continued)*

> (Continued)
>
> Rather than adding to penal legitimacy, privatisation creates new problems in addition to the current crises that the penal system faces.

## Common pitfall

*The debate on penal privatisation is polarised. Ensure that you read sources from all of the different perspectives.*

# DECENCY, MORAL PERFORMANCE AND HUMAN RIGHTS

As a means of dealing with the penal crisis, including prison overcrowding, driving down reoffending rates and protecting the public, new public managerialism has become all-pervasive in penal policy during the last two decades. This has been criticised for promoting performance and cost cutting over procedural justice and well-being. Humanitarian penologists and practitioners have looked to counter the dehumanising aspects of managerialism in three ways:

- promoting decency;
- promoting moral performance;
- promoting human rights.

## DECENCY

The 'decency' agenda was initiated by Martin Narey (HM Prison Service Director General, 1999–2003) and his successor Phil Wheatley. Intended to safeguard the right of prisoners to be treated fairly and respectfully, it focuses on issues of accommodation, equal treatment, suicide prevention and 'constructive activities':

> The decency agenda is intended to run like a golden thread through all aspects of the service's work. Decency means treatment within the law, delivering promised standards, providing fit and proper facilities, giving prompt attention to prisoners concerns and protecting them from harm. It means providing prisoners with a regime that gives variety and helps them to rehabilitate. It means fair and consistent treatment by staff.

(HM Prison Service, 2003a, p. 29)

*Decency would appear to relate to the following:*

- **Physical conditions** *Decent living conditions, cleanliness, access to showers, and a safe, decent and healthy environment.*
- **Staff–prisoner relationships** *Officers treating prisoners as they would treat a family member or as they would like to be treated themselves; developing positive relationships; that prisoners should be treated with dignity and respect; use of language (i.e. serving meals, not 'feeding time') and calling prisoners by their first names.*
- **Legality** *Prisons are lawful and fair, and prisoners receive their legal entitlements.*
- **Anything questioning legitimacy** *Acknowledging institutional racism, prison officer brutality, responding to assaults and maintaining high standards of suicide prevention.*

*The problems with the decency agenda are:*

- *it has no clear definition—'it means all things to all people';*
- *it is nothing new—'old wine in new bottles';*
- *it is too general— it is not focused on the specific experiences of prisoners;*
- *it benefits from no powers of enforcement;*
- *it re-legitimises prison.*

## MORAL PERFORMANCE

The evaluative criteria of 'moral performance' are championed by liberal penologist Alison Liebling. She argues that there have been many positive changes in imprisonment following the rise of performance indicators, including a significant reduction in the suicide rate. Liebling argues that the managerialist agenda can be expanded by undertaking appreciative inquiries (AI) into prison life and by developing Measuring Quality of Prison Life (MQPL) surveys.

### Characteristics of moral performance

Alison Liebling (2004, pp. 154–5) identifies 'what matters' in the moral performance of prisons as:

*(Continued)*

*(Continued)*

- **Relationship dimensions** Respect; humanity; relationships; trust; support.
- **Regime dimensions** Fairness; order; safety; well-being; personal development; family contact; decency.
- **Social structure dimensions** Power; social life.
- **Individual items** Meaning; quality of life.

The idea of moral performance has, however, been criticised on the following grounds:

- the limits of the AI methodology;
- it is predicated on managerialism;
- it benefits from no legal compulsion;
- it works on the terrain of state discourses;
- it fails to connect with broader structural/socio-economic contexts;
- it re-legitimates prisons;
- prisons are profoundly immoral places.

# HUMAN RIGHTS

A third response has been to promote prisoners' human rights. This gained some momentum with the implementation of the Human Rights Act 1998 (HRA) in October 2000, which incorporated the European Convention on Human Rights into English law. Although there have been cases in which the courts have raised standards and improved conditions in prisons, on the whole courts have interpreted the HRA conservatively, while the Prison Service has largely ignored it and given staff little training on it. When the HRA has been discussed in official documents, the Service has outlined how it believes current policies are 'ECHR [European Convention on Human Rights]-proof', vigorously defended them, or emphasised the importance of responsibilities:

> The Government's objective is to promote a culture of rights and responsibilities throughout our society. The Act will make people *more aware of the rights they already have* but also balance these with responsibilities to others.
>
> (HM Prison Service, 2000, p. 1, emphasis added)

The Prison Service has also tended to rely on measures which are not legally enforceable, such as in-house prisoner complaints procedures and the Prisons Ombudsman. The promotion of human rights remains an underdeveloped response to managerial forms of penal performance.

# 'MAKING PUNISHMENT WORK': NOTHING WORKS, 'WHAT WORKS', RESETTLEMENT PATHWAYS OUT OF CRIME, A 'REHABILITATION REVOLUTION'

## NOTHING WORKS

Over the past seventy years, there have been a number of significant and broadly contradictory political changes in penal policy direction. As referred to in the previous chapter, throughout the 1950s and 1960s, a general faith in 'rehabilitation' justified the use of imprisonment on the grounds that prisons were constructive, beneficial places where offenders could be 'diagnosed', 'treated' and 'cured' before returning to the community as productive, law-abiding citizens. However, in the 1970s this sense of penal optimism was challenged by research which found that treatment programmes for offenders were ineffective. Based on the analysis of 231 studies published in the US between 1945 and 1967, it was concluded that 'with few and isolated exceptions, the rehabilitative efforts that have been reported so far have had no appreciable effect on recidivism' (Martinson, 1974, p.25). In fact, the author of the research, Robert Martinson, was circumspect about the implications of the research, suggesting 'it is just possible that some of our treatment programs are working to some extent, but that our research is so bad that we are incapable of telling' (p. 51). Nonetheless, allied to arguments from the political Right that rehabilitation excused criminal behaviour and denied individual responsibility, and political Left that offenders were being pathologised as objects of treatment, the 'nothing works' research, as it came to be known, led to a general sense of despair regarding the reforming potential of imprisonment.

Throughout the 1980s, prisoner rehabilitation was viewed as limited, even counterproductive. Rather than change offenders for the better, the Home Office White Paper *Crime, Justice and Protecting the Public* (1990) described incarceration as an 'expensive way of making bad people worse' (p. 6). The Conservative Government of the day was committed to penal reduction, and the Criminal Justice Act 1991 enshrined the principles of just deserts: that punishment in prisons should be restricted to serious (i.e. violent and sexual) offences and proportionality and determinancy should replace individualised and indeterminate sentencing. Offenders would receive a custodial sentence only if the current offence (previous offences did not qualify) was too serious for a community sentence. Much of the success in containing and reducing prison populations has been attributed to Douglas Hurd, Conservative Home Secretary during the late 1980s. But in 1993, the political landscape changed again when the then Conservative Home Secretary, Michael Howard, argued that prisons 'worked' in terms of incapacitation and deterrence. The Home Office White Paper *Protecting the Public: The Government's Strategy on Crime in England and Wales* (1996) stated simply that 'the Government firmly believes that prison works' (p. 4). Howard advocated increased security, 'decent but austere' regimes and a return to less eligibility.

## Common pitfall

*There are a number of Criminal Justice Acts and laws relating to prisons, probation and sentencing. Ensure that you always check for recent changes to legislation and government White Papers.*

The role of prisons to incapacitate and deter crime received further support with the election of the 'New' Labour Government, albeit with a shift in policy emphasis. The intention now was to *make* prisons work. In 1997, Jack Straw, the first New Labour Home Secretary, made a commitment to constructive prison regimes, stating 'we believe prisons can be made to work as one element in a radical and coherent strategy to protect the public by reducing crime' (Prison Reform Trust, 1998, p. 19). A little later, Lord Justice Woolf (2002, p. 6) argued that '[al]though prison remains very expensive … I now believe that it can be an expensive way of making people better'.

### New penal credo

At the time, Alison Liebling (2004) argued that we have seen the emergence of a *'new penal credo'* (p. 35) centred on the following:

- protection of public as key ideology;
- links with other agencies to maximise effectiveness;
- best value from resources;
- standards for all aspects of work;
- regimes and programmes subject to accreditation;
- reducing reoffending as the key outcome.

The most significant policy document on prisons under the New Labour Government was the Halliday Report, *Making Punishments Work* (2001). The Report called for the virtual abolition of short-term sentences and the end to the proportionality principle that underscored the Criminal Justice Act 1991.

> *Halliday argued that, instead, sentences should reflect previous convictions. This focus was underscored by the unsubstantiated claim that 50 per cent of all 'crimes' were committed by a hard core of 100,000 persistent offenders. In ignoring 'crimes' committed by others such as 'white collar' offenders, this **persistence principle** for sentencing tended to criminalise poor and petty property offenders, and led to greater discrimination in the penal system.*

Halliday advocated that intensive efforts should be made to reduce reoffending by persistent offenders through 'intrusive and punitive sentences'. The opportunity to protect the public would be pursued within an 'appropriate punitive envelope'. He proposed a twin-track approach, distinguishing between tough measures for serious and dangerous offenders, and lenient approaches for ordinary offenders. This 'bifurcated' strategy revisited the debates on policy of the 1970s and 1980s (see, for example, Bottoms, 1977; Hudson, 1993). Halliday also proposed a new generic 'community punishment order' and the need for improved co-operation between criminal justice agencies. The government accepted these proposals in the 2002 White Paper *Justice for All* and the subsequent Criminal Justice Act 2003.

---

### Criminal Justice Act 2003

- Diverts very low-risk offenders out of the court system and punishes them in the community.
- Provides for income-related fines for low-risk offenders.
- Demands community sentences for medium-risk offenders.
- Establishes greater control and surveillance (including satellite tracking) of persistent offenders, combined with help to reduce reoffending.
- Under *Custody plus*, offenders are sentenced to a short spell in prison, followed by a longer period of supervision in the community.
- Under *Custody minus*, offenders who fail to undertake a community punishment are imprisoned.

---

The fulfilment of the changes brought about by the Halliday Report and the Criminal Justice Act 2003 required major organisational changes to the national probation and prison services. The government duly published the Carter Review, *Managing Offenders, Reducing Crime: A New Approach,* on 6 January 2004. Carter promoted rehabilitation through accredited 'What Works' programmes and argued that, for this to be effective, the 'silos' between the 'correctional' services had to be broken down. This was to be done by creating an umbrella organisation that could provide the case management of offenders 'seamlessly' from prison to after release in the community. Without consultation, the government published *Reducing Crime, Changing Lives: The Government's Plans for Transforming the Management of Offenders* (Home Office, 2004a) which introduced NOMS in June 2004.

---

**Improving the way offenders are managed in both custody and the community**

NOMS brings prisons and probation together into one unified service. Its primary aims are to reduce reoffending and protect the public through risk assessment and effective supervision. Ten directors of Offender Management (DOMs) are responsible for commissioning services regionally in prisons and the community, including rehabilitation, from various providers in the market. This principle of 'contestability', in effect, privatises the rehabilitation of offenders. NOMS is rooted in the principles that better management and interagency co-operation will lead to the greater responsibilisation of offenders. It also adheres to the belief that prison is a 'special place' in which we can both punish and rehabilitate serious criminals. NOMS has been heavily criticised. Shortly after its introduction, one undisclosed informant told *The Guardian* 'it's like putting a goat in charge of an orchard' (23 June 2005), while one senior Home Office civil servant suggested that NOMS might really stand for 'Nightmare on Marsham Street' (ibid.). NOMS has undergone significant management restructure, but a contentious issue remains the balance of priority accorded to prisons and probation, and the relationship between them—with the role of probation in NOMS being undefined and subject to continuous change.

---

## 'WHAT WORKS'

Under New Labour, properly managed prisons were seen as an opportunity to responsibilise offenders and reduce the risk of reoffending. Similar themes continue to guide the political ideology of the present Coalition

Government. A sentence of imprisonment is expected to transform serious and persistent offenders by improving their life skills and addressing the drivers that can trigger 'crime'. Prisoners should be given opportunities to make choices that help them learn how to behave responsibly. This responsibilisation process is managed and integrated with other criminal justice agencies and punishments in the community. Reducing the risk of reoffending is tied to the 'What Works' rehabilitative agenda.

Towards the end of the 1970s, research was published which questioned the 'nothing works' consensus. Canadian psychologists schooled in social learning theory argued there was no reason offenders should not be capable of acquiring new attitudes and behaviours just like everyone else. They found that rehabilitation programmes do 'work', especially those that target 'criminogenic needs' such as anti-social attitudes. Based on an understanding that offenders lack or have poorly developed thinking skills (Ross and Fabiano, 1985), 'What Works' roots the causes of offending behaviour in each individual offender's cognitive defects. Programmes are based on a model of effective practice which emphasises that offender rehabilitation should adhere to the following principles:

---

**'What Works'**

- *Classifying risk* so that more intensive programmes are targeted at the higest risk offenders.
- Targeting of *criminogenic needs* that directly support offending.
- *Responding* to offenders' specific learning styles.
- Developing *treatment modality*, including social interaction and cognitive-behavioural skills.
- Being *community based*.
- Maintaining high *programme integrity.*

---

Although it is accepted that 'What Works' community programmes are the most effective, there are a number of accredited 'What Works' programmes in prison, including:

- Reasoning and rehabilitation (R&R)
- Enhanced thinking skills (ETS)
- Making offenders rethink everything (MORE)
- Controlling anger and learning to manage it (CALM)
- Cognitive self-change programme (CSCP)
- Sex offender treatment programmes (SOTPs, of which there are six).

'What Works' rehabilitation has been criticised for being theoretically limited (Ward and Maruna, 2007). Moreover, in terms of practice, as well as implementation problems and methodological constraints, evaluations of 'What Works' rehabilitation have revealed only mixed results (see Harper and Chitty, 2005). Critics have claimed that 'What Works' rehabilitative programmes are epistemologically flawed because 'What Works':

- individualises and pathologises offenders;
- 'others' prisoners as cognitively different;
- demands choice, agency and acting responsibly, all of which, in the prison setting, are virtually non-existent;
- ignores processes of behaviour change which occur irrespective of formal treatment;
- privileges rehabilitation so that, if it fails or is rejected, it is the individual's fault because of his or her own inadequacies;
- leads to further individualisation or redefinition as 'dangerousness' and therefore untreatable;
- focuses on self-governance, and ignores wider social contexts and divisions (such as poverty), doing nothing to change such problematic social circumstances;
- assumes treatment is compatible with a punitive framework of security, control and punishment;
- predicates and justifies improved conditions on reducing offending;
- adds penal legitimacy through the humane cloak of rehabilitation.

## Common pitfall

*Do not confuse 'What Works' with 'prison works'. Both ideologies argue that prison has a utility, but each focuses on very different philosophical justifications.*

## RESETTLEMENT PATHWAYS OUT OF CRIME

Irrespective of the changes in policy emphasis, a consistent role of the Prison Service in recent years has been to reduce reoffending. In this regard, the Social Exclusion Unit Report *Reducing Reoffending by Ex-Prisoners* (2002) recognised the importance of a number of key factors involved in resettlement. These included truancy, unemployment, illicit substance misuse, health, debt, homelessness, social capital and family problems.

**Offender Pathways**

Subsequently, the Home Office's *Reducing Reoffending: National Action Plan* (2004b) identified a number of 'resettlement pathways' out of crime, relating to the following factors:

- Pathway 1 Accommodation
- Pathway 2 Education, training and employment
- Pathway 3 Mental and physical health
- Pathway 4 Drugs and alcohol
- Pathway 5 Finance, benefit and debt
- Pathway 6 Children and the families of offenders
- Pathway 7 Attitudes, thinking and behaviour

Satisfactory accommodation and work outcomes are considered requisites for successful resettlement. However, despite acceptance of these problems and the multiple interventions necessary to address them, little has been achieved to help prisoners secure accommodation and employment after release. Finding adequate accommodation is dependent on finance and the willingness of landlords to accept released prisoners as tenants, while most work and vocational training provided in prisons does not fit the demands of local labour markets.

# A 'REHABILITATION REVOLUTION'

Since coming to power in May 2010, the present Coalition Government has prioritised reform of the criminal justice system, focusing specifically on punishment, sentencing and rehabilitation. Proposals to 'make punishments work' were presented in the Government Green Paper, *Breaking the Cycle: Effective Punishment, Rehabilitation and Sentencing of Offenders* (MoJ, 2010). Promoted by Ministers as a revolutionary programme of criminal justice reform, a number of proposals relate directly to prisons. A current proposal is to re-roll 70 existing adult male local, training and open prisons as community 'resettlement prisons' in which prisoners will be held close to their homes and engage in 'purposeful activities' to prepare for release. Resettlement prisons are not a new idea. In recent years, three specially designated resettlement prisons, Blantyre House, Kirklevington Grange and Latchmere House have accommodated mostly long-term prisoners re-categorised as suitable for open or semi-open prison conditions so they may prepare for release. A doubt, however, is whether resettlement services, including employment, housing, drug and mental health support, can be provided within a prison system which continues to suffer overcrowding. Another proposal is to train prisoners in 'real working conditions' for up to 40 hours per week. Existing non-commercial work undertaken for the internal prison market is to be supplemented by commercial work undertaken by private business for a profit. The financial advantages of 'working prisons' are relatively straightforward. Prison governors will receive additional revenue and the overall costs of imprisonment will be reduced. Furthermore, deductions from prisoner wages may be used to recompense victims for crimes committed against them. Yet the challenges to overcome are considerable:

- The wider public interest must be served by ensuring that prisoners are paid reasonable wages for the work undertaken.
- Measures must be taken to guard against the removal of existing and potential jobs from local labour markets, and for local wages to be undermined in those industries and professions which are suitable to the skill levels of prisoners.
- There are significant costs of setting up and managing work in overcrowded and poor quality prison conditions. The financial advantages to private companies of investing in prison work are by no means certain.
- It is estimated that working prisons will reduce the £13 billion per year costs of recorded crime committed by prisoners after release (National Audit Office, 2010). This will not be achieved unless prison work leads to 'real' jobs of sufficient quality in the community.
- Prison environments and conditions are incompatible with the commercial demands of private business. For example, a social enterprise set up in Coldingley prison in 2005 ended in 2008 because the 'prison ethos and prison rules made securing the profitability of the business ultimately impossible' (Howard League for Penal Reform, 2010).

## "Given the damage being held in prison can cause to offenders and the problems of poverty and social exclusion they face on release, can 'What Works' rehabilitation programmes ever be successful?"

To answer this you need to consider physical and social circumstances internal to prison and also to the wider society. 'What Works' rehabilitation is founded on strategies of risk management and cognitive therapy. Are there human needs not addressed by this agenda? Would cognitive therapy for offenders even be necessary if the social and economic causes of 'crime' were attended to?

## "Is the Prison Service committed to treating prisoners with dignity and respect?"

You need to consider the main Prison Service statements on dignity and respect and whether in practice they have improved prisons since they were introduced. You must also consider what else needs to be done. This will include a discussion of 'decency', the aims of the Prison Service and its statement of purpose, and other policy initiatives such as those focusing on race relations. You should also consider the manner in which the Prison Service has defined prisoner human rights.

---

**TAKING IT FURTHER**

### Economic considerations and the future of prisons and punishment

Governments persuaded by managerialism consider the problems of imprisonment to be located within the prison system itself. Overcrowding, under-staffing, poor security, prisoner disturbances and decrepit environments are addressed through the implementation of new, more efficient systems of prison governance. Within this, meeting the rising costs of imprisonment is a primary guiding factor. Savings made elsewhere, as well as new streams of private capital, increasingly are required to finance existing prison services.

A more radical solution is to use cheaper community alternatives to prison (Scull, 1977). More so than ever, the current economic climate requires that cost efficient decarceration measures are explored (Fox and Albertson, 2010). A current application of economic thinking to penal policy is Justice Reinvestment (JR), an initiative which aims to divert offenders away from custody in order to reduce the cost demands on courts, prisons and probation. As originally advanced in the US, the case for JR is that it frees up funding to help local communities reduce the economic and social deprivation thought to give rise to 'crime' in the first place (Tucker and Cadora, 2003). However, rather than invest in employment, health, education and housing, savings accrued from diverting offenders from custody through JR in the UK to date have been used to fund 'administrative' crime prevention initiatives, including CCTV (Flynn, 2010).

---

# BIBLIOGRAPHY

Any assessment of penal policy is likely to cover a wide range of themes and issues. For an overview of the themes and issues covered in this chapter see:

- **CAVADINO, M, DIGNAN, J and MAIR, G (2013)** *The Penal System: An Introduction*, 5th edn, London: Sage.
- **EASTON, S and PIPER, C (2008)** *Sentencing and Punishment: The Quest for Justice*, 2nd edn, Oxford: Oxford University Press.
- **FITZGERALD, M and SIM, J (1982)** *British Prisons*, 2nd edn, Oxford: Blackwell.
- **JEWKES, Y (ed.) (2007)** *Handbook of Prisons*, Cullompton: Willan.
- **SIM, J (2009**) *Punishment and Prisons: Power and the Carceral State*, London: Sage.

Ideas and principles of new public management are covered in:

- **CLARKE, J and NEWMAN, J (1997)** *The Managerial State: Power Politics and Ideology in the Remaking of Social Welfare*, London: Sage.
- **OSBORNE, SP (ed.) (2010)** *The New Public Governance? Emerging Perspectives on the Theory and Practice of Public Governance*, Abingdon: Routledge.

How the ideas and principles of new public management have impacted on penal policy is described in:

- **HELYAR-CARDWELL, V (ed.) (2012)** *Delivering Justice: The Role of the Public, Private and Voluntary Sectors in Prisons and Probation*, London: Criminal Justice Alliance.
- **McLAUGHLIN, E, MUNCIE, J and HUGHES, G (2001)** 'The Permanent Revolution: New Labour, New Public Management and the Modernisation of Criminal Justice', *Criminology and Criminal Justice*, 1, pp. 301–18.
- **RYAN, M (2005)** *Penal Policy and Political Culture*, Winchester: Waterside Press.

For a critical discussion of criminal justice privatisation see:

- **FEELEY, M (2002)** 'Entrepreneurs of Punishment: The legacy of privatisation', *Punishment and Society*, 4(3), pp. 321–44.
- **GENDERS, E and PLAYER, E (2007)** 'The Commercial Context of Criminal Justice: Prison Privatisation and the Perversion of Purpose', *Criminal Law Review*, pp. 513–29.

- **HARDING, R (1997)** *Private Prisons and Public Accountability*, Milton Keynes: Open University Press.
- **JAMES, AL, BOTTOMLEY, AK, LIEBLING, A and CLARE, E (1997)** *Privatising Prisons: Rhetoric and Reality*, London: Sage.
- **PRISON REFORM TRUST (2005)** *Private Punishment: Who Profits?* London: Prison Reform Trust.
- **RYAN, M and WARD, T (1989)** *Privatization and the Penal System*, Milton Keynes: Open University Press.
- **SHEFER, G and LIEBLING, A (2008)** 'Prison Privatisation: In Search of a Business-like Atmosphere?', *Criminology and Criminal Justice*, 8(3), pp. 261–78.
- **SHICHOR, D (1995)** *Punishment for Profit: Private Prisons/Public Concerns*, London: Sage.

The moral performance agenda is described in:

- **LIEBLING, A (2004)** *Prisons and their Moral Performance*, Oxford: Oxford University Press.

# 2.6 PENAL ADMINISTRATION AND PRISONER POPULATIONS

**Core areas**

the structure of the penal administration in England and Wales
the penal estate
recent and current prison populations
locking up the dangerous or punishing the poor?
prisons and prisoners in Northern Ireland and Scotland

**Running themes**

- Human rights
- Legitimacy
- Less eligibility
- Managerialism
- Pains of imprisonment
- Power to punish
- Public protection
- Social divisions

## THE STRUCTURE OF THE PENAL ADMINISTRATION IN ENGLAND AND WALES

On 9 May 2007, responsibility for prisons, probation and sentencing was moved from the Home Office to the Department of Constitutional

Affairs, which was renamed the Ministry of Justice (MoJ). Before May 2007, the Home Office was the main government body for penal administration. It continues to exist, but is now more focused on security. Lord Falconer of Thoroton was originally appointed to the new combined position of Secretary of State for Justice and Lord Chancellor, and the present Justice Secretary and Lord Chancellor is the Rt Hon Chris Grayling.

---

**The core components of the Ministry of Justice**

- The National Offender Management Service
- The Youth Justice Board
- The Parole Board, HM Inspectorates of Prison and Probation, Independent Monitoring Boards, and the Prison and Probation Ombudsman
- The Sentencing Guidelines Council
- The Office for Criminal Justice Reform
- HM Courts Service—administration of the civil, family and criminal courts in England and Wales

---

The National Offender Management Service (NOMS) deals with the delivery of prison and probation services and commissions offender services from a range of providers in the public and private sectors. The current Chief Executive Officer of NOMS is Michael Spurr, and he chairs the NOMS board, which includes a Director of Public Sector Prisons, a Director of Operational Services, and a Director of Probation and Contracted Services.

The business priorities for NOMS (2012–13) are:

1 Rehabilitation – 'Breaking the Cycle'

2 Re-balancing capacity

3 Commissioning and Competition

4 Organisational Restructure

5 Delivering the punishment and orders of the courts

6 Security, safety and public protection

7 Reducing reoffending

8 Improving efficiency and reducing costs

The HM Prison Service 'statement of purpose' reads:

> Her Majesty's Prison Service serves the public by keeping in custody those committed by the courts. Our duty is to look after them with humanity and help them lead law-abiding and useful lives in custody and after release.

The main aims and priorities for prisons are:

- ensuring that public sector prisons remain safe, secure and decent;
- responding to competition by delivering effective and efficient service level agreements with the Agency;
- developing innovative models of public sector delivery to respond to competition and the payment by results model;
- making prisons place of hard, meaningful work by introducing more work that contributes to paying back victims;
- making prisons drug-free and getting prisoners off drugs for good;
- working to reduce reoffending by creating effective partnerships with providers and other agencies in the public, private and community sectors.

# THE PENAL ESTATE

In 2013, there were 133 prisons in England and Wales. The average annual cost of a prison place for the financial year 2011–12 was £37,648 (£724 per week). Adult prisoners, young offenders and children are held separately. Custodial places for offenders under the age of 18 are commissioned by the Youth Justice Board for England and

Wales (YJB). Young offenders are held in three types of accommodation. Currently there are four privately run Secure Training Centres (STCs) for children aged 12–17; 17 Local Authority run Secure Children's Homes (SCHs) for children aged 10–17; and 11 Young Offender Institutions (YOIs) for offenders aged 15–17. The adult prison estate consists of:

- local prisons for remand prisoners (held in category B conditions);
- training prisons (including both category B and C prisoners);
- high-security prisons (formerly known as 'dispersal prisons') holding both category A and B prisoners;
- open or semi-open prisons (category D prisoners);
- women's prisons (including closed, semi-open and open prisons).

The number of remand prisoners has fallen in recent years, partly owing to restrictions in remand introduced by the Legal Aid Sentencing and Punishment of Offenders Act (2012). In March 2013, around 13 per cent of prisoners were remanded to custody and the average length of time currently spent on remand is two months. It is worth noting that many people on remand do not receive custodial sentences at trial. In the 12 months ending September 2012, only 15 per cent of defendants remanded to custody went on to receive a custodial sentence at magistrates' court, while at crown court 12 per cent were acquitted or not proceeded against. There are also a small number of civil prisoners. These are people who have not broken the criminal law, but have breached procedural rules such as 'contempt of court'.

---

**Who works in prisons?**

The officers of a prison are:

- prison governors (grades 1–5 and governing governor who set budgets);
- prison medical teams (comprising GPs, registered nurses, registered mental health nurses, psychiatrists, pharmacists, dentists, opticians, physiotherapists etc.);
- prison chaplains.

*(Continued)*

*(Continued)*

Other members of prison staff include:

- prison officers, senior prison officers, principal prison officers;
- suicide awareness co-ordinators;
- probation officers;
- psychologists;
- educational (teachers);
- resettlement staff;
- drug workers;
- counselling, assessment, referral, advice and throughcare (CARAT) workers;
- instructors (works unit, physical instructors, farms);
- operational grade support (work on the gate);
- administration (civil servants).

# RECENT AND CURRENT PRISON POPULATIONS

The prison population in England and Wales has doubled since 1993, increasing on average each year by 3.6 per cent. In September 2005, Charles Clarke, then Labour Home Secretary, announced that the government had abandoned its target of keeping the upper limits of the prison population at around 80,000. In December 2011 the prison population reached a new record high of over 88,000 prisoners and from December 2012 it has stabilised at around 84,000, falling by 2,471 (2.9 per cent) over the past 12 months. The reduction in numbers mostly comprises remand and sentenced young offenders. The number of remand prisoners fell by 12 per cent in 2012, the number of young adults aged 18–20 by 15 per cent over the year 2011–12, and the number of children in custody has fallen by over 50 per cent in the last five years. The fall in the number of children in custody is explained, in part, by the introduction of more cost efficient informal criminal justice responses being developed by local authorities (Allen, 2011). As much as this has been welcomed by penal reform groups, it remains troubling that the fall in numbers of white children in custody (37 per cent) outweighs that for black and minority ethnic children (16 per cent). Moreover, the reduction in remand and sentenced young offenders does not reflect overall trends. Projections for the next few years are uncertain. According to the MoJ, by June 2018 the prison population is estimated either to keep on falling to 80,300 or rise to 90,900. Prisoner population figures for July 2013 are presented in Table 2.6.1.

**Table 2.6.1 Prisoner population in England and Wales on 12 July 2013**

| | |
|---|---|
| Male | 80,227 |
| Female | 3,864 |
| **TOTAL** | **84,091** |
| Useable operational capacity | 87,764 |
| Certified normal accommodation | 78,430 |
| Number under Home Detention Curfew supervision | 2,430 |

*Source:* Ministry of Justice, 2013e

Prisoner population figures are considered in relation to the physical capacity of the prison estate to accommodate them. This is done in two ways. The *useable operational capacity* of a prison is the maximum safe limit in terms of control, security and the proper operation of the regime; the sum of the prison estates operational capacity is less than 2,000 places (known as the 'operating margin'). At the end of May 2013 one prison, Swansea, exceeded its operational capacity. A prison is considered over-crowded when the number of prisoners held exceeds its *certified normal accommodation* (CNA). The CNA is the Prison Service's own measure of how many prisoners can be held in decent standards of accommodation. Some prisons suffer the effects of overcrowding more than others. At the end of May 2013, 72 prisons in England and Wales (57 per cent of the estate) were overcrowded. In nine of these, the population was at least 150 per cent of the CNA figure (MoJ, 2013f). Table 2.6.2 presents the figures for the five most overcrowded prisons in July 2013.

**Table 2.6.2 Five most overcrowded prisons in England and Wales on 12 July 2013**

| Prison | Population | No. over CNA | % over CNA |
|---|---|---|---|
| Swansea | 442 | 202 | 184% |
| Wandsworth | 1226 | 496 | 168% |
| Dorchester | 252 | 100 | 166% |
| Leicester | 341 | 131 | 162% |
| Northallerton | 236 | 90 | 162% |

*Source:* Ministry of Justice, 2013g

---

**Prison data snapshots**

These four dates and sets of prisoner figures are worth remembering:

- *December 1992: 40,600 prisoners* The lowest recorded rate of prisoners in recent times.
- *May 1997: 60,131 prisoners* The number of prisoners when the New Labour Government was elected.
- *14 May 2010: 85,009 prisoners* The number of prisoners during the week in which the present Coalition Government was formed.
- *December 2011: current record high of 88,179 reached* Due to the remanding and sentencing of people alleged to have been involved in the city riots which took place in England over August 2011.

(Home Office/MoJ PopulationStatistics)

---

The majority of prisoners serve sentences of less than four years. Women serve far shorter sentences than men. In the year ending 2012, 59 per cent of sentenced women were serving sentences of six months or less. In 2011, the average time served by prisoners serving determinate sentences was 9.5 months. At 31 March 2013, over one-third of the total sentenced prison population were serving determinate sentences of more than four years, with a further one-fifth serving indeterminate sentences (life sentences and indeterminate sentences for public protection— 'imprisonment for public protection' or IPPs).

An effect of increasing sentence lengths has been a rise in the number of older prisoners. People aged 60 and over are now the fastest growing age group in prisons. Over the past year, the number of prisoners in most age groups has fallen, with the exception of prisoners aged over 50, which increased by 5.5 per cent, exceeding 10,000 for the first time. Prisoners aged 60 and over have increased by 103 per cent since 2002.

The most recent figures show that at any one time, approximately 30 per cent of prisoners are convicted of offences related to fraud, theft, burglary or robbery. About 15 per cent of prisoners are convicted of drug offences, which are often linked to property offences, 15 per cent of sexual offences, and 28 per cent of violent offences. The number of people serving sentences for violence against the person, drug-related offences and sex offences have all increased steadily since 1993. Although the number of women serving sentences for violence has also increased, the majority of women prisoners are serving sentences for non-violent offences such as theft and handling stolen goods. (MoJ, 2012d)

## Common pitfall

*Examining the average daily population (ADP) alone can give you a distorted perception. The number of people in various different forms of custody in the UK is much higher than the official statistics suggest, as can be seen from the statistics for individual prisons presented above.*

As previously explained, there is not a direct correlation between levels of crime and fluctuations in prison populations. The rise in prison populations is a political and policy choice, not a response to the official 'crime' rate. Over the time the prison population has increased, the official 'crime' rate has declined.

*According to the official 'crime' statistics and the British Crime Survey (BCS), most 'crimes' are actually going down.*

British Crime Survey (BCS) figures have been on a downward trend since 1995, after a long upward trend since 1981. In May 2013, it was reported that incidents of 'crime' are now 53 per cent lower than they were in 1995, and 19 per cent lower than in 2006/07. Police-recorded figures have also fallen over the same period, with 'crime' levels now 14 per cent lower than in 2007/8, and 38 per cent lower than in 2002/3 (Office for National Statistics, July, 2013).

Only a very small number of reported or recorded crimes end up being processed by the criminal justice system, and only a fraction of these lead to a conviction and to custody. Criminal statistics for 2011 show that of 4,150,097 recorded crimes, just 90,738 (2 per cent) led to a prison reception. This is limited data. Nevertheless, given that politicians often present such figures as accurate and reliable accounts, the decline in 'crime' at the same time as prison populations have increased is significant.

*There are a number of reasons why the prison population has increased over the past two decades, including:*

- longer prison sentences;
- increase in immediate custody rates for indictable offences;
- more people on remand;
- increasing use of determinate sentences of four years or more;
- increase in the number of people serving mandatory life sentences and indeterminate sentences for public protection;
- the collapse of the fine;
- the reduced use of the Home Detention Curfew;
- increasing risk aversion on behalf of parole boards;
- more recalls of people for failure to comply with licence conditions and breaches of community sentences;
- the external pressures of a law and order society that uses punitive rhetoric to exploit people's fears and anxieties to gain political ascendancy;
- internal pressures and the expectations of professionals.

An enduring feature of imprisonment is that recidivism rates for ex-prisoners remain high. In 2013, the MoJ reported that 47 per cent of adults are reconvicted within one year of being released, a figure which increases to 58 per cent for prisoners who have served sentences of less that 12 months. For offenders under the age of 18, the figure is 73 per cent, and for women it is 45 per cent. (MoJ, 2013a)

# LOCKING UP THE DANGEROUS OR PUNISHING THE POOR?

Although we often hear arguments that we punish the dangerous for reasons of public protection, when we look at the facts of who is imprisoned and their social backgrounds, a different picture begins to emerge.

**Prisoner data (at 31 March 2013)**

- Population: 83,769
- Remand population: 10,768
- Male prisoners: 79,900

*(Continued)*

*(Continued)*

- Female prisoners: 3,869
- Age: 34,944 under the age of 30
- Black, Asian and minority ethnic people: 21,462
- Foreign nationals: 10,725

(MoJ, 2013h)

Prisoners are predominately working class. Coming from socially deprived family circumstances and backgrounds, they are more likely to be harmed individuals than seriously dangerous to society.

### Social backgrounds of prison populations (Social Exclusion Unit, 2002)

1  Have been in care or have family difficulties:

- 27 per cent in care as child;
- two-and-a-half times as likely to have had a family member convicted of a criminal offence.

2  Are unemployed or on benefits:

- 5 per cent of general population unemployed, but 67 per cent of prisoners have been unemployed during the four weeks before imprisonment;
- 13.7 per cent of working-age population are in receipt of benefits, but 72 per cent have been in receipt of benefits immediately before entry to prison;
- 75 per cent of prisoners do not have paid employment to go to on release.

3  Homeless:

- 1 in 14 prisoners are homeless at the time of imprisonment;
- 32 per cent of prisoners are not living in permanent accommodation prior to imprisonment.

4  No education:

- 80 per cent have writing skills, 65 per cent have numeracy skills and 50 per cent have reading skills at, or below, the level of an 11-year-old child;

*(Continued)*

*(Continued)*

- 52 per cent of male and 71 per cent of female adult prisoners have no qualifications at all.

5  In poor health:

- 80 per cent of prisoners have mental health problems;
- 46 per cent of sentenced adult male prisoners aged 18–49 reported having a long-standing illness or disability;
- 15 times as likely to be HIV positive;
- 60–70 per cent of prisoners were using drugs before imprisonment.

# YOUNG PEOPLE IN CUSTODY

Children who are criminalised and penalised are generally from vulnerable backgrounds. Rather than presenting a threat to adults, children in secure custody have, more often than not, been harmed by adults. Many children in custody have experienced difficult family relationships, impoverished social backgrounds and have difficulties in coping with the problems with which they are confronted in life. To add to these problems, they are taken away from what is familiar to them and placed in an unfriendly, stigmatising and physically austere environment, which may be overcrowded and which is rooted in conflict, power struggles and bullying. For penal commentators such as Barry Goldson and Debs Coles, such a deliberately painful state of affairs has, quite rightly, been described as 'institutional child abuse' and these critics have called for the abolition of secure custody for children.

### Social backgrounds of children and young people in custody

- 27 per cent of boys and 55 per cent of girls have spent time in care.
- The prevalence of mental health problems for young people in contact with the criminal justice system ranges from 25–81 per cent, being highest for those in custody
- 39 per cent of girls and 34 per cent of boys have a problem with drugs.
- Two out of five girls and a quarter of boys have suffered violence at home.
- 40 per cent have previously been homeless.

*(Continued)*

> (Continued)
>
> - 86 per cent of boys and 82 per cent of girls had been excluded from school.
> - 23 per cent have learning difficulties.
>
> **Recidivism rates**
>
> 73 per cent of children aged 10–17 and 58 per cent of young adults (18–20) are reconvicted within a year of release from custody.

## BLACK AND MINORITY ETHNIC PRISONERS

Imprisonment, detention and immigration policies must be understood within the context of state racism. This analysis considers how 'institutional racism and popular racism are woven into state racism' (Sivanandan, 2001, p. 3). Research shows that the problem of racism in the UK is deeply rooted in the history of the Prison Service. In the 1970s, many officers were members of the overtly racist organisation, the National Front.

> *There is evidence of extreme racism among prison officers, and of the brutal treatment and harassment of minority ethnic prisoners. In 1999, Martin Narey, then its Director General, admitted the Prison Service was 'institutionally racist'.*

It is common for prison staff to be accused of overreacting to disruptive behaviour by Black prisoners and of falsely stereotyping them as 'arrogant, lazy, anti-authoritarian and dangerous'. There have also been dubious statements about Black victims in prison. In 1998, Richard Tilt, former Director General, made the unsubstantiated claim that Black prisoners were more likely to die from positional asphyxia while being restrained because of their genetic disposition to sickle cell anaemia.

Following the murder of Zahid Mubarek by his racist 'cellmate' at Feltham YOI in March 2000, the Prison Service agreed a five-year action plan with the Commission for Racial Equality to improve matters, and race relations training for staff was prioritised. The Commission for Racial Equality published two reports in 2003, which led to the *Prison*

*Service Action Plan* on race relations (HM Prison Service, 2003b). Her Majesty's Chief Inspector of Prisons (HMCIP) published its thematic study *Parallel Lives* in 2005, and a year later, the Keith Inquiry published its two-volume report on *The Zahid Mubarek Inquiry* (2006). *Inter alia*, this made 17 findings of unlawful discrimination against the Prison Service. In 2006, impact assessments were introduced to monitor the effects of prison policies on Black and minority ethnic (BME) prisoners and correct any adverse impacts found. And in 2007, key performance targets were set to monitor and improve race relations in under-performing establishments.

Despite the numerous reports and policies, serious concerns remain about the treatment of BME prisoners. Although the report, *Implementing Race Equality in Prisons – Five Years On* (MoJ, 2008) found substantial improvements, it was acknowledged that the experience of BME prisoners and staff had not been transformed. In 2011, HMCIP reported that almost half of prisons do not have a diversity policy which covers all the main protected characteristics under equalities legislation. In some prisons race relations work is given a low profile and numerous racist incidents continue to be reported, especially the use by staff of inappropriate language and comments. BME prisoners are more likely than White prisoners to be discriminated against over access to jobs and activities, to be segregated from other prisoners, and to be placed on the basic level of the Incentives and Earned Privileges Scheme (HMCIP, 2012).

---

**Black and minority ethnic (BME) prisoners**

- In 1985, there were 8 per cent (men) and 12 per cent (women) from BME groups.
- On 31 March 2013, there were 21,462 ME prisoners (26 per cent of the prison population). This compares to around one in ten of the general population.
- Black prisoners account for the largest number of ME prisoners. Around 10 per cent of the prison population is Black. This compares to less than 3 per cent of the general population.
- Between 1993 and 2003, the White and Asian prison population increased by 48 per cent and 73 per cent respectively, while the BME prisoner population increased by 138 per cent. Between 2006 and 2010, BME prisoners have remained at around 26 per cent of the prison population.

(Home Office/MoJ Management Caseload Statistics)

---

## FOREIGN NATIONAL PRISONERS

The proportion of foreign national prisoners (FNPs) has increased steadily from 8 per cent in 1997 to 13 per cent in June 2011. Around 30 per cent of BME prisoners are foreign nationals. At 31 March 2013, there were 10,725 FNPs, the majority of whom were from just ten countries: India, Jamaica, Lithuania, Nigeria, Pakistan, Poland, Republic of Ireland, Romania, Somalia and Vietnam. (MoJ, 2013h)

The immigration status of FNPs sets them apart from BME prisoners. FNPs are confronted with a variety of problems, concerns and socioeconomic disadvantages. Aside from obvious language barriers, the prospect of deportation and revocation of their immigration status increases anxiety, and the pains of imprisonment. Women FNPs especially—many of whom are victims of human trafficking and have experienced violence, intimidation and rape—receive no support or protection. A lack of strategic management is the root of the problem. In May 2006, the then Home Secretary Charles Clarke resigned in the wake of the failure to consider for deportation over 1,000 FNPs who had been released into the community. Since then, legislation has been passed to facilitate the deportation of FNPs, and it is now government policy to seek to remove FNPs at the earliest opportunity. So-called 'hub' prisons, in which UK Border Agency (UKBA) staff have permanent access to foreign national prisoners, and 'spoke' prisons, in which foreign national prisoners receive regular visits from UKBA staff, have been established to accelerate deportation and reduce the number of FNPs held. The overall lack of support for FNPs has been heavily criticised. The charity Bail for Immigration Detainees (BID) has reported that only 26 per cent of FNPs receive any independent immigration or deportation advice. Furthermore, although foreign nationals constitute some 15 per cent of the overall prison population at any one time, they receive no rehabilitation support whatsoever (BID, 2013).

## WOMEN IN PRISON

Between 2000 and 2010, the women's prison population increased by 27 per cent. This is explained mostly by an increase in the severity of sentences and a greater number of women receiving custodial rather than community sentences. Between 2007 and 2013, however, the number of women prisoners reduced by 475 (11 per cent) (Home Office/MoJ

Management Caseload Statistics). Despite a number of reports highlighting gender differences in offending patterns, sentencing bias and personal and social circumstances, the experiences and differential pains of imprisonment for women have largely been ignored.

---

## Women prisoners

### Populations

- 1965: 841
- 1992: 1,353
- 1999: 3,400
- 2004: 4,672
- 2007: 4,368
- 2010: 4,267
- 2013: 3,893

### Social backgrounds

- Permanently excluded from school: 30 per cent
- Experience of local authority care: 31 per cent
- Unemployed: 66 per cent
- No accommodation: 38 per cent
- Non-violent crimes: 81 per cent
- Misuse of heroin crack or cocaine: 52 per cent
- Domestic abuse: 50 per cent
- Mental, physical or sexual abuse: 53 per cent
- Suffering from some level of psychological disturbance: 78 per cent
- Mothers: 40 per cent
- Black: 25 per cent
- Foreign nationals: 15 per cent
- Attempted suicide before prison: 37 per cent

### Prisons

There are currently 13 prisons for women (including with-male prisons and remand centres).

### Recidivism rates

Figures for 2010 show that 45 per cent of women ex-prisoners reoffend within one year.

---

Women offenders are more likely to be understood through positivistic psycho-biological theories of crime and to be responded to more as psychiatric patients than as offenders.

> *Feminist and other studies have identified the different needs of women offenders and that their experiences of imprisonment are qualitatively different to those of men. Women prisoners are often relatively powerless and vulnerable, and have often been subjected to abuse on the outside.*

There have been many calls to abolish imprisonment for women. Following the government-sponsored *Corston Report: A Report by Baroness Jean Corston of a Review of Women with Particular Vulnerabilities in the Criminal Justice System* (2007), which recommended the scaling back of imprisonment for the majority of women offenders who pose no risk to the public, the United Nations General Assembly, the Women's Justice Taskforce and the National Council of Women have all advocated diverting women offenders from custody. However, little practical progress has been achieved. Six years after the Corston report, an inquiry conducted by the House of Commons Justice Committee (2013) found no evidence that NOMS had identified what the distinct needs of female prisoners were, or taken any action to address them. In continuing to prioritise cost-effective management over any consideration of sentencing, in particular the ongoing imprisonment of women for relatively minor offences, the MoJ has adopted a relatively narrow interpretation of the numerous proposals made to reduce the women's prison population.

# PRISONS AND PRISONERS IN NORTHERN IRELAND AND SCOTLAND

## NORTHERN IRELAND

The Northern Ireland Prison Service (NIPS) is an executive agency within the Department of Justice, established on 1 April 1995. Criminal justice powers were devolved from Westminster to the Northern Ireland Assembly on 12 April 2010. Its main statutory duties are detailed in the Prison Act (Northern Ireland) 1953. Prison rules, providing guidance for the operation of the Prison Service, are made under the Act. The current Director General of the NIPS is Sue McAllister.

---

**Prisons in Northern Ireland**

The NIPS currently has three operational establishments:

- HMP Maghaberry
- HMP Magilligan
- HMP Prison and Young Offenders Centre Hydebank

---

The current NIPS 'statement of purpose' reads:

> The overall aim of the Northern Ireland Prison Service is to improve public safety by reducing the risk of reoffending through the management and rehabilitation of offenders in custody. The Prison Service, through its staff, serves the community by keeping in secure, safe and humane custody those committed by the courts; and by working with prisoners and with other organisations, seeks to reduce the risk of re-offending; and in so doing aims to protect the public and to contribute to peace and stability in Northern Ireland.

Traditionally, the NIPS has had low prison populations. In 1920, there were only 278 people in prison (Tomlinson, 1996). There was, however, a major escalation from the late 1960s, when the prison population rose from below 700 to a peak of 3,000 in 1979. Since then, the population (sentenced and remand) has fallen to around 1,800 prisoners, although there was an increase of 6 per cent in the year 2011–12. The total prison population on 31 March 2012 was 1793. A high proportion of prisoners in Northern Ireland are held on remand. Overall, the figures include 529 remand prisoners (27 per cent), 35 sentenced women prisoners, 138 sentenced young offenders, and 5 juvenile male prisoners. Some 24 per cent sent to prison in 2009 were fine defaulters. See Table 2.6.3 for an overview of the NIPS prisoner population.

**Table 2.6.3  Population details for prisons in Northern Ireland on 31 March 2012**

| Establishments | Sentenced | Remand | Juveniles | Total |
|---|---|---|---|---|
| Maghaberry | 552 | 454 | | 1006 |
| Magilligan | 538 | 0 | | 538 |
| Hydebank Wood (adult female) | 38 | 15 | | 30 |
| Hydebank Wood (young offender male) | 133 | 58 | 5 | 174 |
| **Total** | **1261** | **527** | **5** | **1793** |

*Source:* Northern Ireland Prison Service, 2012

There are 1,883 uniformed grade officers in Northern Ireland supported by some 400 civilian grades. The ratio of staff to prisoners is around two and a half times that of England and Wales, and prison officers are paid on average one-third more. In 2010–11, the annual cost per prisoner place was £73,762.

# SCOTLAND

The Scottish Prison Service (SPS) is an agency of the Scottish Government and was established in 1993. The current Chief Executive of the SPS board is Colin McConnell. The net cost of the Service for the financial year 2012–13 was £353.1 million. The SPS employs over 4,350 members of staff. In recent years, Scottish prisons have suffered from overcrowding, and since 2007 the SPS has paid out over £8.5 million in overcrowding compensation payments. There are currently 14 publicly managed and two privately managed prisons in Scotland. The annual cost per prison place for 2010–11 was £32,146. Prison numbers fell over the year 2012–13 from 8,297 to 7,864. The official capacity of Scottish prisons is 7,844. The population is predicted to rise to 9,500 by 2020.

Young adults make up 10 per cent of the population. Since 2001, the average daily women's population has increased by 69 per cent. In 2009–10, some 38 per cent of prisoners were serving sentences of three months or less. On 6 August 2010, a statutory presumption against short sentences was decreed in the Scottish Parliament. A 2011 prisoner survey found that 50 per cent of Scottish prisoners reported being drunk at the time of their offence, 56 per cent tested positive for drugs, and more than 70 per cent had mental health problems. (Prison Reform Trust, 2012b)

Table 2.6.4 gives an overview of the SPS prisoner population.

**Table 2.6.4   SPS prisoner population on Friday 19 July 2013**

| Status | Number |
| --- | --- |
| Untried male adults | 1,039 |
| Untried female adults | 70 |
| Untried male young offenders | 127 |

*(Continued)*

*(Continued)*

| Status | Number |
|---|---|
| Untried female young offenders | 5 |
| Sentenced male adults | 5,571 |
| Sentenced female adults | 318 |
| Sentenced male young offenders | 397 |
| Sentenced female young offenders | 18 |
| Recalled life prisoners | 78 |
| Convicted prisoners awaiting sentencing | 242 |
| Prisoners awaiting deportation | 4 |
| Civil prisoners | 1 |
| **Total** | **7,870** |

*Source:* Scottish Prison Service, 2013

# "What is the current organisational structure of the Prison Service in England and Wales?"

To answer this question, you will need to look at the MoJ and NOMS websites. You will need to understand how these two bodies interrelate, which will require you to look up recent data on the Internet. Do not be complacent and give out-of-date accounts. That little bit of extra work can make all the difference to your marks.

Prison population projections are used to forecast prison capacity and resource allocation. On the basis that public safety is paramount, governments must respond effectively and cost efficiently to the likelihood of growing prisoner numbers. Projections are based on assumptions about future trends in custody rates, sentence lengths and the anticipated impact of changing legislation, policy initiatives and sentencing guidelines. You might think this is relatively straightforward, but prison population projections are subject to significant uncertainty. Projections made according to 'lower', 'medium' or 'higher' scenarios vary considerably. Armstrong (2012) has argued that the use of statistical forecasts lends a sense of legitimacy to penal policy makers intent on penal expansionism. No matter how inaccurate or inconsistent the numbers, prison population projections make it imperative for governments to act decisively. As a consequence, the case for building more and bigger prisons is normalised.

TAKING IT FURTHER

# BIBLIOGRAPHY

Accounts and descriptions of prison populations in the UK can be found in:

- **BRYANS, S and JONES, R (eds) (2001)** *Prisons and the Prisoner*, London: HMSO.
- **CAVADINO, M, DIGNAN, J and MAIR, G (2013)** *The Penal System: An Introduction*, 5th edn, London: Sage.
- **COYLE, A (2005)** *Understanding Prisons*, Milton Keynes: Open University Press.

On children and young offender populations see:

- **GOLDSON, B (ed.) (2000)** *The New Youth Justice*, Lyme Regis: Russell House.
- **GOLDSON, B and MUNCIE, J (eds) (2006)** *Youth Justice*, London: Sage.
- **SMITH, DJ (2010)** *A New Response to Youth Crime*, Cullompton: Willan.

On 'race' issues in sentencing and prisons see:

- **BOWLING, B and PHILLIPS, C (2002)** *Racism, Crime and Justice*, London: Longman.
- **BHUI, HS (ed.) (2009)** *Race and Criminal Justice*, London: Sage.
- **CHIGWADA-BAILEY, R (2003)** *Black Women's Experience of Criminal Justice*, Winchester: Waterside Press.
- **HOOD, R (1992)** *Race and Sentencing*, Oxford: Oxford University Press.
- **SVEINSSON, K (ed.) (2012)** *Criminal Justice v Racial Justice: Over-representation in the Criminal Justice System*, London: The Runnymede Trust.

And on women's imprisonment see:

- **BOSWORTH, M (1999)** *Engendering Resistance: Agency and Power in Women's Prisons*, Aldershot: Ashgate.
- **CARLEN, P (1983)** *Women's Imprisonment*, London: Routledge.
- **CARLEN, P (ed.) (2002)** *Women and Punishment: The Struggle for Justice*, Cullompton: Willan.
- **CARLEN, P and WORRALL, A (2004)** *Analysing Women's Imprisonment*, Cullompton: Willan.
- **HEIDENSOHN, F (ed.) (2006)** *Gender and Justice*, Cullompton: Willan.
- **WALKLATE, S (2004)** *Gender, Crime and Criminal Justice*, 2nd edn, Cullompton: Willan.

# 2.7 SOCIOLOGIES OF PRISON LIFE

## Core areas

sociological studies of imprisonment
prison conditions
prisoner health

## Running themes

- Human rights
- Legitimacy
- Less eligibility
- Managerialism
- Pains of imprisonment
- Power to punish
- Social divisions

## Key penologists

**Erving Goffman (1922–82)** One of the most influential social thinkers in the twentieth century, Erving Goffman studied sociology and anthropology at the University of Toronto. He undertook his PhD on social interactions in a small island community on the Scottish coast. After studying at the University of Chicago, he spent much of his working life at the University of Pennsylvania. Goffman looked at the mechanics of public behaviour and articulated a general theory of social interaction employing theatre as a metaphor for life. His main writings include *The Presentation of Self in Everyday Life* (1959) and *Asylums: Essays on the Situation of Mental Patients and Other Inmates* (1961), his famous analysis of inmates at a Washington mental institution. Goffman died of cancer at the age of 60 in 1982.

**James B Jacobs (b. 1947)** Currently director of the Center for Research in Crime and Justice at New York University School of Law, James B Jacobs was awarded a PhD from Chicago University in 1975. Jacobs is perhaps best known for his Weberian study *Stateville: The Penitentiary in Mass Society*, which was published in 1977. In this study, he presented an historical examination of the total prison organisation, investigating the role of administrators in authoritarian and legal bureaucratic forms of penal authority, as well as the changing lived realities of prisoners, including the emergence of politicised prison gangs.

**Gresham Sykes (1922–2010)** A key sociological thinker, Gresham Sykes was Professor Emeritus of Sociology at the University of Virginia. Sykes was born at Plainfield, New Jersey, and served in the US armed forces during World War II. He first came to international prominence through his work with David Matza on the techniques of neutralisation. His most influential penological contribution is his book *The Society of Captives*, a seminal and widely cited study of prison sociology, published in 1958 and republished in 2007. Sykes died in 2010 after a long struggle with Alzheimer's disease.

# SOCIOLOGICAL STUDIES OF IMPRISONMENT

Sociologies of prison life investigate the experiences and lived realities of prisoners and prison staff. Prisons are 'unique', 'strange' and 'extraordinary' places which expose like no other the tension between free will and determinism, resistance and compliance. In social science this is often referred to as the relationship between structure and agency. Prison sociologies have generally looked at:

- the extent and nature of the pains of imprisonment;
- the different pains of imprisonment of men and women, and how these pains are compounded by disabilities, racism or homophobia;
- whether modes of behaviour, 'the prisoner code', are imported into or created through the deprivations of prison and/or exported to wider society;
- how prisoners and prison officers develop strategies of 'psychological survival';
- the structure and transmission of informal rules, 'ways of life', cultures and argots;
- the exercise of penal power (legal and coercive), and the management of prison conflicts;
- order, control and the prevalence of violence in everyday prison life;
- the nature of penal controversies and the moral legitimacy of imprisonment.

*Sociological studies have investigated many different aspects of prison life, with authors often combining a number of the above issues in their work.*

Sociologies of prison life remind us of the importance of looking at both the penal environment and how it is impacted upon by the wider social contexts in which imprisonment is situated. There are a number of classic sociological studies of prisons and prisoners. One of the most important early works was Donald Clemmer's *The Prison Community* (1948). This was a study of the maximum-security prison at Menard, Illinois.

> *Clemmer argued that prison subcultures were imported from outside, and reflected the confinement of predominantly male, lower-class and poorly educated populations.*

Clemmer argued there existed a prisoner code emphasising loyalty, which embodied the norms and values distilled from the social backgrounds of prisoners. The code was pro-prisoner and anti-authority, and led to a process of 'prisonisation', which provided a means of protecting prisoners.

A slightly later book, but one that laid the foundations for many subsequent studies, was Gresham Sykes' *The Society of Captives* (1958). Sykes was interested in prisoner subcultures and the exercise of power at New Jersey State Maximum Security Prison, Trenton. Sykes argued that total domination over prisoners was an ideal rather than a reality. A daily round of infractions, disorder and tensions exposed the struggle to maintain order. Because the exercise of power by prison officials lacked legitimacy, prison discipline was a compromise and had to be negotiated on a daily basis. In particular, officers had to offer prisoners rewards to gain their co-operation.

> *Sykes maintained that the prisoner subculture arose as an attempt to mitigate the deprivations that are created by the inherent pains of imprisonment: the deprivations of liberty, goods and services, of heterosexual relationships, autonomy and security.*

Sykes highlighted the ways in which prisoners developed a special language or 'argot', which was a means of communicating with other prisoners the basic tenets of the prisoner code: 'never rat on a con', 'do your own time', 'play it cool', 'be tough, be a man'.

Erving Goffman's *Asylums* (1961; 1991) has also reached classic status. Goffman argued that the 'total institution'—in his study, a mental hospital—stripped an individual of the social and cultural supports of his or her identity. Deprivation is 'symbolized by the barrier to social intercourse with the outside world and to departure that is often built right into the physical plant such as locked doors, barbed wire, cliffs, water, forests, or moors' (pp. 15–16). This led to 'institutionalisation' and a 'disculturalisation', under which people unlearn their normal social skills and sense of self. The inmate's self is recreated through the daily rituals of institutional life: batch living; lack of security and privacy; a strict timetable of routine and activities; sanctions, awards and privileges. The result is that often prisoners are marked by 'personal failure', 'self-pity' and 'time wasted and destroyed' (p. 66), although this process could be reversed when the inmate returned to his or her previous social setting. Goffman also examined power and status in the total institution. He argued that total institutions were inherently conflictual, leading to antagonistic stereotypes between inmates and supervisors, and pressure on staff to ensure compliance from inmates.

## Common pitfall

*Remember that, although we can learn many things by studying similar institutions to the prison, there are also many differences between asylums and other 'total institutions'.*

Most of the classic sociologies of prison life have come from the US but an important English contribution is Stan Cohen and Laurie Taylor's study of the maximum-security wing at Durham Prison. In *Psychological Survival: The Experience of Long-Term Imprisonment* (1972; 1981), they produced a detailed and disturbing account of how long-term prisoners cope with the psychologically devastating consequences of being deprived of their liberty. For lifers in Durham prison, the self came under serious threat, undermined by a sense of futility that brought into question the meaning of life. But adaptation, passivity and powerlessness were not the only outcomes: prisoners could resist by 'asserting their superiority over their guards and ... dealing with attacks on their self-conceptions' (p. 148). Cohen and Taylor pointed not only to the inherent threats of long-term imprisonment, but also to the importance of resistance within an individual's psychological well-being. In a later study of order and resistance in prisons, Sparks et al. observed that, rather than lead to institutionalisation,

in reality prisons quite commonly seethe and boil with human agency, passion and conflict—in ways that are not infrequently magnified and rendered more intense precisely by the constraints and frustrations encountered there.

(1996, p. 68)

This is not to argue that prison causes no damage to the people held there. The 'depth of imprisonment' can and does inculcate a sense of irresponsibility, or 'infantilism', so that ex-prisoners are often unable to develop meaningful and lasting attachments and committments to people on the outside (Shover, 1996).

Building on the work of Jacobs (1977), the importation model of prisoner behaviour has received closer attention over the last few years. Studies have shown how prison life is transformed by demographic, economic and political changes within the wider society. In a well-known study, Israel Barak-Glantz (1981) developed a typology of four models of prison management, some of which respond to and accommodate increasing prisoner involvement and resistance:

- **'Authoritarian'** In this type, virtually all power is in the hands of the warden.
- **'Bureaucratic-Lawful'** This model is characterised by bureaucratisation, decentralisation, the diffusion of power and the atomisation of the inmate community.
- **'Shared-Powers'** This places a premium on keeping physical controls to a minimum and sees the development of prisoner pressure groups.
- **'Inmate-Control'** Under this model, competing gangs—usually based on ethnic origin—control prisons.

## Common pitfall

*Some of the earlier sociological studies looked exclusively at the experiences of men and the operation of male prisons. Some of these theories do not always fit easily with the experiences of women. Much sociological analysis of imprisonment also focuses on the social and cultural context of the US which, in key respects, is very different to that of the UK.*

Some recent sociologies have focused specifically on the issue of 'race' in the US and how prisoners are organised increasingly into ethnically defined gangs characterised by strict internal codes of collective conduct, loyalty and support. For example, the French sociologist and professor of sociology at the University of California, Berkeley, Loïc Wacquant (2000), has argued that througout history African Americans have been defined and made subject to distinct phases of institutional confinement and control which he terms 'peculiar institutions':

- Chattel Slavery (1619–1865)
- The Jim Crow System (1865–1965)
- The Northern Ghetto (1915–1968)
- The Hyperghetto-Carceral Complex (1968–Present)

A consequence of the hyperghetto-carceral complex is that, as large numbers of African Americans have been removed to prison, the social and cultural environments of prisons and ghettos have begun to 'merge and mesh'. The sociology of American prisons has shifted: 'the predatory culture of the street ... has entered into and transfigured the social structure and culture of jails and prisons' (Wacquant, 2001, p. 110), which, in turn, has transformed the urban 'Black Belt' areas to which most African-American prisoners eventually return. In a similar vein, taking black and minority ethnic (BME) relations in Rochester Young Offenders Institution and Maidstone prison in the UK to be informed by postcode as well as ethnic and faith identities, Coretta Phillips (2012) has charted the solidarities and antagonisms that characterise everyday prisoner relations, as well as the tensions of discrimination and inequality faced outside and within prison by diverse groups. Drawing upon ethnographic research undertaken by herself and Rod Earle, Correta Phillips (2012) ultimately identifies racism as one of the key 'pains of imprisonment' for BME prisoners. In so doing Phillips ultimately draws attention to the dehumanisation, humiliation and degradation characterising prison life.

There have also been a number of sociological studies of prison officers. In *Doing Prison Work* (2004), Elaine Crawley examined the social world of prison officers and their families. Her main focus was on the manner in which prison work is impersonal and about the management of human emotions. Just as prisoners become inured to the physical and social environment of prison, staff become pragmatic and disciplinarian. Another influential study is Liebling et al.'s *The Prison Officer* (2011), in which they undertook an appreciative inquiry (AI) into the culture of prison officers and their relationships with prisoners. They argued that prison officers used 'talk' and other hidden skills to develop positive relationships with prisoners. Under-using their powers, and relying on foresight, diplomacy, humour, discretion and personal authority, prison officers performed a peacekeeping function.

In contrast to Liebling et al., David Scott (2006; 2014a) has argued that personal authority is actually deployed to enforce an asymmetrical deference norm and secure prisoner respect. His study identified four working personalities: the careerist, the humanitarian, the mortgage payer, and the disciplinarian—the dominant personality, which was immersed within the principles of less eligibility. Scott details how some prison officers deployed 'techniques of denial' to neutralise acknowledgement of the common humanity of prisoners. Similarly, Kelsey Kauffman (1988) undertook a detailed study of prison officers primarily at Walpole prison in the US. A former prison officer, Kauffman highlighted the importance of solidarity and loyalty among prison officers, and the development of an informal officer code of conduct. She suggested that prison officer cultures effectively 'other' prisoners as lesser human beings. For Kauffman, the occupational culture is composed of functionaries—i.e. officers who have emotionally distanced themselves from prisoners.

More recent ethnographic studies of imprisonment have also focused on professional relations within prisons. For example, Ben Crewe's (2009) study of institutional power in Wellingborough prison has focused on managerialism, staff ethos and prisoner resistance to changing organisational structures. Taking inspiration from the classic study *Society of Captives* by Gresham Sykes (1958), Ben Crewe impressively explores both the working personalities of prison officers and prisoner adaptations. As such, Crewe provides important evidence of contemporary manifestations of the pains of imprisonment—most notably in his notion of 'tightness'—and the responsibilisation of prisoners. And similarly, Deborah Drake (2011) has analysed the impact on high-security prisoners of increasing levels of everyday seclusion and segregation introduced since the Woodcock (1994) and Learmont (1995) inquiries. In this groundbreaking study, Drake asks us to suspend our moral judgements (or at least that of being judgemental) regarding the harms perpetrated by high-security prisoners and instead to focus our attention upon the dehumanising realities that shape their lived experiences in the claustrophobic high-security regimes. Drawing upon her extensive and meticulous ethnographic research, Drake ultimately argues that the only justifiable response to such evidence is penal abolitionism.

> *Read widely and look at the sociological literature from the UK and the US. Much of the classic literature is quite old, so be prepared to look at journal articles for more recent sociological studies of prison life.*

# PRISON CONDITIONS

Prison conditions have been central to the main penological traditions. For those who believe that prisons work through deterrence, prison conditions should be kept austere, because the principle of less eligibility states that prison life must always be worse than living conditions on the outside.

Liberal and humanitarian penologists on the other hand have consistently called for better conditions for prisoners and have advocated minimum legal standards. While abolitionists have argued that, even if prison conditions were to be vastly improved, it would not necessarily lead to greater penal legitimacy. Prisons with good living conditions are still rooted in the deliberate infliction of pain through the deprivation of liberty.

**Table 2.7   Overcrowded conditions in prison**

| Physical conditions inside | Outside contact |
| --- | --- |
| Size of cells | Letters |
| In-cell furnishings | Telephone calls |
| Overcrowding and time in cell | Visits |
| Sanitation | Media |
| Clothes | |
| Showers and personal hygiene | |
| Food | |
| Purposeful activity (work and leisure facilities) | |
| Levels of discipline, control and intimidation | |

As we have seen already, overcrowding has been a major problem for the Prison Service in recent years. The consequences of overcrowding include:

- increase in tension, frustration and threat to disorder;
- negative impact on everything to do with the prison regime, including fewer work and educational facilities;
- prisoners are held in pairs in cells that are designed for one;
- police cells are used to contain prisoners;
- early release of prisoners.

*The Howard League for Penal Reform provides a comprehensive and up-to-date information briefing on prison overcrowding.*

# PRISONER HEALTH

The psychological damage that imprisonment inflicts can have a negative impact on the health of all prisoners. Rather than providing a constructive experience which improves the prospects of prisoners leading a crime-free life after release, prison is damaging to people in ways that increases the likelihood of reoffending. Three 'hot topics' in relation to prisoners' health are mental health, self-inflicted deaths, and illicit substance misuse and the spread of infectious diseases.

# MENTAL HEALTH

The most vulnerable people in prison, as in wider society, are those who are either physically or mentally ill. People with mental health problems are in pain, are often unable to cope with the daily stress of life, have low self-esteem and feel isolated or alienated. Expressions of their suffering include sitting staring into space on association, neglect of personal hygiene, eating disorders and attempts to harm themselves.

---

**Mental health in prison**

There is no shortage of official data on the nature and extent of mental ill health in prison. Recent figures reveal that:

- 70 per cent of prisoners have two or more mental health problems;
- 26 per cent of females and 16 per cent of males say they received treatment for a mental health problem in the year before prison;
- 49 per cent of female prisoners and 23 per cent of males suffer from anxiety and depression. This compares with 19 per cent of females and 12 per cent of males in the general UK population;
- 62 per cent of male and 57 per cent of female sentenced prisoners have a personality disorder;
- 40 per cent of male and 63 per cent of female sentenced prisoners have a neurotic disorder (three times the level of the general population);
- 7 per cent of males and 14 per cent of female sentenced prisoners have a psychotic disorder;
- 10 per cent of male and 30 per cent of female sentenced prisoners have previously been admitted to a psychiatric hospital;
- 35 per cent of girls and 13 per cent of boys aged 13–18 years suffer from depression;
- 47 per cent of all incidents of self-harm are attributed to women.

---

In April 2006, the Department of Health took full responsibility for prisoner health care in prisons. Prison health care services are now commissioned by Primary Care Trusts (PCTs). The aim is to provide equivalence with NHS services in the wider community. But Rickford and Edgar (2005), and others, have argued that there are a number of problems with achieving the goal of equivalence in relation to prisoners with mental health problems:

- there are a higher number of mentally ill prisoners when compared to numbers in the community;
- mentally ill prisoners are confined in the prison hospital or in segregation units;
- historically, lower-quality healthcare services were provided in prisons;
- the prison environment exacerbates the vulnerabilities caused by mental illness;
- staff may treat mentally ill prisoners as lesser humans, neglecting their needs;
- less eligibility continues to influence penal policy and wider culture.

The imprisoning of mentally ill people has been strongly criticised. Mentally ill people are more likely to be a danger to themselves than a danger to others. They are, however, often assessed as being 'difficult', 'problematic' and 'challenging', and some are considered to be suffering from a dangerous and severe personality disorder (DSPD). In 2009, the Bradley Report called for vulnerable prisoners to be diverted to community alternatives including day care provision, and for the Department of Health to refocus mental health primary care services in prison. It also recommended that prisoners with acute mental illness should be transferred out of prison to hospitals. But little progress has been made. In 2012, HMCIP reported that services for patients with common mental health problems were undeveloped and prisoners with personality disorders were often not being diverted to secure NHS facilities. Previously considered untreatable and therefore subject to a diagnosis of exclusion, prisoners with personality disorders are now placed on a treatment pathway. Nevertheless, a number of controversies remain including:

- many prisoners with severe mental illness are placed into segregation units for long periods, sometimes for their own protection;
- personality disorder assessment and diagnosis is unreliable;
- it is a convenient diagnosis that puts individual blame on the prisoner. Some of the most notorious prisoners for control problems have successfully addressed their behaviours—see, for example, Boyle (1977) and Leech (1992).

## Common pitfall

*When looking at prisoner mental health, you will encounter legal, medical and forensic psychology. Make sure that you have a dictionary to help you to understand the technical language used.*

## SELF-INFLICTED DEATHS (SIDS)

Imprisonment is plagued by the deaths of prisoners. The following are three tragic examples.

**Chay Pryor** Chay died in August 2008 aged 18 while on remand in HMP High Down for possession of a broken bottle. Diagnosed with attention deficit hyperactivity disorder (ADHD), Chay had a history of heavy drinking, drugs and self-harm, and had been released from HMP High Down just three months before his death, having served a nine-week sentence for theft, battery and a failure to surrender to bail. On admission to prison, doctors noted Chay's risk of self-harm but reception staff did not take into account his previous medical and prison records and he was not considered a risk. A few days before his death Chay harmed himself, but was assessed as low-risk. On 23 August, Chay asked to speak to a Listener (a prisoner trained to support vulnerable prisoners) and was taken to the Listener's suite where he was left unsupervised. He was later found hanging from a torn bed sheet he had taken from his cell. At the subsequent inquest, it was noted that prior to Chay's death, concerns had been raised about ligature points in the Listener's suite but these had not been acted upon (Prison Reform Trust/INQUEST, 2012).

**Melanie Beswick** Melanie died aged 34 on 21 August 2010 in HMP Send where she was serving a 12-month sentence for fine default. It was her first offence. Melanie suffered from post-natal depression and had a history of self-harm. On the day of her death, Melanie was found motionless in her cell and taken to hospital, from which she was later discharged on the instruction that she required constant attention. Instead, staff at Send placed her on hourly observation. On returning to the prison Melanie asked to speak to a Listener but was told to wait. Less than an hour later she was found hanging from a ligature made from shoelaces attached to the window of her cell. The inquest held in April 2013 found that a failure of communication between the hospital and the prison, and also internally within the prison, contributed to Melanie's death (INQUEST, 2013).

**Helen Wright** While serving a 14-week sentence for theft, Helen was found dead on 7 March 2011 at HMP Bronzefield. She had five young children and was 32 years old. Having struggled with drug dependency for several years, Helen's family had asked for a residential placement but this had not been provided. During her sentence, Helen was put on a detoxification programme, but she died just seven days before she was due to be released. It is now two years since Helen's death, but at the time of writing the inquest into her death has yet to take place (INQUEST, 2013).

> *It is important to recognise the difference between a suicide and a self-inflicted death. A **self-inflicted death** (SID) is when somebody takes his or her own life. This only becomes a **suicide** if the person who died intended to take his or her life rather than to perform an act of self-harm as a cry for help/pain.*

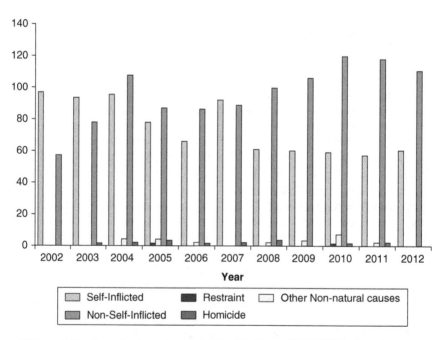

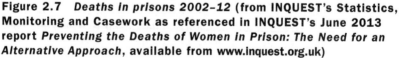

**Figure 2.7 Deaths in prisons 2002–12 (from INQUEST's Statistics, Monitoring and Casework as referenced in INQUEST's June 2013 report *Preventing the Deaths of Women in Prison: The Need for an Alternative Approach*, available from www.inquest.org.uk)**

The number of SIDs in prison has risen dramatically during the last 30 years. In 1983, there were 27 SIDs in prisons in England and Wales. Then, following a steep rise between 2000 and 2004, when there were 95, numbers fluctuated, falling to 61 in 2012. The downward trend has not continued. In 2013, there were 71 SIDs (the highest number since 2007) and four homicides (the highest number since 1998) (INQUEST, 2014). Disproportionate numbers of young people and children also take their own lives in prison. Between 1990 and 2011, 419 young people aged 18 to 24 died in prison, 363 of which were self-inflicted (87 per cent). Over the same period, 31 children aged 14 to 17 died in custody, of which 29 were self-inflicted, one restraint related, and one a homicide. There is also evidence that the experience of imprisonment increases vulnerability to suicide after release. Men released from prison are 8 times, and women 36 times, more likely to take their own life than the general population. (INQUEST, 2013.) Figure 2.7 charts prison deaths during the last 10-year period.

---

**Who is to blame? Explanations of self-inflicted death**

Four main explanations of SIDs have been proposed (Scott and Codd, 2010):

1  *High-risk inadequates, manipulators and attention seekers* The person who has died is personally culpable for their own death. Victims are defined as high-risk inadequates, and 'negative reputations' are established (Scraton and Chadwick, 1987). Reflecting an institutionalisation of the doctrine of less eligibility, prisoners are considered to be lesser beings who do not have the same human rights as those of law-abiding people. Rather than focusing on the Prison Service and the responsibilities of the state to care for those in custody, the person who has died is identified as the problem. These 'weak' people would have committed suicide whether they were in prison or not.

2  *Poor prison conditions* An alternative explanation has looked to locate the cause of such deaths within specific institutional problems, such as overcrowding, poor physical conditions, low feelings of safety, or levels of staffing. From this perspective, the prison environment can be healthy and safe, but becomes dangerous when it falls below certain standards.

3  *People vulnerable to prison environment* Prisons are filled with large numbers of people with poor coping skills who are vulnerable

*(Continued)*

> *(Continued)*
>
> to the unpredictability of prison life. SIDs arise from a combination of 'risky prisoners', who may or may not be psychiatrically ill, and their inability to cope with confinement.
>
> 4  **Inherent harms and pains of imprisonment** All prisoners are vulnerable because isolation, hopelessness and brutality are endemic to prison life. This highly toxic and dehumanising environment cannot be made completely safe or healthy. Its very existence is the negation of humanity, undermining constructions of the self and the meaning of life.

In 2012, the Prison Reform Trust and INQUEST published *Fatally Flawed: Has the State Learned Lessons from the Deaths of Children and Young People in Prison?* This reported on the experiences and treatment of the children and young people who died in prison between 2003 and 2010. It found these children and young people:

- were some of the most disadvantaged people in society and had experienced problems with mental health, self-harm, alcohol and/or drugs;
- had significant interaction with community agencies before entering prison, yet in many cases there were failures in communication and information exchange between prisons and those agencies;
- despite their vulnerability, had not been diverted out of the criminal justice system at an early stage and had ended up remanded or sentenced to prison;
- were placed in prisons with unsafe environments and cells;
- had experienced poor medical care and limited access to therapeutic services in prison;
- had been exposed to bullying and treatment such as segregation and restraint;
- were failed by the very systems set up to safeguard them from harm.

The report also found there had been inadequate institutional responses to the deaths of children and young people in custody.

## ILLICIT SUBSTANCE MISUSE AND INFECTIOUS DISEASES

A 'drug' is a chemical substance that can alter your behaviour, emotions or your psychological or physical disposition. Such substances include LSD (lysergic acid diethylamide), cocaine, alcohol, heroin, tobacco, cannabis, barbiturates, MDMA (3, 4-methylenedioxy-N-methylamphetamine) or ecstasy (XTC), methadone, solvents and caffeine. Despite repeated attempts by the Prison Service to limit the availability of drugs in prisons (high security, low security, big and small), they are accessed and used regularly as an 'anaesthetic' to relieve the boredom and stress of everyday prison life (Matthews, 2009). The most common drug in prisons is cannabis, but 19 per cent of prisoners who have used heroin report first using it in prison (Prison Reform Trust, 2012a).

---

### What do prisoners think about drug use and drug support in prisons?

There are a lot of problems with needles in prison, people making them from anything they find (pens for example) or stealing them from clinical waste bins. There are people who already have an abscess who are continuing to inject in prison.

(Prisoner, cited in Patel, 2010, p. 28)

In prison I learnt how to wash up cocaine and turn it into crack, how to chase the dragon, what speedballs are. All of the jargon that goes along with drug taking became a part of my vocabulary.

(Prisoner, cited in Flynn, 2010, p. 168)

I repeatedly get done for drunk driving. The likelihood of me getting done again is high. The prison should have investigated my issues with alcohol in depth. Even the help I have asked for hasn't come through. I did try to get into detox because of my alcohol issues and they said no. They weren't helpful.

(Prisoner, cited in Prison Reform Trust, 2012a, p. 49)

The screws are so understaffed ... the CARAT team [see below] come on the wing and the screws are like, 'No we're not unlocking anybody because we haven't the staff to supervise you' ... I only saw them once and that was on my second day, then I didn't see them after that in the whole six months I was there.

(Prisoner, cited in Patel, 2010, p. 22)

Prisoners who use illicit substances are labelled as doubly 'deviant', in that they are viewed both as criminals and as drug (mis)users. Illicit substances enter prisons by a variety of sources. Some of the most common routes include being smuggled in through visits, by prison officers, administrators or teachers, or through the delivery of supplies and 'drops' over the fence. A Home Office report conducted in 2005 found that 79 per cent of prisoners had used drugs in prison, with the most popular drugs being heroin and cannabis (Penfold et al., 2005).

---

**Profile of illicit substance (mis)user in prison**

- Young (average age 23)
- Low socio-economic social background
- Male
- Polydrug use (i.e. uses many different drugs)
- Dependent
- Failed treatments
- In poor physical health
- Contracted infectious disease

---

In 2010–11, the Ministry of Justice (MoJ) allocated £71.4 million for drug and alcohol treatment services in prisons. The NOMS Substance Misuse Strategy seeks to:

- reduce supply through security measures and mandatory drug testing programmes;
- reduce demand through targeted interventions for low, moderate and severe substance misusers;
- establish effective through care links to ensure continuity of treatment post release.

---

**The Counselling, Assessment, Referral, Advice and Throughcare Service (CARATS)**

In 1999, the Prison Service introduced the Counselling, Assessment, Referral, Advice and Throughcare Service (CARATS). CARATS is focused on delivering treatments to drug-using prisoners. It has seven interrelated stages:

*(Continued)*

*(Continued)*

1  Make initial contact on reception.
2  Make referrals to enable clinical assessments and detoxification.
3  Undertake a full assessment, based on prisoner needs.
4  Prepare care plans, with regular care reviews.
5  Counselling and group work to address substance misuse.
6  Planning to help management of drug problem on release.
7  Post-release work to establish links with community-based agencies.

An interlinked problem with illicit substance misuse is the spread of infectious and contagious diseases. One of the most significant is the spread of HIV and AIDS in prison. Rates of HIV are higher in prisons than among the wider population, with HIV being 15 times more prevalent than in the community. There are a number of policy options to help contain the spread of HIV and other infectious diseases, and sexually transmitted diseases (STDs), in prisons:

- **Condoms** Prisoners must send a 'Dear Doctor' letter to prison medical officers, who can prescribe condoms and lubricants if they judge there to be a genuine risk of HIV transmission. But the process is slow, there is no confidentiality and condoms are not available in around a quarter of prisons.
- **Disinfecting tablets** Prison Service Instruction (PSI) 53/2003 created provisions for tablets that would disinfect shared needles and syringes to be made available to prisoners (HM Prison Service, 2003c). This was officially introduced in April 2004.
- **Needle exchange programmes** The Prison Service has no plans to introduce needle exchange programmes. This is largely because of security concerns that needles would be used as weapons against other prisoners or prison officers. Evidence available from prisons in which needle exchange programmes have been introduced, however, is that they make prisons safer places because they replace needles that are already in the prison and which may be infected with a disease.
- **Tattooing** There are no plans to provide safe facilities for tattooing.

A report by the Prison Reform Trust/National AIDS Trust (2005) found that one-third of prisons had no HIV policy, one-fifth had no hepatitis C policy, and well over half had no sexual health policy. It also found that HIV-positive prisoners had received inadequate health care and inferior treatment, poor facilities, low levels of medical expertise and badly trained staff who breached the confidentiality of their patients.

## Towards harm reduction

A key theme in responding to the inherent harms of imprisonment is the principle of harm reduction. This involves:

1  Acknowledgement that harmful behaviour is taking place.
2  The need to understand why behaviour occurs.
3  Raising awareness of harms inherent in certain behaviour, but involving the suspension of moral judgement or of a focus on abstention.
4  Reducing the negative consequences arising from the harm.
5  Aiming to increase the safety of all concerned, potentially including safer ways of doing certain harm.
6  Empowering the person who has undertaken the harm.
7  Reducing risks of the harmer repeating behaviour.
8  Focusing on quality of life as measurement of success.

(Prison Reform Trust/National AIDS Trust, 2005)

## "Is prison culture imported into prison from outside or created within prison through the deprivations of prison life?"

This question is asking you to consider the classic works of Clemmer (1948), Sykes (1958), Goffman (1961) and Jacobs (1977) as well as more recent sociologies. You should consider factors created by and within the penal environment, and how behaviour in prison is shaped by wider norms and values in society as a whole. But note: the answer to the question is not necessarily one or the other. Think critically how culture in prisons might be a mixture of factors indigenous to prison as well as imported from outside.

**TAKING IT FURTHER**

Assessing what life is really like in prison requires in-depth research. Perhaps imprisonment can only be understood authentically if researchers inhabit the same everyday surroundings and conditions as those experienced subjectively by prisoners and staff. It is within this tradition that Goffman's (1961) participant observational study of 'inmates' at St Elizabeth's Hospital in Washington DC sought to understand the mechanics of 'total institutions', environments where individuals are cut off from wider society for given periods of time. Goffman observed highly detailed shifts in what he termed the 'moral career' of inmates. For example, at admission to the institution

> loss of identity can prevent the individual from presenting his usual image of himself to others. After admission, the image of himself he presents is attacked in another way. Given the expressive idiom of a particular civil society, certain movements, postures, and stances will convey lowly images of the individual and be avoided as demeaning. Any regulation, command, or task that forces the individual to adopt these movements or postures may mortify his self. In total institutions, such physical indignities abound. (1961; 1991, p. 30)

This is rich analysis but, in concluding that total institutions are structurally consistent and have commonly shared implications for those held in them, it has been criticised for being overplayed. Subsequent sociological analysis has explored differential prison environments and conditions, and the variable experiences of prisoners.

# BIBLIOGRAPHY

Aside from the 'classics', the sociology of imprisonment is well covered in the following publications:

- **BOWKER, L (1977)** *Prisoner Subcultures*, Lexington, MA: DC Heath.
- **CARRABINE, E (2004)** *Power, Discourse and Resistance*, Aldershot: Ashgate.
- **COYLE, A (2005)** *Understanding Prisons*, Milton Keynes: Open University Press.
- **CRESSEY, R (1959)** *The Prison*, New York: Anchor Press.
- **CREWE, B and BENNETT, J (eds) (2012)** *The Prisoner*, London: Routledge.
- **DILULIO, JJ (1990)** *Governing Prisons: A Comparative Study of Correctional Management*, London: Free Press.
- **EMERY, FE (1970)** *Freedom and Justice Within Walls Walls: The Bristol Prison Experiment*, London: Tavistock.
- **FITZGERALD, M and SIM, J (1982)** *British Prisons*, 2nd edn, Oxford: Blackwell

- **FLYNN, N (2010)** *Criminal Behaviour in Context: Space, Place and Desistance from Crime*, London: Routledge.
- **HOBHOUSE, S and BROCKWAY, AF (1922)** *English Prisons Today*, London: Longmans, Green.
- **IRWIN, J (1970)** *The Felon*, Englewood Cliffs, NJ: Prentice Hall.
- **JACOBS, JB (1977)** *Stateville: The Penitentiary in Mass Society*, Chicago, IL: University of Chicago Press.
- **JEWKES, Y (2002)** *Captive Audience: Media, Masculinity and Power in Prisons*, Cullompton: Willan.
- **JEWKES, Y (ed.) (2007)** *Handbook of Prisons*, Cullompton: Willan.
- **JEWKES, Y AND JOHNSON, H (eds) (2006)** *Prison Readings: A Critical Introduction to Prisons and Imprisonment*, Cullompton: Willan.
- **JONES, H and CORNES, P (1973)** *Open Prisons*, London: Routledge Kegan Paul.
- **KING, R and ELLIOTT, K (1977)** *Albany*, London: Routledge Kegan Paul
- **LIEBLING, A, PRICE, D and SHEFER, G (2010)** *The Prison Officer*, 2nd edn, Cullompton: Willan.
- **LOMBARDO, LX (1981)** *Guards Imprisoned: Correctional Officers at Work*, New York: Elsevier.
- **MARUNA, S and LIEBLING (eds) (2005)** *The Effects of Imprisonment*, Cullompton: Willan.
- **MATHIESEN, T (1965; 2012)** *Defences of the Weak: Sociological Study of a Norwegian Correctional Institution*, London: Tavistock.
- **MATTHEWS, R (2009)** *Doing Time: An Introduction to the Sociology of Imprisonment*, 2nd edn, Basingstoke: Macmillan.
- **MORRIS, TP and MORRIS, P (1963)** *Pentonville: A Sociological Study of an English Prison*, London: Routledge Kegan Paul.
- **SCOTT, D (1996)** *Heavenly Confinement? The Prison Chaplain in North East England's Prisons*, London: Lambert Press.
- **SCOTT, D (2014)** *Caretakers of Punishment: Power, Legitimacy and the Prison Officer*, London: Palgrave.
- **SCOTT, D and CODD, H (2010)** *Controversial Issues in Prison*, Milton Keynes: Open University Press.
- **SCRATON, P and MOORE, L** (2014) *The Incarceration of Women: Punishing Bodies, Breaking Spirits*, London: Palgrave.
- **SCRATON, P, SIM, J and SKIDMORE, P (1991)** *Prisons Under Protest*, Milton Keynes: Open University Press
- **SIM, J (1990)** Medical Power in *Prisons: The Prison Medical Service in England, 1774–1989 (Crime, Justice and Social Policy)*, Milton Keynes: Open University Press.
- **SPARKS, R, BOTTOMS, A and HAY, W (1996)** *Prisons and the Problem of Order*, Oxford: Clarendon Press.

- **THOMAS, JE (1972)** *The Prison Officer*, London: Routledge Kegan Paul.
- **TOCH, H (1975)** *Men in Crisis: Human Breakdown in Prison*, Chicago, IL: Aldine.
- **TOCH, H (1977)** *Living in Prison: The Ecology of Survival*, New York: Free Press.

# 2.8 PENAL ACCOUNTABILITY

## Key penologists

**Baron David John Ramsbotham (b. 1934)** Nicknamed 'Rambo', Baron Rmasbotham grew up in County Durham and is the son of the former Bishop of Wakefield. He was a general in the British Army and served in Northern Ireland before being appointed HM Chief Inspector of Prisons for England and Wales (HMCIP) from 1995–2001. A controversial figure, he has had a strained relationship with government. He famously led a Lords' revolt against the abolition of HMIP in 2006 and is author of the highly critical book *Prisongate: The Shocking State of Britain's Prisons and the Need for Visionary Change* (2003). He continues to play an active role in penal affairs. He is currently President of UNLOCK (the National Association of Reformed Offenders); the Vice Chair of both the All Party Penal Affairs Group and All Party Parliamentary Group for Learning and Skills in the Criminal Justice System; Honorary President of the Koestler Award Trust (a prisoner arts project); a Trustee of the International Centre for Prison Studies, and a Patron of the Prisoners Education Trust and African Prisons Project.

**Judge Sir Steven Tumim (1930–2003)** The son of an assize court clerk, Judge Tumim grew up in wartime Oxford, where he had a lonely childhood due to the death of his mother when he was aged only 10 years. He became a county court circuit judge in 1978. As HMCIP from 1987–1995, he proved to be a staunch critic of the government and a passionate advocate of humanitarian penal reforms. He was co-author, with Lord Woolf, of Part II of the investigation into the disturbances at Strangeways prison (1991) and author of a number of tracts on penal reform including *Crime and Punishment* (1997). In retirement, Tumim was Chairman of the Koestler Award Trust, and also served as President of UNLOCK. He died suddenly in December 2003, aged 73.

**Sir Nigel Rodley (b. 1941)** From 1973–90, Sir Nigel Rodley was a senior legal adviser for Amnesty International and, from 1993–2001, he was United Nations (UN) Special Rapporteur on Torture. Educated at Leeds University, Nigel Rodley was awarded a PhD from the University of Essex. His major publications include *The Treatment of Prisoners under International Law* (3rd edn, 2009). He is currently a member of the UN Human Rights Committee and Professor of Law and Chair of the Human Rights Centre, University of Essex. He is also a Member of the United Nations Human Rights Committee, Commissioner of the International Commission of Jurists, and a Trustee of the International Centre for Prison Studies.

# THE EXERCISE OF PENAL POWER

When thinking about punishment—that is, the deliberate infliction of pain—questions of legitimacy are central to any debate. To be legally and democratically accountable is a key part of any legitimate response to dealing with social harms, problems and wrongdoing.

> *It may come as a surprise to you to discover that there is very little literature on prison accountability and that much of what currently exists was written in the 1980s or 1990s. Although prisons throughout history have been subject to inspections, traditionally they tend to be closed worlds which operate according to the discretionary power of prison authorities and resist outside scrutiny or challenge.*

In recent years, accountability for the pro-prison lobby has been largely reduced to concerns around cost-effectiveness and ensuring that the delivery of punishment represents value for money. Liberal penologists have accepted the right of the state to punish, but are concerned that penal power is used correctly. And, although anti-prison critics have questioned the very basis of the power to punish, arguing that no one has the right to harm another person, like liberal penologists, they are interested in how state power is held to account and in the effectiveness of formal mechanisms that are in place to 'guard the guards'.

# THE STEWARDSHIP MODEL: FINANCIAL AND MANAGERIAL ACCOUNTABILITY

The first approach to accountability is to ensure that the sums add up. *Financial* accountability involves scrutiny of Prison Service accounts and is detailed in the Prison Service's annual report. This 'stewardship model' has gained increasing importance with the rise of privatisation and managerialism. Tied to the principles of economy, efficiency and effectiveness, it involves an increasing focus on reducing costs and increasing performance through standards, and through key performance indicators (KPIs) and targets. Such an approach is particularly relevant to private prisons which ultimately are accountable to the share holders of the companies that manage them. The problem is that, under this managerial model, you can find out the cost of everything but end up understanding the value of nothing.

> *The Prison Service is relatively transparent about its finances. This can lead to a discussion of the cost-effectiveness and fiscal logic of penal expansionism.*

# INSPECTION AT HOME: HMIP, IMBS AND THE PPO

There are three domestic forms of penal accountability in England and Wales:

- Her Majesty's Inspectorate of Prisons (HMIP)
- the Independent Monitoring Board (IMB)
- the Prison and Probation Ombudsman (PPO)

While at first appearing to provide a strong form of accountability, questions have been raised about the power of these institutions to hold the government to account, their independence and in whose interests they serve. Critics point to the difference between paying 'lip service' and legitimating imprisonment, and genuine forms of penal accountability.

# HER MAJESTY'S INSPECTORATE OF PRISONS FOR ENGLAND AND WALES (HMIP)

HMIP reports on the conditions of those held in adult prisons, young offender institutions and immigration centres. Appointed by the Secretary of State for Justice, the current HM Chief Inspector of Prisons (HMCIP) is Nick Hardwick. Section 5A of the Prison Act 1952 sets out the responsibilities for his role (see s. 57 of the Criminal Justice Act 1982). HMIP was established by the May Committee in 1979 and has had some high-profile chief inspectors, including Judge Stephen Tumim, Baron David Ramsbotham and Dame Anne Owers. HMIP carries out full inspections, full follow-up inspections and short, unannounced, follow-up inspections. Alongside individual inspections, HMCIP also produces an annual report and regular thematic studies on prison issues. For example, during the year 2011/12, reports were published on the care of looked after children, resettlement provision for children and young people, and alternatives to custody for women offenders (HMCIP, 2012).

---

**Healthy prisons**

Since a 1999 thematic review of suicides in prison, HMIP has used 'healthy prison' criteria to assess the moral legitimacy of a penal regime. The four key tests are:

- **Safety** Prisoners, particularly the most vulnerable, are held safely.
- **Respect** Prisoners are treated with respect for their human dignity.
- **Purposeful activity** Prisoners are able, and expected, to engage in activity that is likely to benefit them.
- **Resettlement** Prisoners are prepared for release into the community and helped to reduce the likelihood of their reoffending.

(HMCIP, 1999)

---

HMIP has only limited powers and can neither hold the government or The National Offender Management Service (NOMS) to legal account nor enforce changes. A common response of the Ministry of Justice (MoJ) is to delay the publication of inspection reports so that prison governors are given time to rectify serious problems highlighted. It is also common for prison officials to respond publicly to the positive elements of reports while ignoring the criticisms. Consequently, often there is some incongruity between the findings of reports and the official press statements released in response to them. See example below.

---

### Inspection reports and official responses

In 2013, an unannounced inspection of HMP Thameside in London found that substantial improvements were required to key aspects of the prison regime including safety, purposeful activity and resettlement. Furthermore, levels of assault were also too high and prisoners lacked confidence in staff to deal with and protect them from violence. In total, the report (HMCIP, 2013b) concluded that 'the prison regime was one of the most restricted we have ever seen'. In a press statement released on 14 May 2013, Michael Spurr, Chief Executive of NOMS responded:

> I am pleased the Chief Inspector acknowledges the progress being made, with strong staff prisoner relationships, a high quality of accommodation and an innovative use of interactive technology. Decisive action has been taken already to address the concerns raised in this report and I am confident that Thameside is well placed to deliver a safe, secure and decent regime for the prisoners it holds.

---

HMIP does provide an important shaming function, consistently producing damning reports of dreadful prison conditions which sometimes receive considerable press and public attention. But independence from government remains crucial to its work. Recently, Nick Hardwick has highlighted constraints on communication arising from the administration by the MoJ of the HMIP website, and restrictions placed on the recruitment of staff. In the introduction to the HMCIP Annual Report (2012), he stated:

> As it was for my predecessors, preserving the Inspectorate's independence has been a time-consuming and frustrating battle throughout the year. It is perhaps time to consider whether the independence of bodies such as the Inspectorate could be better preserved by a more direct relationship to Parliament and its institutions.

## Common pitfall

*There are a large number of inspection reports published each year and it is easy to lose motivation when examining so many documents. To avoid overload, read the annual report and then individual reports that have been highlighted in the media. Also, look at the thematic reports that are published regularly by the HMIP, such as those on suicide, race relations or mental health.*

## INDEPENDENT MONITORING BOARDS (IMBS)

IMBs comprise unpaid volunteers who are appointed by the MoJ to monitor the day-to-day life of penal institutions in their local area. Every prison has an IMB.

Known as 'Boards of Visitors' (BoVs) until 2004, IMBs have a long history in prisons in England and Wales.

Until the early 1990s, IMBs had a disciplinary function, as well as a monitoring role. That disciplinary role had, however, been legally challenged since the 1970s and was officially ended by the Woolf Report (1991). To address claims that BoVs were 'in the pocket of the government', the organisation changed its name to the 'Independent Monitoring Board'. Current members of IMBs are charged with ensuring that proper standards of care and decency are maintained in prisons, and can also deal with confidential requests from prisoners. IMB volunteers are supposed to have unrestricted access to all areas of a prison 24 hours a day and can talk to any prisoner or detainee they wish. To continue in their role, IMB volunteers must regularly attend their given prison and each IMB must produce an annual report. IMBs can play an important role as a whistleblower, highlighting brutality in prison through its annual report, but it has no formal powers to hold an institution to account; it has only an advisory function. IMBs are *not* independent, and impartiality is also hampered through the close relationships that volunteers often develop with prison staff. Unsurprisingly therefore, prisoners do not always trust IMB volunteers, seeing them as working in the interests of the prison rather than those of the prisoners. Although there are exceptions, owing to the voluntary, unpaid status of the post, most members of the IMB are middle-aged and middle class, and therefore do not represent the wider community or have much in common with the social backgrounds of prisoners.

## THE PRISON AND PROBATION OMBUDSMAN (PPO)

The PPO investigates complaints from prisoners in both public and private prisons and, since 2001, those subject to probation supervision and immigration detainees. Appointed by and reporting to the Secretary of

State for Justice, the Ombudsman does not have any statutory powers and no executive authority to enforce decisions made. The Ombudsman's powers are limited to making recommendations to the chief executive of NOMS, and it cannot comment on any decisions made by Ministers. The role was introduced in 1994 on the recommendation of the Woolf Report (1990), but, after a row between Sir Peter Woodhead, then Ombudsman, and Michael Howard, then Home Secretary, in 1996 a number of powers were taken away. New terms of reference were introduced in 2001, but these still impose considerable restraints. Since 2004, the Ombudsman has also investigated all deaths in prisons:

> The Ombudsman will examine complaints to consider whether they are eligible. To be eligible the internal complaints procedure of the prison must have been exhausted first. To assist in this process, where there is some doubt or dispute as to the eligibility of a complaint, the Ombudsman will inform the Prison Service or the National Probation Service Area Board of the complaint and, where necessary, the Prison Service or area board will then provide the Ombudsman with such documents or other information as the Ombudsman considers are relevant to considering eligibility.

> (Home Office, cited in Livingstone et al., 2008, p. 50)

The current Ombudsman is Nigel Newcomen. The Ombudsman produces annual reports and has carried out high-profile investigations into controversial incidents, such as the suicide in prison of the serial killer Harold Shipman and the disturbances at Yarlswood immigration centre in 2001. In 2011–12, the Ombudsman received 5,294 complaints, 4,726 about the Prison Service, 433 about the Probation Service and 135 about the United Kingdom Border Agency (UKBA). Around half the complaints received were deemed eligible for investigation, and of these 23 per cent of the prison cases and 22 per cent of the probation and UKBA cases were found in favour of the complainant.

# LEGAL ACCOUNTABILITY: PRISON RULES, PRISON LAW AND THE HRA 1998

---

### The Prison Act 1952

The authority of penal administrators is derived largely, but not exclusively, from the Prison Act 1952, a statutory framework that confers

*(Continued)*

---

> *(Continued)*
>
> massive discretionary powers upon penal officials. It is essentially enabling legislation, outlining who is legally empowered to perform duties relating to the operation and management of prisons.

Section 47 of the Prison Act 1952 provides for the Secretary of State for Justice to make rules for the regulation and management of prisons and for the classification, treatment, employment, discipline and control of persons required to be detained therein, while the resulting Prison Rules 1999 outline the procedures, policy objectives and obligations of the prison authorities. Both the Prison Act 1952 and the Prison Rules 1999 have been criticised for being anachronistic and maximising the discretion of the prison authorities. For example, Lord Denning, in *Becker v Home Office* (1972), famously claimed that 'the prison rules are regulatory directions only. Even if they are not observed, they do not give rise to a cause of action' (cited in Scott, 2006, p. 122). This implied that prison rules did not give rights to prisoners. Recently, however, there have been movements to recognise that prison rules and also other non-statutory instruments, such as Standing Orders, Prison Service Orders (PSOs) and Prison Service Instructions (PSIs), do, in fact, infer certain obligations onto the state and legal rights for prisoners. Yet there remains a reluctance on the part of the authorities to revise the regulatory framework of procedural justice in prisons in order to more clearly delineate prisoner rights in law.

---

### A legal right

An assertion is a legal right when the claim is protected and sanctioned through the law. Consequently, prisoners' legal rights can be understood as those legally enforceable claims that require the accomplishment or restraint of certain actions on the part of the Prison Service.

---

Although coming to such a definition is relatively straightforward, determining the content and interpretation of such rights for prisoners has proved to be much more controversial. Indeed, even the very acknowledgement that prisoners possess some legal rights has been highly contested. For example, up until the 1970s, prisoners were considered to possess only privileges and, once the gate closed behind them, were viewed as being beyond normal legal remedies.

The policies of penal administrators were uncritically supported or condoned by a highly conservative, non-interventionist legal discourse, with a self-imposed deference to the executive. While some cases were successful, prisons were left to themselves, becoming lawless and discretionary institutions with which the use of arbitrary powers by staff could go largely unchecked. This attitude gradually began to change in the 1970s and 1980s, with a gradual shift towards the recognition that prisoners do have some legal rights. The current basis of prisoners' residual legal rights can be found in Lord Wilberforce's definitive statement in *Raymond v Honey* (1982), within which he stated that a prisoner 'retains all civil rights which are not taken away expressly or by necessary implication' (cited in Scott, 2006, p. 123).

---

### Human Rights Act 1998

- *Article 2* Right to life
- *Article 3* Prohibition of torture
- *Article 4* Prohibition of forced labour and slavery
- *Article 5* Right to liberty and security
- *Article 6* Right to a fair trial
- *Article 7* No punishment without law
- *Article 8* Right to respect for private and family life
- *Article 9* Freedom of thought, conscience and religion
- *Article 10* Freedom of expression
- *Article 11* Freedom of assembly and association
- *Article 12* Right to marry
- *Article 14* Prohibition of discrimination
- *Article 16* Restrictions on political activities of aliens
- *Article 17* Prohibition of abuse of rights
- *Article 18* Limitations on use of restrictions on rights

### First Protocol

- *Article 1* Protection of property
- *Article 2* Right to education
- *Article 3* Right to free elections

### Sixth Protocol

- *Article 1* Abolition of death penalty
- *Article 2* Death penalty in time of war

On 2 October 2000, the Human Rights Act (HRA) 1998 was implemented. The HRA incorporates the European Convention on Human Rights (ECHR) into English law. Under the HRA, all new primary legislation, and existing procedures and practices of public authorities, including public and private prisons, must be compatible with the principles of the ECHR. Despite great hopes that the HRA would lead to an expansion of prisoners' legal rights, in the years since it was introduced and despite a handful of victories for prisoners, very little has changed. In the period both before and after the introduction of the HRA, cases have been most successful when they:

- fall within an area of traditional judicial intervention, such as those of legal advice and access, or release and discipline;
- raise concerns regarding natural justice, due process or procedural issues;
- aim to provide greater transparency in the decision-making process of penal administrators.

Where prisoners' claims have failed—the most common finding—the domestic courts in both private and public law have often justified such a decision through submitting to the arguments that such a restriction is required because of necessary implications, or by showing support for the convenience of those administering imprisonment. In judgments relating to interference with Convention rights, prison authorities have maintained the courts' sympathy in terms of their requirements for discretionary decision making, or on the basis that the restriction is necessary on grounds of prison security, order, the needs of victims of crime, the prevention of crime and even administrative convenience. This has meant that cases on personal issues such as correspondence, family contact and reviews of detention have been more likely to succeed than cases on structural issues such as prison conditions.

---

**Absolute rights of a prisoner**

When we ask the question 'What absolute rights are invested in prisoners?', the answer remains fairly brief. Prisoners in England and Wales have the absolute right to commence legal proceedings at an impartial and independent tribunal, and must be allowed uninhibited access to legal advice, whether through legal visits or correspondence. (Scott, 2013)

Prisoner rights jurisprudence can be developed to make a substantial impact on prisoners' lived realities, but the domestic courts must first recognise that no human being should have to live in the appalling circumstances in which many prisoners find themselves today.

## Common pitfall

*To understand the legal rights of prisoners fully requires some understanding of the law. If you are a social science or humanities student, ensure that you get guidance from the law librarian before you start to look at recent case law.*

# INTERNATIONAL AND REGIONAL PROTECTION: THE ECTHR, THE CPT AND THE UN

Outside of the domestic forms of accountability, there are regional and international bodies to which prisoners can appeal to uphold legal rights, and to hold the state and its penal authorities to account. At the regional level (Europe), there are the European Court of Human Rights (ECtHR) and the Committee for the Prevention of Torture (CPT); and at the international level, there are various bodies that have been established by the United Nations (UN).

## THE EUROPEAN COURT OF HUMAN RIGHTS (ECTHR)

The ECtHR was established in Strasbourg in 1951 by the European Convention on Human Rights (ECHR). Prisoner petitions to the ECtHR have been successful since the 1970s. It was expected that, with the introduction of the HRA, the ECtHR would be less significant in defining and upholding prisoners rights, but, because the UK courts have conservatively interpreted the HRA, the ECtHR has continued to be the main progressive legal avenue for prisoners. Recent successes have included cases on mandatory sentences (Stafford, 2002), inquiries into deaths in custody (Edwards, 2002), governor adjudications (Ezeh and Connors, 2002), the right to vote (Hirst, 2005), the right of male prisoners to artificially inseminate their wives (Dickson, 2007), and most recently the right of life sentence prisoners to receive a review of whole life tariffs and be considered for release (Vinter et al., 2013). The main drawback of the

ECtHR, and of the ECHR generally, is that it has a very restrictive under-standing of human rights and has largely supported prisoners when procedural, rather than substantive, rights have been breached. Moreover, there is no obligation on governments to uphold the rulings of the European Court (Scott, 2013).

> *A notable recent example in which the Government resisted a successful legal challenge concerns the blanket ban on the right of prisoners to vote, which was judged to breach Article 3 of Protocol 1 of the European Convention on Human Rights. The decision to comply with the judgment remains with Parliament however, and in response Prime Minister David Cameron has said: 'no one should be under any doubt; prisoners are not getting the vote under this government' (Telegraph, 2012).*

# THE EUROPEAN COMMITTEE FOR THE PREVENTION OF TORTURE (CPT)

The CPT was created by Article 1 of the European Convention for the Prevention of Torture and Inhuman or Degrading Treatment or Punishment (1987). The Committee, comprising penal experts from across Europe, visits penal establishments among the countries of the Council of Europe that have ratified the Treaty. The focus of the CPT includes all places of detention (prisons and juvenile detention centres, police stations, holding centres for immigration detainees and psychiatric hospitals) and aims to highlight cases in which it feels that confinement is inhuman, degrading or amounting to torture. All visits are undertaken after prior notification, and this notification may be made directly before the visit is about to take place. CPT delegates should have unlimited access to designated places of detention and the right to move inside without restriction. The primary goal of the CPT is the prevention of torture and it reports directly to the government of the member State under investigation. The CPT does not provide for the public shaming of abusing States, but is instead guided by the principles of co-operation and confidentiality. Only if a country fails to co-operate will the CPT make a public statement. The CPT has visited the UK on six occasions—investigating the conditions of terrorist suspects at HMP Belmarsh, and in 2008 called upon the authorities to 'consider fresh approaches towards eradicating overcrowding as a chronic feature of the prison system' (CPT, 2009). The CPT has been said to be a 'toothless tiger', however, and its reports have done little to add to the jurisprudence on torture, inhuman and degrading treatment or to improve the lived realities of prisoners in the UK.

## Common pitfall

*The CPT reports are important, but you will find that they follow a very similar pattern. Report writers are heavily reliant upon 'cut and paste', so be selective of the reports you read.*

## UNITED NATIONS (UN)

The UN is an international body that has produced a number of major declarations, charters, standards and principles outlining international law on prison conditions. The 1948 United Nations Declaration and the 1966 Convention on Civil and Political Rights feature Articles that condemn torture and cruel, inhuman or degrading treatment. The 1966 Convention also states that 'all persons deprived of liberty shall be treated with humanity and with respect for the inherent dignity of the person'. In 1955, the UN introduced the Standard Minimum Rules for the Treatment of Prisoners, and in 1988 published the 'Body of Principles for the Protection of All Persons Under Any Form of Detention or Imprisonment'. In addition, the UN has a Special Rapporteur and Committee for the Prevention of Torture (see above).

*The problems with international laws are that they are rarely used by domestic courts or prisoners in the UK, they are focused on procedural issues, and they have set prison standards so low it is difficult to bring a case against present conditions.*

## "Does Her Majesty's Chief Inspector of prisons have enough power to hold the Prison Service to account?"

You must first outline the main role and duties of HMCIP, and then identify the powers it has to hold the Prison Service to account. Provide a critical scrutiny and assess whether the current powers are limited. Identify the main themes of some recent reports, and how Ministers, prison governors and the media have responded to these reports. Also look at the comments of the current and former HMCIPs. To conclude, provide some indication of what would be necessary to a HMIP that could hold the Prison Service to account.

Read an official report of your local prison by either HMIP or the IMB. What does the report say about the prison? Is it critical? Does it indicate whether previous recommendations have been acted upon? Does the report get to the heart of the running of the prison and the problems encountered there? How were the findings reported in the local press? What was the official response to the report? To what extent do you think the prison and NOMS have been held accountable by it?

*TAKING IT FURTHER*

# BIBLIOGRAPHY

Prisoners' rights and prison accountability are covered in the following publications:

- **CREIGHTON, S and ARNOTT, H (2009)** *Prisoners: Law and Practice*, London: Legal Action Group.
- **CREIGHTON, S, KING, V and ARNOTT, H (2005)** *Prisoners and the Law*, 3rd edn, Haywards Heath: Tottel.
- **EASTON, S (2011)** *Prisoners' Rights: Principles and Practice*, London: Routledge.
- **EASTON, S and PIPER, C (2008)** *Sentencing and Punishment: The Quest for Justice*, Oxford: Oxford University Press.
- **FIELD, S (2012)** *Prison Law Index: The Definitive Annual A–Z Index of Prison Law Cases and Materials*, 2nd edn, Stockport: prisons.org.uk.
- **FITZGERALD, M and SIM, J (1982)** *British Prisons*, 2nd edn, Oxford: Blackwell.
- **HARDING, R (1997)** *Private Prisons and Public Accountability*, Milton Keynes: Open University Press.
- **LIVINGSTONE, S, OWEN, T and MACDONALD, A (2008)** *Prison Law*, 4th edn, Oxford: Oxford University Press.
- **MAGUIRE, M, VAGG, J and MORGAN, R (eds) (1985)** *Accountability and Prisons: Opening Up a Closed World*, London: Tavistock.

- **OBI, M (2008)** *Prison Law: A Practical Guide*, London: The Law Society.
- **RODLEY, N (1999)** *The Treatment of Prisoners under International Law*, 2nd edn, Oxford: Clarendon Press.
- **Scott, D. (2013)** 'The politics of prisoner legal rights' in *The Howard Journal of Criminal Justice*, 52 (3): 233–250.
- **VAGG, J (1994)** *Prison Systems: A Comparative Study of Accountability in England, France, Germany and The Netherlands*, Oxford: Clarendon Press.
- **VAN ZYL SMIT, D and SNACKEN, S (2011)** *Principles of European Prison Law and Policy*, Oxford: Oxford University Press.

# 2.9 PROBATION AND COMMUNITY PENALTIES

## Core areas

'advise, assist, and befriend': the origins and history of probation
the current and future role of the National Probation Service
perspectives on criminal desistance
towards decarceration?

## Running themes

- Alternatives to prison
- Legitimacy
- Managerialism
- Penal reform
- Power to punish
- Rehabilitation
- Risk

## Key penologists

**Professor Sir Anthony Bottoms (b. 1939)** Tony Bottoms was Wolfson Professor of Criminology at the University of Cambridge from 1984 to 2006, and is now Emeritus Wolfson Professor of Criminology at Cambridge and Honorary Professor of Criminology at the University of Sheffield. He is a leading figure in both criminology and penology, and has written extensively on prisons and alternatives to custody. His most recent books on penology include (with Richard Sparks and Will Hay) *Prisons and the Problem of Order* (1996) and *Alternatives to Prison: Options for an Insecure Society* (2004), the latter in collaboration with Sue Rex and Gwen Robinson. He was elected Fellow of the British Academy in 1997.

**Professor Stan Cohen (1942–2013)** Stan Cohen was Martin White Professor of Sociology at the London School of Economics from 1996 to 2006. Cohen grew up in South Africa and was an undergraduate at the University of Witwatersrand. He worked as a social worker in London before undertaking a PhD at the London School of Economics. Cohen taught at the University of Durham and the University of Essex, before he moved with his family to Israel in 1980. In Israel, he was a human rights activist and Director of the Institute of Criminology at the Hebrew University. Perhaps the most influential writer on crime and punishment of his generation, Stan Cohen has written on 'moral panics', prisons, social control, human rights and the techniques we deploy to deny the suffering of others. He was elected as a member of the British Academy in 1987 and received the Sellin-Glueck Prize from the American Society of Criminology in 1985. His book, *States of Denial: Knowing About Atrocities and Suffering* (2001), was voted best book of the year by the British Academy in 2002. He died in 2013 after being diagnosed with Parkinson's disease in 1996.

**Professor Andrew Scull** Distinguished Professor of Sociology and Social Science at the University of California since 1994, Andrew Scull studied as an undergraduate at Oxford University from 1966–9 and was awarded a PhD from Princeton University in 1974. He is one of the leading writers on history, psychiatry, medicine and social control. His books include *Decarceration: Community Treatment and the Deviant – A Radical View* (1977), *Museums of Madness* (1979), *Social Control and the State* (1983) with Stan Cohen, *Undertaker of the Mind: John Monro and Mad-Doctoring in Eighteenth-Century England* (2001) with John Andrews, and *Durkheim and the Law* (2nd edn, 2013) with Steven Lukes.

# 'ADVISE, ASSIST AND BEFRIEND': THE ORIGINS AND HISTORY OF PROBATION

The Probation Service performs a key role within the penal system. In recent times, it has become increasingly aligned with the Prison Service and both are now tied through the National Offender Management Service (NOMS). Probation does, however, have a very different history to that of the prison.

Probation arose in the nineteenth century as a result of voluntary, ad hoc and informal attempts to provide support, friendship and spiritual and practical guidance for offenders. Much of this work was guided by religious conviction and motivated by moral feeling and Christian charity. One of the most significant forms of philanthropy came from the police court missionaries who were employed by the Church of England Temperance Society in the 1870s to help to rehabilitate alcoholics. The Victorian middle and upper classes believed there was a strong association between drink, sin, 'crime' and other forms of vice. This lent support to the idea that, through a programme of individual supervision and being treated with decency and dignity, it was possible to change offenders for the better.

Probation for offenders was first introduced in 1877, but the most significant piece of legislation came with the Probation of Offenders Act

1907. Guided by the principle of reform advocated a few years earlier by the Gladstone Committee of 1895, the Act empowered every court to appoint at least one probation officer whose role it was to 'advise, assist and befriend' offenders. Probation officers had a direct supervisory role, and were there to help the offender lead an industrious, peaceful, well-behaved and lawful life. But from the beginning, probation was also about deterrence and control. Seen as a way of easing prison overcrowding, 'probationers' were required to comply with certain conditions, for example to report to supervisors, avoid certain places and refrain from alcohol, otherwise they would be returned to court.

After these first few years, probation adopted a more secular, scientific approach. The Criminal Justice Act 1948 led to a greater professionalisation of the Probation Service, laying down guidelines for assessment, diagnosis, treatment, training and improved links with the courts, and introducing new probation hostels, allowing for their administration through new probation committees. There were 54 probation committees, comprising magistrates, judges, civil servants and representatives of the local community. Throughout the 1950s and 1960s, probation work with offenders was based increasingly on individual understandings of criminal behaviour and social and psychological treatment solutions to it. However, during the 1980s and 1990s, as faith in rehabilitation declined, a new approach to 'punishment in the community' was adopted, which affirmed supervision and control as its primary purpose. Today, probation services are delivered through a range of 'alternatives to custody' and rehabilitation is delivered only if it demonstrates a reduction in reoffending.

> It is important that you examine closely the changes between the historic role of probation and its current deployment in the criminal justice system. This can also help you to track wider changes in crime control.

# THE CURRENT AND FUTURE ROLE OF THE NATIONAL PROBATION SERVICE

The organisational structure of the Probation Service has undergone considerable change over recent years. In April 2001, the National Probation Service of England and Wales (NPS) was launched.

Northern Ireland and Scotland have their own probation services. At present the NPS has 42 operational areas that are equivalent to the boundaries of the Police and Crown Prosecution Services. These are served by 35 Probation Trusts which receive funding from NOMS to which they are accountable for overseeing offenders released from prison on licence and those on community sentences. The end result of this is that NOMS now manages both the Prison and Probation Services, and that, through the principle of 'contestability', the delivery of community penalties has been opened up to market testing. Following the Halliday Review of sentencing (2001), the Criminal Justice Act 2003 tied punishments served in prison and the community together, indicating that the most significant difference between prison and probation officers should now be in where they perform their correctional duties, rather than in their task or work ethos. Rather than befriending offenders, probation officers today are expected to assess and manage the risk they present to public safety. The role of the NPS is to:

- provide pre-sentence reports to the courts;
- supervise offenders in the community;
- manage offender programmes and reduce the risk of reoffending;
- safeguard the welfare of children;
- facilitate crime prevention initiatives;
- undertake work in prison.

The work of the NPS is extensive. In the year 2011–12, 215,666 people started court orders and pre-release supervision and 267,441 court reports were prepared. In June 2012, a total of 111,735 people were supervised by the Probation Service, 70,814 on pre-release and 41,294 on post-release supervision in the community. The most recent report of HM Inspectorate of Probation (2013) has highlighted good practice in much of the work undertaken by the Probation Service. For the year 2012–13, it found that 75 per cent of work with adults was of a sufficiently high level of quality to minimise risk of harm, 74 per cent to reduce the likelihood of reoffending, and 79 per cent supported compliance and enforcement. However, on the downside it also reported significant shortcomings in adult offending work carried out in prisons, noting that 'the opportunity provided by a period of custody to focus on and change aberrant behaviour was ... in a significant proportion of cases, being lost' (2013, p. 24).

Look at the NPS website, and read the NPS and NOMS annual reports. You will also find the annual reports of HM Inspectorate of Probation useful, as well as statements and briefings published by the National Association of Probation Officers (NAPO). Quarterly offender management statistics including probation tables are published by the Ministry of Justice (MoJ).

Non-custodial sanctions can be divided between those that require supervision and those that do not.

Examples of current penalties with *no supervision* include:

- warnings;
- formal cautions;
- conditional cautions;
- conditional discharge;
- fines;
- fixed penalty notices;
- binding over.

There are also community penalties that require some form of state supervision or control. These community penalties gained increasing political importance during the 1970s and 1980s, and were tied in with the ideas of 'bifurcation'—i.e. the attempt to distinguish between serious and dangerous offenders, who should be imprisoned, and lesser offenders who should be dealt with through discharges, financial penalties and community sentences (Bottoms, 1977).

The deployment of community penalties has been significantly changed following the Criminal Justice Act 2003. A new generic community sentence was introduced in April 2005. There are three punishment bands: low, medium and high. The new community sentence combines a number of requirements in order to punish, rehabilitate, protect society or provide some form of reparation to the victim. The full list of requirements includes:

- unpaid work for up to 300 hours;
- specific activities such as developing skills or making amends to victims;
- undertaking a particular programme to help change offending behaviour;
- prohibition from doing particular activities;
- adherence to a curfew so an offender is required to be in a particular place at certain times;

- an exclusion requirement so that an offender is not allowed to go to particular places;
- a residence requirement so that an offender is obliged to live at a particular address;
- mental health treatment with the offender's consent;
- a drug rehabilitation requirement with the offender's consent;
- an alcohol treatment requirement with the offender's consent;
- supervision by the Probation Service;
- for offenders under the age of 25, an attendance requirement so that an offender must go to a probation centre at specific times.

Probation officers have undertaken work in prisons since 1966, but the two 'correctional' services have become more closely intertwined in recent times. Correctional work with offenders in prisons and post-release in the community is now called 'Integrated Offender Management'. The term is intended to emphasise the importance of control and supervisory work with offenders. The momentum for the changes has been driven by the sentencing implications of the Halliday Report (2001), the emphasis on cognitive behaviouralism and risk, and the belief that problems in the criminal justice system can be solved through more effective management and the introduction of competition. Seeking to steer a course between punitiveness and welfare, encapsulated in the couplet 'tough on crime, tough on the causes of crime', the New Labour Government promoted accredited rehabilitation interventions and programmes premised on the 'What Works' agenda, cognitive behaviour programmes in particular.

## Common pitfall

*The terms 'intervention' and 'programme' are often used interchangeably, but writers on offender rehabilitation sometimes define and use them differently. Whereas an 'intervention' usually denotes any kind of rehabilitative work with offenders including one to one and group work, a 'programme' may be used definitively to describe a set of inter-related activities (delivered to either individuals or groups) which are planned and sequenced in such a way as to achieve a specific objective.*

Programmes accredited on the basis of research demonstrating they reduce reoffending has been the policy of preference ever since. The Probation Service is once again set to undergo considerable change to its role and governance. The MoJ white paper, *Transforming Rehabilitation: A Strategy for Reform* (2013c) sets out a series of reforms to extend competition of probation services via a new commissioning model. Intended to ensure that 'the money we spend on rehabilitating offenders has the greatest possible impact', the strategy will:

- open up community orders and licence requirements for low and medium risk offenders to a diverse market of private and voluntary sector providers. Through making payments on the basis that a sufficient reduction in reoffending is quantitatively evidenced—'payment by results'—providers will be incentivised 'to focus relentlessly on reforming offenders';
- extend post-release supervision to offenders serving custodial sentences of less than 12 months;
- reposition public sector probation as the body accountable for supervising only those offenders who pose the highest risk of reoffending. No longer responsible for commissioning or providing offender rehabilitative services directly to offenders, the Probation Service will prioritise public protection through advising courts on sentencing, conducting initial risk assessments of offenders, and monitoring arrangements of contracted providers to manage on-going risk. Accordingly, public sector probation is to be reorganised as a single National Probation Trust.

The proposals have raised a number of concerns about the experience and expertise of new private sector companies to work safely and effectively with offenders. In particular, there have been concerns expressed about the payment by results funding mechanism:

- Rehabilitating offenders is uncertain in both theory and practice. There is no reason to expect that rehabilitation programmes delivered by the private sector on the basis of payment by results will improve matters.
- Given the upfront costs required to deliver rehabilitation funded through payment by results, the market is likely to be dominated by a small number of large, well-resourced private companies, thereby marginalising the contribution of the Probation Service and smaller voluntary sector organisations, and hampering the sharing of good practice built up over many years.
- Evidencing success according to a simple binary measure of non-offending, and providing payment on this basis, is likely to encourage providers to 'cherry pick' those offenders least likely to reoffend, and to reject the most problematic repeat offenders.

# PERSPECTIVES ON CRIMINAL DESISTANCE

'What works' rehabilitation has been criticised for adopting an essentially narrow and limiting view of human behaviour. Researchers interested in life-course 'desistance' perspectives have argued that the cognitive-behavioural model of rehabilitation:

- is relevant to high-risk offenders only;
- is insufficient on its own to achieve lasting change;
- fails to reveal anything about other processes by which offenders cease to reoffend;
- is treated with suspicion and not engaged with by offenders.

> *The verb 'to desist' means to stop doing something. Criminal desistance research is interested in the processes by which offenders stop offending. Such processes occur over time and normally involve lapses back into offending. 'Primary desistance' is the achievement of a temporary offence-free period. 'Secondary desistance' is the achievement of a permanent state of non-offending.*

An important policy implication of research on criminal desistance is that informal relationship building with offenders is often more effective than formal treatment. In a study of 199 probationers, Farrall (2002) found that, although over half had made progress towards giving up 'crime', successful desistance could be attributed to specific interventions in only a few cases. Therefore, research is needed to investigate how, why, when, and under what circumstances offenders stop offending by themselves, such as by acquiring relevant skills, forming pro-social relationships and gaining social capital education and employment. Research should also seek to expose the factors that block desistance. In particular, the propensity of imprisonment to:

- disrupt the maturation process;
- reduce agency—the purpose and intent of offenders to change;
- disrupt pro-social bonds such as employment and stable relationships;
- reinforce association with criminal peers.

Desistance research has been received favourably within the academic community but, to date, it has not influenced in any significant way future probation policy.

# TOWARDS DECARCERATION?

What is the wider social and political context of the changes Probation Service practice has undergone in recent years? When talking about 'non-custodial penal sanctions', we are referring to what is known as 'decarceration'. The decarceration movement had considerable influence among both academia—popularised by the influential social theorist, Andrew Scull—and among penal practitioners in the 1960s and 1970s. Decarcerationists called for the closing down of asylums, prisons and reformatories, and their replacement by alternatives rooted in the community.

---

**The destructuring impulse**

**Cognitive**

1 Prisons are costly and ineffective: community penalties are cheaper than prison sentences.
2 Community alternatives must obviously be better—or, at the very least, no worse.
3 In times of overcrowding, community sanctions might ease the pressure on the Prison Service.

**Theoretical**

1 Insights under labelling theory point to the counterproductivity of control systems.
2 Informal social controls—i.e. family, community, school, economic system—work.
3 We should aim for 'reintegration' (the new panacea).

**Ideological**

1 There are criticisms of bureaucracy and the penetration of formal controls.
2 There are many doubts about expertise and state intervention.
3 We need to focus on 'less harm' rather than 'more good'.

(Cohen, 1985)

---

Underscored by a humanitarian ideology, the decarceration vision called for an inclusionary, rather than an exclusionary, mode of social control. But Stan Cohen (1985) identified that, even in its heyday, the decarceration movement proved to be nothing more than a smokescreen for more insidious forms of social control. In fact, in the 1970s, the original structures of social control became stronger, extending their reach, intensity and intrusion, and drawing new 'deviants' into the clutches of their centralised and bureaucratic penalties. The little decarceration that did take place revolved around the mentally ill. This decarceration was actually in response to fiscal pressures and the retrenchment of welfare policies, and alternatives to custody became simply add-ons to the current mechanisms of social control.

Cohen points to problems around the following factors:

- **Net widening** Alternatives to prison can bring new people into the system who have committed minor offences.
- **Thinning mesh** It becomes harder to escape from state controls.
- **Blurring of boundaries** It becomes more difficult to determine institutional and non-institutional forms of control.
- **Penetration** New forms of control go deeper into the social body.

Penalties in the community have become a new way of introducing control into the penal system, thus expanding the 'net' for those at the bottom end of the system.

During this time, the prison became defined more negatively—as a warehouse for incorrigibles and hard cases—but continued to expand on a new incapacitative set of logics; overall, the system enlarged itself due to the proliferation of 'soft' community alternatives. This principle of bifurcation and increased community interventions leads, for Cohen, to yet 'another round in the game of blaming the *victim*' (1985, p. 126):

> From the foundation of the control system, a single principle has governed every form of classification, screening selection, diagnosis, prediction, typology and policy. This is the structural principle of binary opposition: how to sort out the good from the bad, the elect from the damned, the sheep from the goats, the amenable from the non-amenable, the treatable from the nontreatable, the good risks from the bad risks, the high prediction scorers from the low prediction scorers; how to know who belongs in the deep end, who in the shallow end, and who is hard and who is soft.

(Cohen, 1985, p. 86)

*You can make important connections between notions of **dangerousness**, the principle of **bifurcation** and recent debates on **governmentality, risk and actuarial justice**. No longer premised on retribution, deterrence or reform, imprisonment combined with new mechanisms of supervision and surveillance employed beyond the prison walls, are justified in the interests of public safety. Mandatory minimum sentences, indeterminate sentences, and sentences of Imprisonment for Public Protection; along with community based exclusion and activity requirements: curfews, unpaid work, electronic monitoring, drug and alcohol treatment requirements and Multi-Agency Public Protection Arrangements are each underpinned by the principles of incapacitation, risk management and control.*

Alternatives, then, may not be used as alternatives, but may instead be about making social controls better. It is certainly understandable to be sceptical about alternatives to prison. Thomas Mathiesen (1974) argued that we should not offer a blueprint of the alternative, and should only critique and provide an alternative after the prison system has been dismantled. Mathiesen believed in alternatives, but that penal critics must be strategic to avoid state manipulation. The limitations of this position are that, if critics do not offer a plausible alternative to prison, then they are unlikely to convince the public that they are serious. There must be plausible answers and solutions to social problems, and the reconstruction of the possibility of a better way of dealing with conflicts than that which we currently have now.

The above problems should not lead to nihilism, pessimism or the rejection of alternatives. Stan Cohen puts it best when he states:

> I believe that the ideology of doing good remains powerful … This is the essence of humanistic civilisation: to exert power and to do good at the same time.

(1985, p. 114)

## Common pitfall

*Criticism of the 'alternative' has sometimes been described as 'left pessimism' or 'nihilism'. This is probably unfair, because many of the critics of alternatives— such as Mathiesen and Cohen—have continued, in their work and activism, to call for humanitarian changes and a more sophisticated understanding of the positives and limitations of alternatives to custody.*

## "What is 'decarceration'? Is there evidence that UK and US governments adopted this policy in the 1970s?"

You will first need to define the term 'decarceration'. Then, look at the evidence of a movement away from using state institutions to deal with human problems. You will find the work of Scull (1977) useful here. Consider also those who have raised question marks against the decarceration thesis. The most detailed and sympathetic to the original argument is Cohen (1985). You may wish to conclude by considering alternative explanations of changes in the 1970s.

### TAKING IT FURTHER

### Beyond the criminal law: antisocial behaviour

Antisocial behaviour is defined as including a variety of 'complex, selfish and unacceptable activities' (Home Office, 2006) that blight the quality of life of people in the community. It is claimed that it provides a breeding ground for future criminal activity. As advanced by the New Labour Government, antisocial behaviour entails:

- rowdy and nuisance behaviour;
- yobbish behaviour and intimidating groups taking over public spaces;
- groups of youths behaving aggressively in shopping precincts;
- neighbours who do not clean up after their dogs;
- vandalism, graffiti and fly-posting;
- people dealing and buying drugs on the street;
- people dumping rubbish and abandoning cars;
- begging and antisocial drinking;
- the misuse of fireworks.

The Labour Government believed that the causes of antisocial behaviour include poor parenting, low educational achievement, truancy, community breakdown, early involvement in drug and alcohol misuse, vandalism, lack of social commitment and peer pressures that condone illegalities. Interventions aimed at tackling antisocial behaviour included:

- warning letters and interviews, contracts and agreements;
- individual support orders;
- agreements, contracts and fixed penalty notices;
- youth-specific interventions;

- antisocial behaviour orders (ASBOs);
- 'crack house' closure orders;
- possession proceedings against a tenant.

---

Central to the interventions was the Respect Action Plan, launched by Tony Blair, then Prime Minister, in January 2006. For Blair, the Plan aimed to 'eradicate the scourge of antisocial behaviour', based on his belief that the latter is caused by a breakdown of respect in society and where 'the self-reinforcing bonds of traditional community life do not exist in the same way' (Home Office, 2006). The Plan aimed to tackle antisocial behaviour and to reclaim communities for the law-abiding majority.

---

**Provisions of the Respect Action Plan**

- Increase fixed penalty notices for antisocial behaviour from £80 to £100.
- Extend the use of conditional cautions, so that offenders might be required to undertake unpaid community service.
- Provide a lower threshold for seizure of suspected proceeds of crime from £5,000 to £1,000.
- Create new powers to 'shut and seal' premises (including homes) that are a constant source of antisocial behaviour.
- Provide a network of intensive support schemes for problem families, with sanctions to cut Housing Benefit.
- Extend parenting schemes and a national parenting academy to train social workers.
- Allow schools to apply for parenting orders for families of pupils who seriously misbehave in school.
- Give police community support officers the powers to take part in truancy sweeps.
- Introduce national youth volunteering schemes and expand mentoring projects.

(Home Office, 2006)

---

The antisocial behaviour agenda has not been without its critics. A specific concern is that persistent, petty and mostly young offenders responsible for relatively low level anti-social behaviour increasingly have been drawn into the criminal justice system and in some cases imprisoned for breaching the conditions of orders imposed on them. We would appear to be witnessing the growing disciplinary powers of state control beyond the legal boundaries of the criminal justice system, and this presents a serious threat to our civil liberties. Specifically, fixed penalty notices raise concerns centring on the denial of due process rights and the manner in which 'justice' is defined exclusively as successful prosecution. Further, the concept of antisocial behaviour is rooted in individual and social pathologies that ignore wider social structures. Finally, there is no discussion of the antisocial behaviour of the rich and powerful, which may be more dangerous and damaging to society as a whole.

The present Coalition Government has been critical of the Antisocial Behaviour agenda without making any commitment to abandon it. Indeed, the recent Anti-social Behaviour, Crime and Policing Bill (2013) has reclassified anti-social behaviour as 'crime'. The ASBO and six related orders are to be replaced by two orders: the Criminal Behaviour Order and the Crime Prevention Injunction. Intended to make the system simpler, more enforceable and focused squarely on the needs of victims and local communities, it appears that the new system is designed to further extend the reach of criminal justice interventionism into civil society.

# BIBLIOGRAPHY

Critical analyses of the decarceration agenda include:

- **BOTTOMS, A, REX, S and ROBINSON, G (eds) (2004)** *Alternatives to Prison: Options for an Insecure Society,* Cullompton: Willan.
- **BROWNLEE, I (1998)** *Community Punishment: A Critical Introduction,* London: Longman.
- **CAVADINO, M, DIGNAN, J and MAIR, G (2013)** *The Penal System: An Introduction,* 5th edn, London: Sage.
- **COHEN, S (1985)** *Visions of Social Control,* Cambridge: Polity Press.
- **GARLAND, D and YOUNG, P (eds) (1983)** *The Power to Punish: Contemporary Penality and Social Analysis,* London: Heinemann Education.
- **RAYNOR, P and VANSTONE, M (2002)** *Understanding Community Penalties,* Milton Keynes: Open University Press.
- **WORRALL, A and HOY, C (2005)** *Punishment in the Community,* Cullompton: Willan.

Probation practice and offender management is discussed in:

- **CANTON, R (2011)** *Probation: Working with Offenders*, Cullompton: Willan.
- **GELSTHORPE, L and MORGAN, R (eds) (2007)** *Handbook of Probation*, Cullompton: Willan.
- **MAIR, G (ed.) (2004)** *What Matters in Probation*, Cullompton: Willan.
- **MAIR, G and BURKE, L (2011)** *Redemption, Rehabilitation and Risk Management: A History of Probation*, London: Routledge.

Offender rehabilitation, reintegration and resettlement is discussed in:

- **FARRALL, S and CALVERLEY, A (2006)** *Understanding Desistance from Crime: Theoretical Directions in Resettlement and Reintegration*, Maidenhead: Open University Press.
- **FLYNN, N (2010)** *Criminal Behaviour in Context: Space, Place and Desistance from Crime*, London: Routledge.
- **HUCKLESBY, A and HAGLEY-DICKINSON, L (eds) (2007)** *Prisoner Resettlement: Policy and Practice*, Cullompton: Willan.
- **MARUNA, S (2001)** *Making Good: How Ex-convicts Reform and Rebuild their Lives*, Washington, DC: American Psychological Association.
- **MARUNA, S and IMMARIGEON, R (2004)** *After Crime and Punishment*, Cullompton: Willan.
- **ROBINSON, G and CROW, I (2009)** *Offender Rehabilitation: Theory, Research and Practice*, London: Sage.
- **WARD, T and MARUNA, S (2007)** *Rehabilitation*, London: Routledge.

# 2.10 FUTURE DIRECTIONS AND ALTERNATIVE VISIONS

## Core areas

penal expansionism and 'prison works'
penal standstill
penal reductionism
penal abolitionism
thinking critically about penal legitimacy
radical alternatives

## Running themes

- Alternatives to prison
- Human rights
- Legitimacy
- Pains of imprisonment
- Power to punish
- Social divisions
- Social justice

## Key penologists

**Charles Murray (b. 1943)** Currently associated with the American Enterprise Institute, Charles Murray was born and raised in Newton, Iowa. He obtained a degree in history from Harvard and a PhD from the Massachusetts Institute of Technology. He first came to prominence with his controversial book *Losing Ground: American Social Policy, 1950–80* (1984), and co-authored (with Richard Herrnstein) the even more controversial *The Bell Curve: Intelligence and Class Structure in American Life* (1994), the most successful criminology book of the 1990s in terms of sales. A self-avowedly populist commentator on penal affairs, Murray has written widely on crime and human intelligence, crime and 'the underclass', social welfare and the family, and is a leading advocate of imprisonment as an effective form of deterrence. His work has been heavily criticised by liberal and left-wing penologists.

**Professor Andrew Rutherford (b. 1940)** Andrew Rutherford is Emeritus Professor of Law and Criminal Policy at the University of Southampton. He was an undergraduate at Durham University (1961) and was awarded a Diploma in Criminology from Canterbury in 1962. From 1962 until 1973, he was an assistant and deputy governor in the Prison Service. One of the leading penal reductionists of recent years, between 1984–99 Rutherford was Chairman of the Howard League for Penal Reform and since 2001 has been a member of the Parole Board of England and Wales. His main publications include *Prisons and the Process of Justice: The Reductionist Challenge* (1984), *Criminal Justice and the Pursuit of Decency* (1993) and *Transforming Criminal Policy* (1996).

**Professor Joe Sim (b. 1952)** A leading member of the European Group for the Study of Deviance and Social Control and penal pressure group INQUEST, Joe Sim is one of the most influential penal campaigners and abolitionists of his generation. Currently Professor of Criminology in the School of Social Science at Liverpool John Moores University, he previously worked at the University of Stirling and for the Open University, at which he was awarded a PhD under the supervision of Professor Stuart Hall. Joe Sim has published a number of books, including *British Prisons* (with Michael Fitzgerald, first published in 1979), *Prisons Under Protest* (1991, with Phil Scraton and Paula Skidmore), and *Punishment and Prisons: Power and the Carceral State* (2009). His book *Medical Power in Prisons* (1990) is widely regarded as one of most important works on imprisonment in the last three decades.

# PENAL EXPANSIONISM AND 'PRISON WORKS'

Andrew Rutherford (1984) has argued that 'penal expansion' takes place when:

- prisoner populations rise;
- prisons are overcrowded;
- the proposed solution is to build new prisons;
- there is an increase in numbers of prison staff;
- there is greater security across the penal estate.

In recent times, all of these factors have been evident in penal policy in England and Wales.

---

**Average daily population (ADP) of prisoners in England and Wales every ten years from 1884–2004**

- 1884     25,866
- 1894     17,127
- 1904     21,360

*(Continued)*

---

(Continued)

- 1914    15,743
- 1924    10,750
- 1934    12,238
- 1944    12,635
- 1954    22,421
- 1964    29,600
- 1974    36,867
- 1984    43,295
- 1994    48,621
- 2004    74,658

(Rutherford, 1984; HM Prison Service, 1995, 2005)

The figures above clearly indicate that the prison population in England and Wales has been rising since the 1940s. In 1940, the ADP was 9,377 prisoners; on 26 July 2013, the ADP stood at 84,052. Between 1974 and 1993, the prison population has kept pace with rises in 'crime' rates but, in recent times, incarceration rates have gone well beyond the (falling) recorded 'crime' figures. Despite such sustained increases, there is nothing inevitable about growing prison populations. (For further details see MoJ, 2013i.)

Prison populations are political choices, made by government, by means of the laws it introduces and the subsequent interpretation of these laws by the judiciary. Most penologists have been very concerned about the massive rise in prison populations (see Figure 2.10). But some politicians—such as Michael Howard, the Conservative Home Secretary in the 1990s—and other, mostly American, right-wing thinkers—such as Charles Murray, Lawrence Mead and James Q Wilson—have argued that 'prisons work' and that we should send more people to prison for longer periods of time. For some, imprisonment is a practical inevitability. Because the causes of 'crime' are too uncertain and too complicated to address in any meaningful way, imprisonment is the only possible response to the actions of 'wicked people' (Wilson, 1975).

*Charles Murray (1997) has adopted a specifically utilitarian perspective. He contends that, if used sufficiently, prison can work on the grounds of deterrence and incapacitation. Murray maintains there is a clear link between the recorded 'crime' rate and imprisonment rates.*

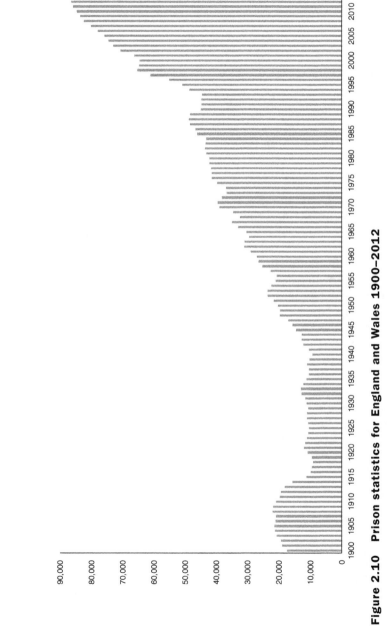

**Figure 2.10  Prison statistics for England and Wales 1900–2012**

*Source:* Offender Management Caseload Statistics, 2012 Tables, Ministry of Justice

Charles Murray (1997) suggests that, from 1955–93, the risk of being sent to prison was cut by 80 per cent. Contrary to expectations, during this period prison numbers actually declined, largely due to the failings of prosecutors.

## Common pitfall

*Remember that official criminal statistics are social constructions that are there to serve the administration of the system. They are not hard or true facts that provide a comprehensive view of criminality and wrongdoing in a given society. Care should also be taken when analysing prison statistics.*

Murray (1997) goes on to argue that the UK should 'reverse the great decline in imprisonment' and that it should look to the US for evidence that this can contain official 'crime'. He explains how, in 1974, there were 218,205 prisoners in the US, but that the 'crime' rate was out of control; the massive increase in the use of custody, containing 2 million prisoners in 2000, has held the official 'crime' rate in check. When translated to England and Wales, Murray argues that, to reverse the decline in prison, the average daily population must reach 275,000 (over a quarter of a million) prisoners. Then, says Murray, we must keep the prison rate high, because that is the only way in which we can contain 'crime' rates. However, even such a massive increase in imprisonment will not singularly reduce 'crime', because the real cause of 'crime' is welfare dependency. To reduce 'crime', we must remove welfare benefits for the unemployed.

Not many penologists take the great decline argument seriously, but its simplicity may be seductive to politicians, some members of the public and even some penology students.

**Prison does not work ...**

The criticisms made against Charles Murray (1997) include:

- His analysis is overly simplistic and does not meet normal scholarly standards.
- The 'crime' rate is a social construction and we cannot use this as an accurate measure of actual level of crimes.

*(Continued)*

*(Continued)*

- 'Crime' and imprisonment rates fluctuate from country to country, and the relationship between 'crime' and punishment is very complex.
- Equating 'crime' and welfare dependency takes no account of shifting occupational structures in causing poverty.
- There is no evidence that prisons actually do deter.
- Imprisonment creates more problems than it solves and may actually lead to increases in 'crime' rather than to its reduction.
- If there is a lesson to be learnt from the US incarceration binge, it is that prisons do not work.

# PENAL STANDSTILL

The first alternative to penal expansionism is to attempt to keep the prison population at around its current population. In the mid to late 1980s, 'penal standstill' was the dominant rhetoric in official penal policy. Andrew Rutherford (1984, pp. 54–5) has identified the following aspects of penal standstill:

- Exhortations by politicians to reduce custody.
- The development of non-custodial sanctions to replace imprisonment.
- A construction programme that is intended to replace existing prisons.
- Greater discretion to reduce sentence length.
- A ceiling placed on ADP of prisoners.
- Pragmatism and realism characterising the aims of imprisonment.

## Common pitfall

*It is easy to confuse **standstill** policies with penal **reductionism**.*

# PENAL REDUCTIONISM

A large number of penologists have promoted 'penal reductionism'. These range from administrative penologies, which are often philosophically close to both the standstill and reductionist models, to more socialist-inspired penologies, which advocate radical agendas that are not that dissimilar to those of penal abolitionists.

> All penal reductionists share a commitment to decent prison conditions, the acknowledgement of prisoners' procedural and due process legal rights, and consider imprisonment to be merely a suspension of offender liberties. Following the famous dictum of Sir Alexander Paterson, one of the foremost prison administrators in the early part of the twentieth century, 'people are sent to prison as punishment, not for punishment' (Ruck, 1951, p. 13).

Penal reductionists highlight how prison populations in England and Wales were drastically cut at the beginning of the twentieth century. In 1908, the throughput for prisons was 200,000, with an ADP of 22,029. By 1918, the ADP had dropped to 9,196 and, in 1938, the ADP was 11,086, with a throughput of less than 40,000 (Prison Service Annual Statistics). Through the promotion of genuine alternatives—such as probation, the abolishment of imprisonment for debt and allowing time for fines to be paid by offenders—the prison population was dramatically reduced. Underscoring this change was a political commitment to reducing prison numbers.

Although penal reductionists sometimes direct attention towards social problems, such as poverty or racism, reform of the criminal justice system has normally been their central focus. Penal reductionists raise concerns centring on:

- high prison populations;
- overcrowding;
- high costs of imprisonment;
- inadequate living conditions;
- culture of criminal justice staff;
- denial of prisoner legal rights.

Penal reductionists are often reluctant advocates of the prison and are unable to conceive of responses to social harms that do not rely upon this 'detestable solution'. Penal reductionists call for:

- a reduction in the physical capacity of prisons to 20,000–40,000;
- imprisonment to be restricted for serious crimes only;
- legal enforced minimum standards;
- greater penal accountability;
- less punitive sentencing;
- the creation of more non-imprisonable offences;

- the early release of prisoners;
- development of alternatives to prison.

The aims of penal reform are to create greater scepticism about the benefits of prison, to moderate its use and to muster the political will to change (see Loader, 2010).

The limitations of penal reductionism include that it:

- is confined within a liberal political ideology that naturalises the prison;
- demonstrates no consideration of how imprisonment is intimately connected with structural divisions and definitions of social harms;
- does not question the power to punish and that reforms support the legitimacy of imprisonment;
- does not fully take into account the knowledge of prisoners.

*There are a number of different approaches to penal reductionism. Although they largely argue for similar things, there are often major inconsistencies and differences between theorists and how they advocate penal reforms. A classic example is the debate between Andrew Rutherford, and Roy King and Rod Morgan. Both camps are reductionists but King and Morgan (1980) argued for the principle of normalisation—that prison life should be as normal as possible—while Rutherford (1984) is highly critical of this, arguing that prisons can never be normal places.*

# PENAL ABOLITIONISM

There are many similarities between penal reductionism and 'penal abolitionism'. The main difference, however, is that abolitionists have questioned the role and function of the prison in advanced capitalist societies, and the actual necessity of human suffering through incarceration. Rene van Swaaningen argues that

> at its core, criminal law … is based on … repressive assumptions … From the beginning it has been seen to create problems instead of solving them. A penal reaction after the fact is not preventive but de-socialises an ever-increasing number of people. Therefore it would be better to abolish penal means of coercion, and to replace them by more reparative means. This briefly is the abolitionist message.

(1986, p. 9)

Abolitionists have been concerned with both the micro-realities of imprisonment, such as the lived experiences of prisoners, the inherent brutalities and dehumanisation of prison life, and the unfettered discretion of prison officers. Alongside this is a concern with the broader macro socio-economic contexts through which social harms are both understood and defined as 'crime', and which legitimise the current focus on, and indeed existence of, the process of penalisation.

Penal abolitionism has been criticised on the following grounds:

- **Irresponsibility** It advocates releasing 'dangerous' prisoners and does not provide an agenda to protect victims or to deal with 'crimes' of the powerful.
- **Irrelevance** It does not engage with current political debates and so does not help the powerless, because it is easily defined out of the debate.
- **Idealism** It provides unrealistic, modernist visions of alternatives, which can be dangerous and rooted in left-wing 'fantasy'.

In fact, penal abolitionism does none of the above. Abolitionists generally promote responsible, relevant and realistic accounts of the penal system.

## RESPONSIBILITY

A responsible approach to wrongdoing must ask the following questions:

Do prisons help the victims of crime?
Do prisons help the offender or do they make the behaviour of the offender worse?
Do we imprison the people who cause the greatest harm?

Penal abolitionists can be seen to pursue the following goals in relation to social harms:

- **Justice for all** Our society is profoundly unequal, with major deficiencies surrounding social justice. What governments should do is look to provide justice, inclusion, integration, safety and security for all citizens, whether they are 'victims' or 'offenders'. This means doing something to address wrongdoing that actually works, rather than imprisonment, which generally makes the situation worse.
- **The reduction of dehumanisation and unnecessary suffering** Abolitionists fight against dehumanisation, unnecessary human suffering and the infringement of humanity, both inside and outside of the prison. They

argue that suffering, pain and harm should be reduced wherever and whenever possible for all concerned, and believe that punishment (the intentional infliction of suffering) is largely an immoral act.

- **Responsibilisation of the powerful** Our prisons are largely filled with poor, vulnerable, harmed, relatively powerless property offenders. Responsibilities should be tied to power and the actions of the powerful should be legally and democratically accountable.

# RELEVANCE

A relevant approach to penal policy today would ask:

What are the implications of the current political climate for penal reform?
What reforms do prisoners advocate?
What is the most plausible and relevant form of struggle?

To this end, the following are critical factors:

- **Reflexivity in a negative political climate** Current political realities are shaped by the Thatcherite settlement, which prioritises neoliberal political economy, and under which governmental sovereignty relies on a strong, potent and authoritarian state that can ensure security. This breeds a hostile social, economic and political context; in response, abolitionists have called for a moratorium on prison building and the protection of prisoner human rights.
- **The need to legitimate the experiences of prisoners** Abolitionists root their legitimacy in the meanings that prisoners have given to their own lived reality. They have attempted to present a picture of real life: an accurate portrayal of the subjects' understandings, meanings and interpretations of the social world. Abolitionists have presented reforms that have accurately reflected the protests and resistance of the subjugated and the grass roots movements. The adoption of the 'view from below' opened up space in which abolitionists could acknowledge and provide solidarity to prisoners. Contemporary abolitionists have, however, also retained some distance to allow critical judgements of prisoner meanings that are rooted in discriminatory beliefs.
- **Competing contradiction and human rights** Thomas Mathiesen (1974) argued that abolitionism must attain the 'competing contradiction', because this was the only way to avoid being either co-opted by the state or being defined as irrelevant. The 'competing contradiction' is competitive because it is relevant to the material conditions of the confined and

a contradiction because it is in opposition to the broader goals of the penal system. Human rights, legal guarantees and positive (welfare) rights for citizens can achieve the competing contradiction, and have been central to recent abolitionist debates. In addition, prisoners have often understood their struggles against the brutalising nature of imprisonment through a human rights and legal framework.

# REALISM

A realistic approach to dealing with social problems would ask:

Do prisons reduce 'crime' or solve moral conflicts?
Do prisons really protect society?
Do alternatives work?

Penal abolitionists respond with the following:

- **The punitive sanction really does not work** There will always be moral conflicts, but the term 'crime' should be replaced with alternative terms, such as 'problematic behaviours' or 'troublesome actions' that are understood in terms of harm. The criminal and penal law fail to solve problems or protect the vulnerable. They should not be used to regulate human interactions and so should be drastically reduced, or abolished.
- **Law is an arena for resistance** Abolitionists recognise that the law is neither 'innocent' nor 'evil'; rather, the law is an arena of struggle and can lead to emancipation or repression. The rule of law is a means of protection and coercion, a mechanism for establishing democratic freedoms and legitimating terror. Abolitionists have selectively endorsed penal reforms. Their aim has been to challenge and exploit the contradictory nature of both the law and the state, and to bring about reforms that will have a positive impact on the concrete everyday existence of marginalised and excluded groups.
- **A real commitment to justice and alternatives that really do work** A mandatory response is required for problems, conflicts and wrongdoing, but the forms of redress do not necessarily have to involve the deliberate infliction of pain. Abolitionism is rooted in both deconstruction (critique) and reconstruction (alternatives). Abolitionist alternatives have ranged from promoting alternative ways of thinking that reject the punitive rationale, to concrete projects that look to work with offenders, to radical socialist political transformations that challenge the dominant forms of governmental sovereignty and political economy.

> *It is important to consider all of the perspectives surrounding prisons and punishment. It is easy to construct a 'straw man', by failing to include all of the arguments surrounding a particular position, and then tear it down in what appears to be a compelling way—but penologists and practitioners will neither believe nor advocate positions that do not have some form of intellectual coherence. All published works should be taken on their merits. You should allow your imagination to take hold and try to think like a penologist. Look at prisons, from the perspective of right-wing, liberal and abolitionist standpoints: all three have their strengths and weaknesses, and you should explore them thoroughly.*

# THINKING CRITICALLY ABOUT PENAL LEGITIMACY

The claims of penal authorities to legitimacy are predicated upon the current distribution and application of punishment, and upon successfully attaining political validity and a sense of moral rightfulness in a given society, and lead to acquiescence, obedience and consent from both those imprisoned and from the general public. Failure to attain such moral or political validity can be assessed in two ways: as creating a legitimacy 'deficit' or as leading to a 'crisis' of penal legitimacy.

> *A prison service can be considered as suffering from a **legitimacy deficit** when the absence of legitimacy is believed to derive from weak justifications for its current aims, objectives and/or stated purposes, if it appears to be inadequate in terms of fulfilling its desired goals and stated intentions, or if the authority of those who apply penal power is significantly undermined.*

The current appliance of the power to punish can be considered to be illegitimate when it creates too many inherent infringements of human rights, when dehumanising penal regimes are endemic to operational practice, when it inevitably exceeds certain tolerable pain thresholds, or when it is entirely misapplied and inappropriately punishes certain categories of harm or wrongdoers. There are subsequently two dimensions to this 'crisis of penal legitimacy' (Fitzgerald and Sim, 1982): political legitimacy and moral legitimacy.

Fitzgerald and Sim provide a classic statement of the crisis of *political* legitimacy:

[T]he sanction of imprisonment is invoked consistently against marginal, lower class offenders. In so doing, imprisonment serves a class-based legal system, which first, defines the social harms which are singled out for punishment, and second, invokes different types of sanctions for different categories of social harm.

(1982, p. 24)

For abolitionists such as Joe Sim, imprisonment cannot be understood outside of social context—i.e. the social divisions and structural inequities of society around racism, sexism and poverty. Because we lock up the poor, the vulnerable and the powerless, rather than the most dangerous, prisons do not do what they claim to do. In this sense, they are politically illegitimate.

The *moral* legitimacy of imprisonment has also been questioned. For Barbara Hudson and a number of abolitionists from Continental Europe, imprisonment must be understood within the wider debates on punishment (the intentional imposition of suffering). The very deployment of the punitive rationale and punishment itself, rather than the liberal reductionist concerns with prison conditions or standards, become the central focus of a moral critique. For many abolitionists, the deliberate infliction of pain is inherently morally problematic and so the penal system also faces a crisis of moral legitimacy.

The term 'neo-abolitionism' was first introduced by Dutch abolitionist Rene van Swaaningen. Some neo-abolitionists and abolitionists argue that prisons are profoundly immoral and represent the negation of humanity on the bases that:

- the label 'prisoner' constructs a dehumansing context;
- the pains of imprisonment are structured, and present inherent threats to human dignity and respect;
- prisons are a spatial matrix that is predicated on violence and legalised terror;
- prisons dehabilitate people.

The prison is an inherently harm-creating environment that has direct implications for the health of those confined. For anti-prison critics, penal institutions are detestable solutions that we can live without—and this implies their deligitimation.

Abolitionists and neo-abolitionists point to the crises of both moral and political legitimacy.

# RADICAL ALTERNATIVES

Radical alternatives to prison have taken three forms:

- **Political** The promotion of norm-creating social policies that are rooted in social justice (recognition and respect as fellow humans, and the equitable redistribution of wealth), democratic accountability and human rights.
- **Cognitive** A new way of thinking about social problems that is focused on redress, reparation and restoration in relation to harm done.
- **Practical** Concrete alternatives that include offenders and attempt to address offenders' needs. These can be preventative—such as providing investment into youth clubs, constructive employment opportunities and social inclusion— or through promoting restorative justice and community activities that empower, improve skills, meet needs and invest in offenders as human beings.

## "Are abolitionist perspectives plausible in a time of penal expansionism?"

First, you need to explain what you mean by both 'penal abolitionism' and 'penal expansionism'. Then discuss the main themes of the abolitionist perspectives. Highlight the criticisms made against abolitionism, paying particular attention to current political realities and the impact of abolitionism upon penal policies. You may wish to conclude with a defence of abolitionism, looking at its use of reflexivity, and more limited goals and aims, such as the promotion of prisoner human rights.

There are a number of different penal reductionist perspectives. Table 2.10 details six different approaches.

**TAKING IT FURTHER**

**Table 2.10  Six approaches to penal reductionism**

| Approach perspective | Literature |
| --- | --- |
| The Cambridge School | Alison Liebling (2004) *Prisons and their Moral Performance: A Study of Values, Quality and Prison Life* |
| Fabian socialists | Vivien Stern (1989) *Imprisoned by Our Prisons: A Programme for Reform* |

*(Continued)*

**Table 2.10    (Continued)**

| Approach perspective | Literature |
| --- | --- |
| Left realist | Roger Matthews (2009) *Doing Time: An Introduction to the Sociology of Imprisonment* |
| Normalisation | Roy King and Rod Morgan (1980) *The Future of the Prison System* |
| Radical liberal | Andrew Rutherford (1984) *Prisons and the Process of Justice: The Reductionist Challenge* |
| Radical pluralists | Michael Cavadino, James Dignan and George Mair (2013) *The Penal System: An Introduction*, 5th edn |

# BIBLIOGRAPHY

Books which discuss possible future directions of prisons and punishment include:

- **EASTON, S and PIPER, C (2008)** *Sentencing and Punishment: The Quest for Justice*, 2nd edn, Oxford: Oxford University Press.
- **FITZGERALD, M and SIM, J (1982**) *British Prisons*, 2nd edn, Oxford: Blackwell.
- **JEWKES, Y (2007)** *Handbook of Prisons*, Cullompton: Willan.
- **KARSTEDT, S, LOADER, I and STRANG, H (2011)** *Emotions, Crime and Justice*, Oxford: Hart.
- **MATTHEWS, R (1999)** *Doing Time: An Introduction to the Sociology of Imprisonment*, London: Palgrave.
- **McLAUGHLIN, E and Muncie, J (eds) (2002)** *Criminological Perspectives: Essential Readings*, 2nd edn, London: Sage.
- **RUTHERFORD, A (1984)** *Prisons and the Process of Justice: The Reductionist Challenge*, Oxford: Oxford University Press.
- **RYAN, M (2005)** *Penal Policy and Political Culture*, Winchester: Waterside Press.
- **SMITH, P (2008)** *Punishment and Culture*, Chicago, IL: University of Chicago Press.
- **TONRY, M (ed.) (2006)** *The Future of Imprisonment*, Oxford: Oxford University Press.
- **VAN SWAANINGEN, R (1997)** *Critical Criminology: Visions from Europe*, London: Sage.

Other books and articles which adopt an abolitionist stance include:

- **DE HAAN, W (1990)** *The Politics of Redress: Crime, Abolition and Penal Abolition*, London: Sage.
- **DE HAAN, W (1991)** 'Abolition and Crime Control: A Contradiction in Terms', in K Stenson and D Cowell (eds), *The Politics Of Crime Control*, London: Sage.
- **DAVIS, AY (2003)** *Are Prisons Obsolete?* New York: Seven Stories Press.
- **DAVIS, AY (2005)** *Abolition Democracy*, New York: Seven Stories Press.
- **GOLASH, D (2005)** *The Case Against Punishment*, London: New York University Press.
- **MATHIESEN, T (2006)** *Prison On Trial*, 3rd edn, Winchester: Waterside Press.
- **ROLSTON, B, TOMLINSON, M, MOORE, J and SCOTT, D (eds) (2014)** *Beyond Criminal Justice*, Bristol: EGSDSC.
- **RUGGIERO, V (2010)** *Penal Abolitionism*, Oxford: Oxford University Press.
- **SCOTT, D (2009)** 'Punishment', in A Hucklesby and A Wahidin (eds), *Criminal Justice*, Oxford: Oxford University Press.
- **SCOTT, D (2013)** 'Visualising an Abolitionist Real Utopia: Principles, Policy and Praxis', in M Malloch and W Munro (eds), *Crime, Critique and Utopia*, London: Palgrave.
- **SCOTT, D (ed.) (2013)** *Why Prison?* Cambridge: Cambridge University Press.
- **SCOTT, D (2014)** *The Caretakers of Punishment: Power, Legitimacy and the Prison Officer*, London: Palgrave.
- **SCRATON, P (2007)** *Power, Conflict and Criminalisation*, London: Routledge.
- **SIM, J (1994)** 'The abolitionist approach: a British perspective', in A Duff, S Marshall, RE Dobash and RP Dobash (eds), *Penal Theory and Practice: Tradition and Innovation in Criminal Justice*, Manchester: Manchester University Press.
- **SIM, J (2009)** *Punishment and Prisons: Power and the Carceral State*, London: Sage.

And books which advance alternative prison and punishment perspectives are:

- **JOHNSTONE, G (2011)** *Restorative Justice: Ideas, Values, Debates*, 2nd edn, London: Routledge.
- **ZEHR, H (2005)** *Changing Lenses: A New Focus for Crime and Justice*, 3rd edn, Scottdale, PA: Herald Press.

# PART III*

# STUDY WRITING AND
# REVISION SKILLS

---

*in collaboration with David McIlroy

# 3.1 HOW TO GET THE MOST OUT OF YOUR LECTURES AND SEMINARS

**Core areas**

use of lecture notes
mastering technical terms
developing independent study
note-taking strategy
developing the lecture
seminars should not be underestimated

It is the responsibility of your tutors to provide module booklets detailing lecture topics and recommended readings. It is a good idea to become familiar with your module outlines as soon as possible. Before you go into each lecture, you should briefly remind yourself of where it fits into the overall scheme of things.

*It is a good idea to acquaint yourself with the main recommended textbooks before the start of the module. Purchase them, if possible, secondhand from the university bookshop or online.*

# USE OF LECTURE NOTES

It is important that you do not view lectures as providing all the information needed about a given topic. Lectures provide a basic outline only. Full and complete knowledge of a subject only comes from reading. It is always beneficial to do some preliminary reading before a lecture, otherwise you will find it difficult to participate in class discussions. If lecture notes are provided in advance (e.g. electronically), read these over and bring them with you to the lecture. Some lecturers provide full notes, some make skeletal outlines available, and some do not issue notes at all. If notes are provided, take full advantage and supplement these with your own notes as you listen. Some basic preparation will equip you with a great advantage: you will be able to 'tune in' and think more clearly about the lecture than you would have been able to had you not undertaken the preliminary work.

> *Lecturers are likely to draw on key readings only. Make a note of any supplementary reading and other theories and studies signposted to you in the lecture so that you can fill in the gaps.*

# MASTERING TECHNICAL TERMS

New words can be threatening, especially if you have to face a string of them in one lecture. Uncertainty about new terms may impair your ability to benefit fully from lectures and hinder your comprehension of the subject matter when reading. The use of technical terms in penology is unavoidable, but when you have employed a term a number of times yourself it will not seem as daunting as it did initially.

## CHECKLIST FOR MASTERING TERMS USED IN LECTURES

✓ Read lecture notes before the lectures.
✓ List any unfamiliar terms.
✓ Read over the listed terms until you are familiar with their sound.
✓ Try to work out meanings of terms from their context.
✓ Write out a sentence that includes the new word (do this for each word).

✓ Meet with other students and test each other with the technical terms.
✓ Jot down new words you hear in lectures and check out their meaning soon afterwards.

*Your confidence will greatly increase when you begin to follow the flow of arguments that contain technical terms, especially when you can freely use the terms yourself, both in speaking and writing.*

# DEVELOPING INDEPENDENT STUDY

The issues raised in your lectures are designed to inspire you to undertake deeper independent study. Invariably, your aim should be to build on what you are given, and you should never merely return the bare bones of the lecture material in a piece of coursework or in an exam.

*It is always refreshing for a lecturer or examiner to receive assignments or exam answers that contain references to studies that he or she has not highlighted in a related lecture or has not previously encountered.*

# NOTE-TAKING STRATEGY

Note taking in lectures is an art that you will only perfect with practice, and by trial and error. The problem will always be to try to find a balance between concentrating on what you hear, and making sufficient notes that will enable you later to remember and reflect on what you have heard. You should not, however, become frustrated by the fact that you will not immediately understand or remember everything that you have heard.

## GUIDELINES FOR NOTE TAKING IN LECTURES

To develop a note-taking strategy that works best for you; work at finding a balance between listening and writing. This may entail listing a few key words to summarise the issues discussed in the lecture. Remember that:

- too much writing may impair the flow of the lecture for you;
- too much writing may impair the quality of your notes;
- some limited notes are better than none;
- good note taking facilitates deeper processing of information;
- it is essential to 'tidy up' notes as soon as possible after a lecture;
- reading over notes soon after lectures will consolidate your learning.

## DEVELOPING THE LECTURE

Lectures are sometimes criticised as a form of 'passive learning'. Some lecturers, however, make their lectures more interactive by using handouts or posing questions during the lecture and giving students time to reflect on these. As a student, you can also make the lecture more interactive by:

- trying to interact with the lecture material by asking questions;
- highlighting points that you would like to develop independently;
- tracing connections between the lecture and other parts of your study programme;
- restructuring the lecture outline into your own preferred format;
- thinking of ways in which aspects of the lecture material can be applied;
- designing ways in which aspects of the lecture material can be illustrated;
- making a note of interesting questions if the lecturer invites questions;
- following up on issues of interest that have arisen out of the lecture.

## SEMINARS SHOULD NOT BE UNDERESTIMATED

Seminars have a unique contribution to learning. They provide an opportunity to revisit and explore topics in more depth. Seminars can:

- identify problems of which you had not previously thought;
- clear up confusing issues;
- allow you to ask questions and make comments;
- help you to develop friendships and teamwork;
- enable you to refresh and consolidate your knowledge;
- help you to sharpen your motivation and redirect your study efforts.

There are a number of ways in which you can benefit from seminars. The checklist below is a useful tool to help you gain the maximum benefits.

# CHECKLIST OF STRATEGIES FOR BENEFITING FROM YOUR SEMINAR EXPERIENCE

✓ Do some preparatory reading.
✓ Familiarise yourself with the main ideas to be addressed.
✓ Make notes during the seminar.
✓ Make some verbal contribution, even if it is only a single question.
✓ Trace learning links from the seminar to other topics on your programme.
✓ Continue discussion with fellow students after the seminar has ended.

If you are required to give a presentation as part of a seminar, the following points will be helpful.

- Map out where you are going and be selective in what you choose to present.
- Have a practice run with friends.
- If using visuals, check out beforehand that all equipment works.
- Space out your points clearly on any visuals (i.e. make them large and legible).
- Time your presentation in relation to your visuals (e.g. five slides for a 15-minute talk = 3 minutes per slide).
- Make sure your presentation synchronises with the slides on view.
- Project your voice so all in the room can hear.
- Inflect your voice and do not stand motionless.
- Spread eye contact around the audience.
- Avoid the twin extremes of a fixed gaze on certain individuals or of never looking at anyone.
- It is better to fall a little short of time allocated than to run over.
- Summarise your main points at the end.

# 3.2 WRITING A DISSERTATION

## THE RESEARCH PROCESS

A dissertation is an independent piece of work that you will be expected to complete, probably in the third year of your undergraduate degree or towards the end of a taught postgraduate degree. The length of your dissertation can range from 8,000 to 20,000 words. If you are doing a research degree, the word length will be even longer. Undergraduate dissertations are normally 10,000 words. Although this may sound a lot at the start, by the time you come to submit your dissertation, you will probably wish it could be much longer. A dissertation is an original piece of work negotiated between you and your dissertation supervisor. It is an opportunity for you to explore a topic in which you have developed a particular interest. It should therefore prove to be the most enjoyable piece of work you complete on your degree.

The art of writing a dissertation is to identify the appropriate themes and issues that need to be incorporated into your work. This is often the hardest part, and so it is important that you give the focus of your topic and access to relevant literature a great deal of thought. With the support of your supervisor, you will need to select a working title, devise a literature review, organise chapter structures and set deadlines.

> *It is important, in a large project (such as a dissertation), that you choose a topic you are really interested in and for which you can maintain your motivation, momentum and enthusiasm.*

# PREPARATION AND FOCUS

It is sensible to choose a dissertation topic which has been covered already in other modules and you have a prior overview of the general literature. You will need to convince your supervisor that there is enough material readily available for you to undertake the project. Always start with the most broad and straightforward books, and then work your way into the specialist area. Focus is all-important. You should ask yourself what exactly you want to examine in your dissertation: a common mistake is to try to do too much. This is natural and you will probably find that, as you progress with your project, you will refine the topic to a much smaller issue, or combination of issues.

> *Time is also very important. If you are an undergraduate student, you should start thinking about your dissertation in your second year, and as a postgraduate on a taught course, it is worthwhile thinking about your dissertation as soon as you start your course.*

Dissertations usually involve the collection and analysis of either 'primary' data, produced through empirical research (interviews or participant observation for example), or 'secondary' data, produced through a review of relevant literature (theoretical analysis or official reports, for example). Undergraduate students should probably undertake literature reviews rather than empirical research. This is because doing empirical work well is quite difficult, and there are also clear ethical issues that need to be addressed in the design and application of the dissertation.

# CHAPTER STRUCTURE

Once you have established a clear focus, a good chapter structure is key to success. There are no hard and fast rules about how dissertations should be structured, but a penology dissertation might be organised in the following way:

## 1 Introduction to study and context to research question (Word count: 5–10 per cent)

What is the focus of your study and why is it important?
How can the research issue be understood in context?
What theoretical position have you adopted?
What methodologies have you used to access literature or data? (If you are doing empirical research instead of a literature review, you will need to provide a detailed account of the methodology used.)
What is the broad structure and content of the dissertation?

## 2 Definitions, data and historical contexts (Word count: 15–20 per cent)

What are the major historical developments?
What is the official definition and data on the given issue?
Should these social constructions be problematised?

## 3 Theories and explanations (Word count: 15–20 per cent)

What are the dominant ways of thinking about the issue?
Are there competing explanations?
Are there gaps and omissions in the literature?

## 4 Policy (Word count: 15–20 per cent)

What are the main penal policies on the issue?
What are their strengths and weaknesses?

## 5 Case studies (Word count: 15–20 per cent)

What are the main cases linked to your research focus?
What do problems, concerns or good practices highlight?

## 6 Evaluation of case studies/effectiveness of current responses (Word count: 15–20 per cent)

How does the case study link to the main research question?
How is a given problem investigated or examined by the government?

## 7 Conclusion (Word count: less than 5 per cent)

How have you answered the research question or explored the topic focus? What are the implications of your findings?

> When working out your chapter structure, you should be looking to provide a platform for the central focus of the dissertation. Chapters should be building blocks that are leading the reader towards a case study, empirical evidence and ultimately your evaluation of the material presented and conclusions.

In many dissertations, your evaluation and conclusions can be combined into one chapter. This will allow you a greater percentage of the word count in the preceding chapters.

---

### Structure of a dissertation

**Example question and research focus:** 'Is the dual purpose of imprisonment to punish and reform offenders defensible?'

- *Introduction* Outline of chapter structure and context of the dissertation including justification for the historical tradition of punishment and reform (Gladstone, 1895); the prevention of crime and reduction of reoffending.
- *Chapter 1* Overview of different theories and justifications for rehabilitation in prison: utilitarian, rights based, social and individual.
- *Chapter 2* Now counterbalance the justifications for punishment and reform against the incompatibility arguments; including retributivist principles, disciplinary perspectives and liberal arguments, and highlighting the corrosive effects of imprisonment. Discuss problems of definition, and also diversity issues: age, 'race', gender.
- *Chapter 3* Analysis of practice developments: impact of prison crisis dilemmas: overcrowding, security issues, 'humane containment'.
- *Chapter 4* Critical appraisal of rehabilitation policies: 'nothing works', 'What Works'.
- *Chapter 5* Case studies of rehabilitation programmes in prison: e.g. anger management programmes, sex offender treatment programmes,

*(Continued)*

---

*(Continued)*

education and work programmes. Ensure that you have access to recent critical evaluations of the case studies you choose.

- **Conclusion** Answer the question you have identified as the central focus of the dissertation—what does this tell us about penal legitimacy and the justifications for imprisonment?

## SUPERVISION

Supervision is very important. Supervisors provide intellectual support, help you keep on track and can also help with basic referencing and layout tips. You will have regular meetings with your supervisor. In the first or second meeting, you should be able to offer:

- a clear topic area;
- a specific focus or question;
- a list of references that you can access, having already undertaken some preliminary reading;
- an idea of how you are going to structure your dissertation;
- the deadlines of when you are going to submit your chapters.

It is the responsibility of the supervisor to ensure that he or she is available to see you over the year, but it is down to you to make sure that you use that time constructively. This means giving him or her plenty of time to read plans or drafts before meetings. What your supervisor will not do is edit drafts of your work or correct your grammar.

*Many universities recommend receiving six hours of supervision over the course of a year. This would mean seeing your supervisor for a 30-minute meeting every two weeks over semesters one and two.*

## FROM FIRST THOUGHTS TO FINAL DRAFT

Completing the first draft of the dissertation is the hardest part. You should always try to finish your dissertation with a few weeks to spare. This will allow you to proofread your dissertation and spot any small mistakes or contradictory arguments. When reading a dissertation, you should initially focus on the content, rather than on sentence structure or referencing problems. Everything takes longer than you think: you may expect to finish a chapter in a couple of weeks, but it will probably take twice as long. Remember that writing academically involves being able to explain and apply all of the concepts you use. Write in a clear and understandable way and explain what you mean. Do not take the reader's knowledge for granted. You are being tested on what you know and how you came to your conclusions.

> *Hard work will pay off: rewrites, especially if you follow the guidance of your dissertation supervisor, will lead to better marks. Remember that your supervisor is also likely to be one of your markers.*

## CHECKLIST FOR YOUR DISSERTATION

- ✓ Undertake preliminary reading and ensure that enough material is available.
- ✓ Have a clear focus and structure.
- ✓ Set yourself deadlines from the beginning.
- ✓ Make the most of your supervision.
- ✓ Complete a first draft at least a month before the deadline.
- ✓ Ensure that the final draft has been proofread and is properly referenced.

# 3.3 ESSAY-WRITING HINTS

## GETTING INTO THE FLOW

When writing an essay (or dissertation chapter), one of your first aims should be to get your mind engaged with the subject. Before you begin to write, it is a good idea to 'warm up' for your essay by jotting down key themes and ideas. This will allow you to think within the framework of your topic and will be especially important if you are coming to the subject for the first time.

## THE 'TRIBUTARY' PRINCIPLE

A 'tributary' is a stream that runs into a river as it wends its way to the sea. Similarly, in an essay, you should ensure that every idea you introduce is moving towards the overall theme you are addressing. Your ideas should be relevant to subheadings, and subheadings to main headings.

Every idea you introduce should 'feed' into the flowing theme. Avoid 'distributaries', ideas that run away from the main stream of thought and leave the reader confused about their relevance. It is one thing to have grasped your subject thoroughly, but quite another to convince your reader that this is the case. Your aim should be to build up ideas sentence by sentence and paragraph by paragraph, until you have communicated your clear purpose to the reader.

> *It is important that you do not include irrelevant material and that you stay focused on the essay question. You can make linking statements that show a wider understanding of the issues, but you must ensure that you explain how they contribute to your answer and why you consider them to be relevant.*

All subjects have central concepts that sometimes can be usefully labelled by a single word or term. Course textbooks may include a glossary of terms, and these provide the essential raw materials upon which you can build mastery of a topic. Ensure that you learn the terms and their definitions, and then link key terms and words together.

### "Write an essay answering the question 'Are our prisons accountable?'"

You might decide to draft your outline points in the manner shown in Figure 3.2 (or you may prefer to use a mind-map approach).

## ADDRESSING PENAL CONTROVERSIES

In higher education, students are required to make the transition from descriptive to critical writing. You should imagine the critical approach to be like a law case that is being conducted, in which there is both a prosecution and a defence. Your concern should be for objectivity, transparency and fairness. No matter how passionately you feel about a cause, you must not allow information to be filtered out because of personal prejudice. An essay should not be made a crusade in which contrary arguments are ignored or not addressed in an even-handed manner. You should demonstrate awareness that opposite

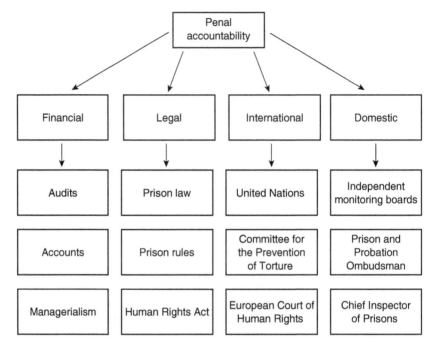

**Figure 3.2  Considering penal accountability**

views are held and represent them as accurately as possible. This does not mean that your own views are not important. You are entitled to adopt a position on a particular subject and feel strongly about it. Indeed, such feelings may well be a marked advantage if you can bring them under control and channel them into balanced, effective writing. Below is an example of a controversial issue that may stir up heated debate.

## "Offer arguments for and against the privatisation of prisons."

### For

'Private companies provide criminal justice services at the same or improved levels as the public sector, but at lower cost.'

'Privatisation unleashes "entrepreneurial energy": private companies are more innovative in management and delivery.'

'Competition – market testing, competitive tendering – results in better standards of delivery, in contrast to the monopoly position of the state.'

'Private companies are able to avoid industrial conflict and opposition to new practice developments by public sector unions.'

'Private companies are more open to public scrutiny, as operational standards are specified in contracts, and penalties imposed if they are breached.'

'To address problems of prison overcrowding, private finance pays the costs of new high technology, modern prisons which otherwise would not get built.'

## Against

'Punishment should be a function of government. Privatisation weakens the bond between the citizen and the state – "the social contract".'

'The private sector is more interested in doing well financially than doing good morally.'

'Private companies are removed from democratic control. They are responsible to their shareholders, not to government.'

'Obligations to shareholders may conflict with the need to improve services and conditions.'

'Profits are to be made by recruiting fewer staff, paying lower wagers and investing less in training. This can increase risks to staff and prisoners.'

'Private companies have a vested interest in seeing prison populations rise.'

'Competition is not guaranteed. By monopolising the market, large firms are free to negotiate higher prices.'

# STRUCTURING AN OUTLINE

In academic writing, structure and order facilitate good communication. You might plan for an 'Introduction', a 'Conclusion' and three main sections, each with several subheadings (see example below). Alternatively, you may decide not to include headings in your final presentation—i.e. you may use them only initially to structure and balance your arguments. Either way, a good structure will help you balance the weight of each of your arguments against the others and arrange your points in the order that best facilitates the fluent progression of your argument.

## "Write an essay answering the question 'Does prison work?'"

### 1 What do we mean by the term 'prison works'?

i) Define the term 'prison works'. Does it have validity in relation to debates on retribution, deterrence and incapacitation?

ii) Outline the political context and rise of the 'prison works' movement in the 1990s.

iii) Highlight the main advocates of this perspective in the UK, such as Michael Howard.

### 2 The implications of the 'prison works' agenda: penal expansionism

i) Discuss the definition of 'penal expansionism' provided by Andrew Rutherford (1984).

ii) Examine recent data on prison populations to assess the extent of penal expansionism.

### 3 The defence of this perspective

i) Investigate the main arguments defending 'prison works', such as those of Charles Murray and the pressure group Civitas.

ii) Overview the claims made regarding the relationship between 'crime' rates and levels of imprisonment.

### 4 What criticisms can be made against this argument?

i) Consider the accuracy of the data deployed to defend rising rates of imprisonment.

ii) Detail the philosophical, sociological and administrative evidence concerning deterrence and incapacitation.

# IDENTIFYING KEY QUESTIONS

When you are constructing a draft outline for an essay or project, you should formulate the major questions you wish to address. It is useful to make a list of all the issues you might wish to tackle. The ability to design a good question is an art form that needs to be cultivated. To illustrate the point, consider the example below. For criminal justice to be legitimate it must have legitimacy in the eyes of the public. But gauging public opinion on public issues such as prisons and punishment is difficult. The beliefs human beings have are susceptible to widely different meanings and understandings. Some penologists have suggested that in recent years public opinion has become more punitive, and this is reflected in more authoritarian penal policies. How do we know this is true? You might, as your starting point, pose the following questions:

## "Are contemporary penal policies influenced by popular punitiveness?"

What is the definition given of 'popular punitiveness'?

To what extent is it understood in the strict sense as privileging the infliction of pain and attributes of cruelty and revenge over other justifications of punishment: incapacitation, deterrence and reform?

What are the main social scientific explanations that have been advanced for the emergence of punitiveness in public life?

What evidence is there for its popularity? Refer to opinion polls, the British Crime Survey, for example.

What policy evidence is there that governments have become more punitive over recent years? Refer to increases in prison populations, harsher sentencing, decline of welfare, etc.

In what ways do new community based measures signify punitiveness in contemporary penality? Refer to specific examples and explain what is distinctively punitive about them.

In implementing new sentencing, prison and community based policies, how often, and in what detail, have governments referred specifically to popular punitiveness in official statements and reports as justifications for the approach taken?

# REST YOUR CASE

It should be your aim to give the clear impression that your arguments are not based on hunches, bias, feelings or intuition. In exams and essay questions, it is usually assumed that you will appeal to theoretical perspectives and research evidence to support your claims. Therefore, when you write your essay or dissertation, you should ensure that it is liberally sprinkled with recognised citations. By the time the assessor reaches the end of your work, he or she should be convinced that your conclusions are evidence-based. A fatal flaw would be to make claims for which you have provided no authoritative source.

> *Make sure to spread your citations across your essay, rather than compressing them into a paragraph or two at the beginning and end.*

Some examples of how you might introduce your evidence and sources are:

'According to Liebling (2004) ...'
'Sim (2008) has concluded that ...'
'Cohen (2001) found that ...
'It has been claimed by Garland (1990) that ...'
'Hudson (2003) asserted that ...'
'A review of the evidence by Codd (2008) suggests that ...'

## CAREFUL USE OF QUOTATIONS

Although it is desirable to present a good range of citations, it is not appropriate to simply paste together what others have said, with little thought for interpretative comment or coherent structure. As a general point, avoid very lengthy extracts: short ones can be very effective. Aim to blend quotations as naturally as possible into the flow of your sentences. Also, it is good to vary your practices: sometimes by using short, direct, brief quotations (citing page number, as well as author and year), and at other times by summarising the gist of a quotation in your own words (citing the author's name and year of publication, but leaving out quotation marks and page number).

> *A good guide for deciding whether to include a quotation is to consider its originality, or if you find the prose is so beautifully or powerfully written that you could not hope to put it better yourself.*

Referencing practice may vary from one discipline to the next, but some general points that contribute to good practice are:

- names and dates in text should correspond exactly with those listed in the 'References' or 'Bibliography';
- 'References' should be listed in alphabetical order by the surname (not the initials) of the author or first author;
- any reference you make in the text should be traceable by the reader (i.e. he or she should clearly be able to identify the source).

## A CLEARLY DEFINED 'INTRODUCTION'

In an 'Introduction' to an essay, you have the opportunity to define the problem or issue that is being addressed and to set it within context. Resist the temptation to elaborate on any issue at this stage. The introduction should provide a taster of what is to follow, in order to whet the reader's appetite and mark out the boundaries of your discussion.

*If you leave the introduction and definition of your problem until the end of your writing, you will be better placed to map out the directions taken.*

## THE 'CONCLUSION': ADDING THE FINISHING TOUCHES

In the 'Conclusion', you should aim to tie your essay together in a clear and coherent manner. It is your last chance to leave an overall impression in your reader's mind. Therefore, at this stage, you will want to do justice to your efforts and not sell yourself short. This is your opportunity to identify the strongest evidence points and where the balance of probability lies. The conclusion to an exam question often has to be written hurriedly under the pressure of time, but with an essay or dissertation you can refine and adjust the content to your satisfaction. Do not underestimate the value of an effective conclusion. 'Sign off' your essay in a manner that summarises succinctly your arguments and brings closure to your subject.

## TOP-DOWN AND BOTTOM-UP CLARITY

An essay gives you the opportunity to refine each sentence and paragraph according to the 'tributary' principle. From a 'top-down' perspective —i.e.

that of starting at the top with your major outline points—clarity is facilitated by the structure drafted in your outline. You can ensure that the subheadings are appropriately placed under the most relevant main heading, and that both subheadings and main headings are arranged in logical sequence. From a 'bottom-up' perspective— i.e. that of building up the details that 'flesh out' your main points—you should check that each sentence is a 'feeder' for the predominant concept in a given paragraph. When all this is done, you can check that the transition from one point to the next is smooth, rather than abrupt.

## CHECKLIST: SUMMARY FOR ESSAY WRITING

- ✓ Before you start, 'warm up' by giving yourself thinking time.
- ✓ List the major concepts and link them in fluent form.
- ✓ Design a structure (outline) that will facilitate balance, progression, fluency and clarity.
- ✓ Pose questions and address these in a critical way.
- ✓ Demonstrate that your arguments rest on evidence, and distribute cited sources across your essay.
- ✓ Provide an 'Introduction' that sets the scene and a 'Conclusion' that rounds off the arguments.

# 3.4 REVISION HINTS

**Core areas**

compile summary notes
keep organised records
use past papers
employ effective memory aids
alternate between methods
revise with others

Strategy for revision should be on your mind from your very first lecture at the beginning of your academic semester. You should be like a squirrel that stores up nuts for the winter: do not waste any lecture, tutorial, seminar or group discussion by letting the material evaporate into thin air; get into the habit of making guidelines for revision after each learning activity. Keep a folder, file or small notebook in which to write out the major points you have learned in each session. By establishing this regular practice, what you have learned will become consolidated in your mind, enabling you to 'import' and 'export' material both within and across subjects.

*If you do this regularly and do not make the task too tedious, you will be amazed at how much useful summary material you have accumulated when it comes to revision time.*

## COMPILE SUMMARY NOTES

It is useful and convenient to have a notebook or cards on which to write outline summaries that provide an overview of your subject at a glance. You might use treasury tags to hold different batches of cards together, allowing for inserts and re-sorting. Such practical resources can easily be slipped into your pocket or bag and produced when you are on the bus or train, or sitting in a traffic jam. A glance over your notes will consolidate your learning and encourage you to think further about your subject. It is also useful to make a note of questions that you would like to explore in greater depth at a later time.

## KEEP ORGANISED RECORDS

People who have a fulfilled career usually have developed the twin skills of time and task management. You can use your academic training to prepare for your future career in this respect. Ensure that you do not fall short of your potential simply because these qualities have not been cultivated.

One important tactic is to keep a folder for each subject and to divide this topic by topic, keeping your topics in the same order in which they are presented in your course lectures. Use subject dividers to separate the topics. At the front of the folder, compile an index of the contents, listing each topic clearly as a way of identifying each new section. Notes may come from lectures, seminars, tutorials, internet searches, personal notes etc.

*Academic success has as much to do with good organisation and planning as it has to do with ability. The value of the material you accumulate on your academic programme may be diminished if you do not organise it into an easily retrievable form.*

## USE PAST PAPERS

Revision will be limited if it is confined to memory work. While you should read over your revision cards or notebooks, it is also essential that you become familiar with how essay and exam questions are likely to be framed. If they are accessible to you, build up a good range of past essay and exam papers (especially recent ones) and add these to your folder.

## EMPLOY EFFECTIVE MEMORY AIDS

Use devices that help you recall information that might otherwise be difficult to retrieve from memory. 'Visualisation' is one technique that can be used to aid memory: for example, the 'location method' involves visualising a familiar journey and 'placing' facts you wish to remember at various landmarks along the journey—e.g. a bus stop, a car park, a shop, a store, a bend, a police station, a traffic light etc. This has the advantage of associating information you have learned with material already firmly embedded and structured in your memory. Therefore, once the relevant memory is activated, a dynamic 'domino effect' will be triggered. There is, however, no reason why you cannot use a whole toolkit of memory aids.

---

**Memory aids**

Memory can be enhanced when information is processed in a range of modalities, such as hearing, seeing, speaking and visualising. Some examples are:

- *Alliteration's artful aid* Phrase a key learning point in such a way that it forms a series of words all beginning with the same letter.
- *The 'peg' system* 'Hang' information onto a term (an 'umbrella' term) so that when you hear that term, you will remember the ideas connected with it.
- *Acronyms* Take the first letter of all of the key words and make a word from these. These are widely used in penology. Recent examples include NOMS (the National Offender Management Service) and CARATS (the Counselling, Advice, Referral, Assessment and Throughcare Services).
- *Mind maps* These allow you to draw lines that stretch out from the central idea to develop subsidiary ideas in the same way.
- *'Rhymes and chimes'* Associate words that rhyme and words that end with a similar sound (e.g. criminalisation, penalisation, incarceration).

---

# ALTERNATE BETWEEN METHODS

It is not enough, however, merely to present a list of outline points in response to a question (although it is better to do this than to do nothing if you have run out of time in an exam). Your aim should be to add substance, evidence and arguments to your basic points. Work at finding a balance between the two methods—outline revision cards might be best reserved for short bus journeys, whereas extended reading is better employed for longer revision slots at home or in the library.

244 PRISONS & PUNISHMENT

# REVISE WITH OTHERS

Group work is deemed advantageous by educationalists, and teamwork is held to be a desirable employability quality. If you can find a few other students with whom to revise, this will provide a fresh approach to your learning. First, ensure that others carry their own workloads and are not merely using the hard work of others as a short-cut to success. This collective approach will allow you to assess your strengths and weaknesses (showing you where you are offtrack), and to benefit from the resources and insights of others. Before you meet up, design some questions for the whole group to address. The group might also go through past essay and exam questions to identify what is an effective response to each question— but remember: it should not be the aim to provide standard and identical answers that each group member can mimic.

# 3.5 EXAM HINTS

## HANDLING YOUR NERVES

Exam nerves are not unusual: anxiety arises because of the perception that your performance is being evaluated, that the consequences are likely to be serious, and that you are working under the pressure of time. If you focus on the task at hand, rather than on feeding a downward negative spiral in your thinking patterns, it will help you keep your nerves under control. It has been said that stress is the body's call to take action, but anxiety is a maladaptive response to that call.

*Try to interpret your nervous reactions positively—being nervous shows you care. Symptoms are more likely to be problematic if you interpret them negatively, pay too much attention to them, and allow them to interfere with your exam preparation or performance.*

## TIME MANAGEMENT

The all-important matter as you approach an exam is to develop the belief that you can take control of the situation. As you work through the list of issues that need to be addressed, you will be able to tick them off one by one. One of the issues about which you will need to be clear before the exam is the length of time that you should allocate to each question. Sometimes, this can be quite simple (although it is always necessary to read the rubric carefully: for example, if two questions are to be answered in a two-hour paper, you should allow one hour for each question. If it is a two-hour paper with one essay question and five shorter answers, you might allow one hour for the essay and 12 minutes each for the shorter questions—but you must check the weighting for the marks on each question. You will also need to deduct whatever time it takes to read over the paper and to choose your questions. More importantly, give yourself some practice on papers similar to those you are likely to face (i.e. past papers).

*Do not forget that excessive time on your 'strongest' question may not compensate for very poor answers to other questions.*

## TASK MANAGEMENT

Decide on the questions you wish to address and then plan your answers. Some students prefer to plan all outlines and draft work at the beginning, while others prefer to plan and address one answer before proceeding to address the next question.

*The exam is like conducting an argument, but one in which you have the opportunity to get your views across without interruption.*

Decide on your strategy before you enter the exam room and stick to your plan. After you have completed your draft outline, allocate an appropriate time for each section. This will prevent you from treating some aspects excessively, while falling short on others. Careful planning will help you to achieve balance, fluency and symmetry.

> *Remaining aware of time limitations will help you to write succinctly and stay focused on the task, while preventing you from dressing up your responses with unnecessary padding.*

# ATTEND TO PRACTICAL DETAILS

This short section is designed to remind you of the practical details that should be attended to in preparation for an exam. There are always students who turn up late, go to the wrong venue, arrive for the wrong exam, or do not turn up at all! Check and recheck that you have all of the details of each exam correctly noted.

## CHECKLIST: PRACTICAL EXAM DETAILS

- ✓ Check that you have the correct venue and know where it is.
- ✓ Ensure that the exam time you have noted is accurate.
- ✓ Allow sufficient time for your journey.
- ✓ Bring an adequate supply of stationery and a drink.
- ✓ Fill in required personal details before the exam begins.

# THE ART OF 'NAME DROPPING'

When answering an exam question, you will be required to cite studies as evidence for your arguments and link these to the names of researchers, scholars or theorists. It will help if you can use the correct dates, or at least the decades. Try to be original in demonstrating your sociological imagination. A marker will have dozens, if not hundreds, of scripts to work through and he or she will know if you are just repeating the same phrases from the same sources as everyone else.

> *Give the clear impression that you have done more than the bare minimum and that you have enthusiasm for the subject.*

# A POLITICIAN'S ANSWER

Politicians are renowned for refusing to answer questions directly or for evading them through raising other questions. A humorous example is that of a politician being asked: 'Is it true that you always answer questions by asking another?' To which the politician replied: 'Who told you that?' The point here is that, in an exam, you must make sure you answer the set question, although there may be other questions that arise out of this that you might want to highlight in your conclusion. As a first principle, you must answer the set question and not another you had hoped to answer.

## "Explain and critically analyse Rusche and Kirchheimer's (1939) argument that economic forces shape penal policy and practice."

### Directly relevant points

A traditional Marxist perspective – base and superstructure.
   Negation of relationship between 'crime' and punishment.
   Labour market thesis (the link between imprisonment and unemployment).
   Economic change and functions of punishment.
   A reductivist perspective.
   Historicial evidence is contradictory.
   Alternative labour market perspective: the 'exchange of equivalents'—money for time, 'the prison and the factory' (Melossi and Pavarini, 1981).

### Less relevant points

Broader themes of Marxist social theory.
   Deterrence and the symbolic role of imprisonment.
   Alternatives to imprisonment.
   Foucauldian elaborations.
   The development and decline of state welfare.
   Poverty as a social problem.

Although some of the 'less relevant points' listed may be relevant overall, they are not as directly relevant to the given question. Ensure that you focus on the actual question.

# MISSING YOUR QUESTION

Students have often been heard, after an exam, to complain bitterly that the topic they had revised so thoroughly had not been tested in the exam. The first response is, of course, that students should always cover enough topics to avoid selling themselves short—the habit of 'question spotting' across past papers is always a risky game to play. The reality may be, however, that the question was there, but not in the precise words the student expected it to be. The simple lesson, then, is to always read over the exam paper carefully, slowly and thoughtfully.

# WRITE IT DOWN

If you write down the question that you have chosen to address and, perhaps, quietly mouth it to yourself, you are more likely to process fully its true meaning and intent. Think of how easy it is to misunderstand a question that has been put to you verbally, because you have misinterpreted the tone or emphasis.

# PURSUE A CRITICAL APPROACH

In degree courses, you are usually expected to write critically rather than merely descriptively, although it may be necessary to use some minimal descriptive substance as the raw material for your debate. Given that most questions require some form of critical evaluation of the evidence, you will need to address issues one by one from different standpoints. What you should *not* do, however, is digress and discuss irrelevant and abstract information.

# ANALYSE THE PARTS

A good essay cannot be constructed without reference to its component parts. Although breaking down a question into component parts is not sufficient for an excellent essay, it is a necessary starting point.

## "Discuss the view that the purpose of punishment is to prevent 'crime'."

This is not a straightforward question. First you need to define 'crime', articulating its social construction. Then you need to critically analyse the three utilitarian principles of incapacitation, deterrence and reform. Prioritise these in the order you prefer. To conclude, assess utilitarian principles against the alternative symbolic view of punishment.

## "Critically appraise the development of punishment in the community."

This also is not straightforward. You will need to consider changes to probation policy and practice, especially its new supervisory role. You should address the broad historical, economic and political factors which have contributed to the 'dispersal of discipline', 'decarceration', 'net widening' and the recent 'responsibilisation' and 'respect' agendas. Perhaps finally consider whether communities have benefitted from the change in policy direction and the extent to which there is opposition to it.

# WHEN ASKED TO 'DISCUSS'

In a 'discussion', as you raise one issue, another might arise out of it. In a discussion, your aim should be not only to identify and define all of the parts but also where they fit (or do not fit) into the overall picture.

## CHECKLIST: FEATURES OF A RESPONSE TO A 'DISCUSS' QUESTION

- ✓ It contains a chain of issues that lead into each other in sequence.
- ✓ It has clear shape and direction, which is unfolded in the progression of the argument.
- ✓ It is underpinned by reference to findings and certainties.
- ✓ It identifies those issues for which doubt remains.

# IF A 'CRITIQUE' IS REQUESTED

One example that might help to clarify what is involved in a 'critique' is the hotly debated topic of the imprisonment of women. It would be important, in the interest of balance and fairness, to present all sides and shades of the argument. You would then look at whether there is available evidence to support each argument, and you might introduce issues that have been coloured by gender, prejudice, tradition, religion and legislation. You would aim to identify those arguments that are based on emotion and intuition, and to get down to those arguments that really have solid evidence-based support. Finally, you would need to flag up where the strongest evidence appears to lie and also to identify issues that appear to be inconclusive. It would be expected that you should, if possible, arrive at some certainties.

# IF ASKED TO 'COMPARE AND CONTRAST'

When asked to 'compare and contrast', you should be thinking in terms of similarities and differences. You should ask what the two issues share in common and what features of each are distinct.

## "Compare and contrast penal reductionist and abolitionist approaches to the penal system."

### Similarities

Both promote humanitarian changes to dealing with offenders.

Both highlight the pains of imprisonment and penal controversies, such as the punishment of the mentally ill, self-inflicted deaths and racism in prison.

Both promote the human rights of offenders.

Both highlight the necessity of democratic and legally accountable means of dealing with offenders.

Both call for alternatives to prison.

### Contrasts

The legitimacy of punishment and the punitive rationale are conceived differently in each approach.

Reductionists focus mainly on changing the criminal justice system, whereas abolitionists highlight socio-economic and political contexts.

There are differences in the proposed content of human rights.

Reductionists believe that prisons can be reformed, whereas abolitionists point to the inherent brutalities of imprisonment.

Abolitionists call for radical alternatives, while reductionists look to probation and more mainstream community penalties.

# WHEN ASKED TO 'EVALUATE'

When thinking about how to approach a question that asks you to 'evaluate' a theory or concept in penology, you should consider:

- Has the theory stood the test of time?
- Is there a supportive evidence base that is not easily overturned?
- Are there questionable elements that should be challenged?
- Does more recent evidence point to a need for modification?
- Is the theory robust and likely to be around for the foreseeable future?
- Might it be strengthened through being merged with other theories?

It should be noted that the words presented in the above examples might not always be the exact words that will appear on your exam script—you might, for example, find 'analyse', 'outline' or 'investigate' etc.—but the best advice is to check over past exam papers and to familiarise yourself with the words that are most recurrent.

# PART IV
# ADDITIONAL
# RESOURCES

# GLOSSARY

**Abolitionism**   A theoretical and political perspective holding that the penal system creates, rather than provides solutions to, **social problems**. Abolitionists call for new understandings of the social harms that we face and for **radical alternatives** to current ways of responding to **wrongdoing**.

**Actuarialism**   An insurance technique that can be deployed to manage 'crime' by analysing the distribution of **risk** within aggregate populations.

**Administrative penology**   A way of theorising and analysing punishments intimately associated with, and often funded by, the government.

**Authoritarian populism**   An explanation of how punitive and repressive laws can gain widespread consent among the public.

**Bifurcation**   The attempt to reserve imprisonment for serious and dangerous offenders, while at the same time giving low-risk offenders **community penalties**.

**Bloody code**   How capital punishments were deployed in eighteenth-century England as a means of exercising ideological control.

**Carceral society**   The argument made by Michel Foucault (French philosopher) that changes in the penal system in the nineteenth century were not inspired by humanitarian benevolence but rather by the deepening and expansion of disciplinary **power**.

**Causation**   The assertion that one event or set of circumstances inevitably cause(s) another event or set of circumstances to occur.

**Civilisation**   The advancement of society to a higher level of **moral**, cultural and social values. Emile Durkheim and penologists following in the tradition of Norbert Elias have applied the civilisation process to forms of **punishment**.

**Community penalties**   Non-custodial penal sanctions.

**Comparative analysis**   The selection and study of two or more cases to highlight similarities and differences. This can involve comparing penal systems and forms of **punishment** in different countries.

**Contestability**   The opening up of the provision of **rehabilitation** for offenders to contest from both the public and private sectors.

**Correlation**   When two or more phenomena occur at the same time, but are not necessarily linked.

**'Crime'**   The term applied to refer to certain social harms, illegalities and forms of **wrongdoing**. A 'crime' is a **social construction** that is shaped by specific legal, historical and spatial contexts. The constitution of what a 'crime' entails is essentially contested, and depends on the theoretical and political position of the definer.

**Criminalisation**   The application of the 'criminal' label.

**Criminal justice system**   The collective name given to state agencies that respond to illegal behaviours. These include the police, the courts, and **probation** and prison services.

**Crisis**   A term indicating that, if action is not taken soon to address current problems and difficulties, a breakdown or disaster will occur.

**Critical race theory**   The analysis and transformation of the role of racial discrimination in systems of criminal justice.

**Culture**   The norms and values of a given society or institution.

**Dangerousness**   A social and historical construction that has referred to a number of different groups of offenders. Today, it generally refers to violent, sexual and persistent property offenders.

**Dark figure**   The very large amount of **'crime'** and harm in society that is not covered in official statistics.

**Decarceration** Moving away from imprisonment as the central penal sanction.

**Decency** A humanitarian ethos to prison work introduced by former Director General Martin Narey. This is a vague concept that implies treating prisoners as fellow human beings, developing relationships with prisoners, ensuring that prisoners receive their lawful entitlements, and a commitment to reducing racism, self-inflicted deaths and prison officer brutality.

**Dehumanisation** A process under which the basic prerequisites of human life are undermined and deliberately removed, resulting in alienation and profound human suffering.

**Democracy** The unhindered participation of all people in processes of shared decision making. In a democracy, all human voices are deemed valid and of equal worth in the creation of social norms.

**Denunciation** When a '**crime**', social harm, or wrong is symbolically denounced, often through **punishment**.

**Deterrence** The philosophical justification of **punishment** that looks to deter individuals or wider members of society from future lawbreaking through efficient and effective penal sanctions.

**Deviance** Social behaviour that deviates from the dominant cultural norms and values.

**Enlightenment** The philosophical movement maintaining that man and woman can use human reason and rational thought to explain social phenomena.

**False negatives** Linked to the philosophical justification of **incapacitation**. This arises when an **offender** is predicted not to reoffend, but does so.

**False positives** When an **offender** is predicted to reoffend, but does not do so. This is difficult to assess because the offender has been incapacitated.

**Feminism** A sociological, philosophical and political tradition that calls for the fair and equitable treatment of women. There are a number of feminist perspectives, including liberal feminism, Marxist feminism, radical feminism, Black feminism, post-modern feminism and socialist feminism.

**Functionalism** When a given social institution, such as prison, is defined as meeting certain prerequisite needs for society to function successfully. This 'functional fit' does not necessarily have to correspond with the official aims of the given institution. Marxist and Foucauldian theories are sometimes referred to as 'left functionalism', because they highlight the way in which prisons function in the interests of the powerful.

**Globalisation** The increasing homogeneity of global economies, and its implications for national politics and **culture**.

**Governmentality** A highly influential theoretical perspective derived from the later works of Michel Foucault. Governmentality theorists focus on governing technologies and mentalities that privilege **risk** and security. The major drawback is that this perspective is largely descriptive.

**Governmental sovereignty** The political criteria that defines the legitimate goals and role of the government.

**Harm reduction policies** These are policies that prioritise the safety of those who engage in risky and potentially harmful practices. The overall goal is reducing harm—such as the spread of HIV through infected needles—rather than reducing the prevalence of a given activity.

**Hegemony** The dominant idea or means of interpretation. It implies intellectual and **moral** leadership, and is crucial in the creation of consent.

**Humane containment** An aim of imprisonment which claims that, although prisons cannot be justified through **rehabilitation**, prisons should treat those they contain as humanely as possible.

**Human rights** A concept that is based on the recognition of the innate dignity of a fellow human beings. Human rights provide a politically acceptable **moral** framework through which we can critique the infamies of the present, acknowledge human suffering and promote tolerance of diversity. They also have a latent function in promoting the positive obligations and legal duties of the powerful to protect the rights of citizens.

**Human Rights Act (HRA)**   The Human Rights Act 1998, which came into force on the 2 October 2000.

**Ideology**   A set of beliefs, values and ideas that shape the way in which people understand the world. For neo-Marxists, ideology is important in winning the battle for hearts and minds on how we should respond to wrongdoers.

**Incapacitation**   A philosophical justification of **punishment** that calls for the removal of the **offender**'s physical capacity to offend. This can be done through the death penalty, banishment or **incarceration**.

**Incarceration**   The process of placing people into institutions such as the prison.

**Just deserts**   A justification of sentencing that is tied to the philosophical justification of **retribution**. In short: you get the **punishment** you deserve by receiving a sentence that is proportionate to the offence you have committed.

**Key performance**   The targets that the prison service sets; indicators/ targets each financial year.

**Labelling theory**   A sociological theory that examines the social consequences of applying negative labels to individuals and groups. Rooted in the symbolic interactionism of George Herbert Mead, penologists have focused on the stigma and **dehumanisation** that is created through the 'prisoner' label.

**Labour market**   A term used to describe the relations between the buyers (capitalists) and sellers (workers) of labour **power**. Penologists have been particularly interested in the division of labour (Durkheim) and the consequences of unemployment for the form that **punishment** takes in a given society (Rusche).

**Late modernity**   A term used to describe changes in the **labour market**, families, communications, **mass media** and **culture** in Western societies since the 1970s.

**Law and order society** The famous argument made by sociologist Stuart Hall that concerns about '**crime**' and lawbreaking have become central to current forms of political debate.

**Legitimacy** The **moral** and political validity of a given state of affairs. This is a contested concept, with some penologists arguing legitimacy is dependent on: (1) whether people *believe* something is legitimate; (2) whether a set of circumstances adheres to *people's beliefs*; or (3) whether validity should be based on *normative criteria*, such as meeting the requirements of **social justice** and **human rights** standards.

**Less eligibility** A doctrine under which the conditions of imprisonment must not be higher than the living conditions of the poorest labourer. This perspective is tied to the philosophical justification of **deterrence**.

**Managerialism** Highly influential credos that claimed that changes in the management of the criminal justice would lead to improved performance and lower costs.

**Marxism** Sociological, political and philosophical perspective, rooted in the work of Karl Marx, that argues against the logic of capitalism, calling instead for forms of **political economy** and **governmental sovereignty** that are rooted in meeting human needs.

**Mass media** Institutions of communication that broadcast, or distribute, information. The media include newspapers, magazines, the Internet, television, radio and cinema.

**Methodology** The techniques deployed to undertake empirical studies to glean knowledge of social practices. Research methodology can include observation, interviews and questionnaires.

**Ministry of Justice** A government department established in May 2007 to head the correctional services (prisons and **probation**) in England and Wales.

**Modernity** A period of time since the eighteenth century that is closely associated with the rise of industrial society, liberal democratic governance and the intellectual drives of the **enlightenment**.

**Moral**   Refers to the 'right thing to do' in a given set of circumstances.

**Moral panic**   A term introduced by Stan Cohen in the 1970s to explain how society sometimes over-reacts to a person, or group of people, who have challenged societal norms, and calls for a disproportionate increase in **social control** and repression.

**Neo-abolitionism**   A modernist and humanist perspective that integrates the insights of symbolic interactionism with the political analysis of criminologies that are inspired by neo-Marxism and the **moral** framework of penal **abolitionism**.

**Neoliberalism**   A term that describes a set of ideologies that privilege the free market. Neoliberalism promotes minimal state intervention for the provision of social welfare, but argues that we should retain a strong authoritarian state.

**NOMS**   The National Offender Management Service.

**Normalisation**   This term has been applied in two very different ways in **penology**. Roy King and Rod Morgan used this term in the 1980s to argue that prison life should be as *normal* as possible in relation to that on the outside. This use of the term is closely linked to debates on prison conditions. The French philosopher Michel Foucault, however, used the term 'normalisation' to highlight how penalties have been used in an attempt to make offenders normal. This use of the term is closely associated with the ideas of **bifurcation** and **rehabilitation**.

**OASys**   Offender assessment system—used by **probation** officers to assess **risk**.

**Offender**   The term used to describe a person who has breached societal rules or laws.

**Offender pathways**   Current government initiative around **resettlement** that aims to identify the criminogenic and social needs of offenders, and to provide policies that can address each one of these factors.

**Pains of imprisonment**   A term used to describe the inherent deprivations of prison life. Gresham Sykes (1958) described the 'pains of imprisonment' for male prisoners as the deprivation of liberty, heterosexual sex, goods and services, autonomy and security. Women prisoners are likely to experience other pains in addition to these.

**Panopticon** A prison design by Jeremy Bentham that aimed to maximise prisoner surveillance as a means of instilling discipline.

**Parole** A word derived from the French term *parole d'honneur*, meaning to give your word of honour. Parole was first introduced in the English penal system through the 'ticket of leave system' in the nineteenth century.

**Penal accountability** The principle that responses to wrongdoers should be premised upon the rule of law, legal guarantees and procedural safeguards rooted in the principles of fairness, transparency and equality. Legal accountability places ethical boundaries and preclusions on the extent of state interventions.

**Penal controversy** This is a strongly disputed and contentious form of penal practice that leads to questions about its **moral** and/or political **legitimacy**.

**Penal expansionism** Referring to an approach based on increasing prison numbers and prison capacity. This approach currently shapes **penal policy** in England and Wales.

**Penalisation** The application of the penal sanction.

**Penality** The study of the ideas, principles, policies and practices of the penal system, alongside their broader socio-economic, historical, intellectual and political contexts. Penality looks to understand **punishment** and regulation, both within and beyond state institutions.

**Penal performance** The measurements used to assess if a prison is meeting the standards set by the prison service. This can be linked to managerial targets or based on 'Measurement of the Quality of Prison Life' surveys, which aim to assess the **moral** performance of imprisonment.

**Penal policy** A collective term for government and **criminal justice system** documents detailing the main aims, principles and ideas that shape the practices of penal institutions.

**Penal reductionism**   Calls for a massive reduction in prisoner numbers and the penal estate. Penal reductionists often argue that the capacity for imprisonment should be at no higher than 20,000 places.

**Penitentiary**   A term used to describe the first convict prisons of the UK in the nineteenth century. Drawing upon the meanings of the Christian term 'penitence', the penitentiary was intended to be an institution that would lead those incarcerated to repent of their **wrongdoing**.

**Penology**   The sociological and philosophical study of penal institutions. In recent times, in the UK, its primary focus has been on evaluating the practices and **legitimacy** of imprisonment.

**Persistency**   A term largely applied today to prolific property offending by working-class boys.

**Persistency principle**   A belief that offenders should be punished not only based on their current offence, but also on past offending. This approach has gained increasing influence with the changes to sentencing following the Halliday Report (2001) and the Criminal Justice Act 2003.

**Political economy**   The manner in which the economy is organised in a given society.

**Political theory**   The study of the organisation and exercise of power, including that of the state and government.

**Positivism**   The belief that scientific knowledge and methods can be used in the social sciences to study humans. Positivism has significant implications for research ethics and **methodology**. Although it has been intellectually discredited in the academy, positivistic studies still have political and policy influence.

**Postmodernism**   A theoretical perspective and 'state of mind' that is rooted in the belief that we have seen an end to meta-narratives (big stories) and a loss of confidence in social progress. Without absolute values, we can no longer have certainty in knowledge or uncover the truth.

**Poverty**   Refers to the inability to meet necessary needs and to live a full human life.

**Power**   A term that refers to an ability to make somebody do something that they would not normally do.

**Power/knowledge**   A term introduced by Michel Foucault to describe the manner in which people in positions of **power** have the ability to present certain realities as the truth.

**Pressure group**   This is an organisation that looks to: lobby parliament for changes in the law; inform the general public on a particular matter; and/or provide specialist support to members of the public who have been affected by a particular problem, such as the families of those who die in custody. A pressure group will reflect certain political beliefs and values.

**Prison disturbances**   The term sometimes used to describe prisoner rebellion, revolts and riots. Used most famously by Lord Woolf in 1991.

**Prisoner populations**   This can be measured by various means: the average daily population; the rate per 100,000 of the overall population; examining the numbers who are sentenced to prison each year. These are not objective data, but are produced for the needs of the penal system itself.

**Prison works**   The argument popularised by Michael Howard and Charles Murray that, if used ruthlessly enough, prison might act as a means of **deterrence** and **incapacitation**.

**Probation**   A state institution that was set up to befriend offenders, but which, in recent times, has become focused on **risk assessment**.

**Punishment**   The deliberate infliction of pain.

**Punitiveness**   The extent to which **punishment** and the punitive rationale is embedded within an individual or **culture**.

**Radical alternatives**   The argument made by penal abolitionists that we need to rethink how we respond to **social problems**. Radical alternatives include promoting forms of redress, social policies that are rooted in the principle of **social justice** and which look to address structural inequities, and positive community interventions that give young people (the staple diet of the **criminal justice system**) constructive things to do with their time.

**Rational choice theory** Intimately tied with the philosophical justification of **deterrence**, this perspective is predicated on the assumption that human beings make rational decisions before they break the law. Severity and certainty of sentence are supposed to impact upon this decision-making process.

**Recidivism rates** The level of reoffending.

**Reform** (1) A philosophical justification of **punishment**, which claims that punishment—and specifically imprisonment—can be used to change the prisoner into a better person. Today, this meaning of reform is used interchangeably with **rehabilitation**. (2) Reform is now often used to refer to changes made to penal regimes and attempts to make prisons more humane environments.

**Rehabilitation** A philosophical justification of **punishment**, which claims that punishments can be used to restore an **offender** to his or her previous competency. Although tied to a medical model, the term is used in the broader sense as a means of helping offenders to desist from 'crime'.

**Relative surplus population** A group of people who are unemployed, but who can join the workforce in times of economic growth. The term is largely used by Marxist penologists.

**Remand** The term used to refer to the time during which a person is held in prison awaiting trial. Remand prisoners are often held in worse conditions than those of convicted prisoners.

**Resettlement** The current policy aiming to help prisoners to reintegrate back into the community on release from prison.

**Responsibilisation strategies** An argument that, under neoliberal forms of governance, the powerless are given responsibilities rather than rights. Responsibilities are removed from the state for providing security and safety for the general public.

**Restorative justice** A way of responding to crimes, problems and harms that is rooted in the principles of mediation and reparation. Since the Crime and Disorder Act 1998, restorative justice has become an important part of government policy.

**Retribution** The philosophical justification of **punishment**, which claims that people deserve to be punished for their past crimes. Rooted in the principles of 'two wrongs make a right', the philosophy explains why we need to respond to **wrongdoing**, but does not explain why that must entail the deliberate infliction of pain.

**Risk** A means of calculating danger, harm, injury, damage or loss. This is now the dominant way of conceiving **social problems**.

**Risk assessment** Assessment of an **offender**'s likelihood to perform future criminal activity.

**Risk society** An influential argument made by German sociologist Ulrich Beck that society is now more characterised by the distribution of ills than it is by the distribution of goods.

**Scapegoating** A term that refers to the practice of wrongly blaming somebody for a **'crime'** or harm. People from minority ethnic groups and poor backgrounds are most likely to be scapegoated.

**'Security, control and justice'** An approach to **penal policy**, as advocated by Lord Justice Woolf in 1991.

**Social construction** The manner in which meanings are defined, judged and applied to social life. Understandings of social phenomena are shaped by time, place, **culture** and historical contexts.

**Social control** A very broad term, which relates to the mechanisms that are deployed to ensure that people conform to social expectations. This includes informal social controls, such as the family and schooling, and formal social controls, such as the police and prisons.

**Social exclusion** Often used in place of the term **'poverty'**, social exclusion refers to many ways in which people can be barred from participating in society's social, economic, political and cultural systems.

**Social harm perspective** A radical argument that moves beyond those harms defined by the criminal law to take seriously all harms that impact upon people, from cradle to grave.

**Social justice** This principle requires the equitable redistribution of the social product, allowing individuals to meet their necessary needs. Alongside this, it requires a rebalancing of **power**, the reducing of vulnerabilities, and the fostering of trust, security and social inclusion. This principle supposes that all wrongdoers and social harms are dealt with fairly and appropriately. It also implies recognition and respect for the shared humanity of offenders.

**Social problems** Refers to issues that are understood as problematic within their social and historical context. What is included in the definition of social problems depends, at any given time, on the influence of those who have the **power** to define.

**Socio-economic context** The social and economic circumstances surrounding a person's lived realities.

**Sociology** An academic discipline that studies society. Sociological theories inform a number of penological studies and the 'sociology of **deviance**'.

**Sub-proletariat** A term used by Marxist penologists in place of the term 'underclass', which implies a permanent class that exists below the proletariat. The sub-proletariat consists of economically marginalised and socially excluded people at the bottom of the social hierarchy. They are often members of the **relative surplus population** (unemployment) and are the people most likely to end up in our prisons.

**Transcarceration** When people are moved from one institution, such as the mental asylum, to another, such as the prison.

**Treatment and training ideology** The term used to describe the dominant rationale of the prison service in England and Wales from the 1920s until the 1970s.

**Utilitarianism** The philosophy that social policies should be based on the principle of the greatest happiness of the greatest number of people. It has been challenged, because it raises considerable problems for the **human rights** of minority groups.

**Victim**   The term used in the **criminal justice system** to describe the person who has been harmed through a criminal act. The word 'victim', however, has been challenged and many feminists have argued that the term 'survivor' is a more accurate description.

**Welfare through punishment**   The argument that social welfare is now provided to the poor and vulnerable only after they have been caught up within the penal web.

**What Works**   An approach to **rehabilitation** that is rooted in the principles of cognitive behaviouralism. The 'What Works' agenda dominates current accredited programmes in prisons in England and Wales.

**Woman-wise penology**   A feminist approach that is championed by Pat Carlen, who argues that responses to women who offend should be rooted in principles of empowerment.

**Wrongdoing**   A **moral** term used to describe inappropriate, harmful and potentially illegal behaviour.

# REFERENCES

Allen, R (2011) *Last Resort? Exploring The Reduction in Child Imprisonment 2008–11*, London: Prison Reform Trust.

Allen, R (2012) *Reducing the Use of Imprisonment: What Can We Learn From Europe?*, Report for the Criminal Justice Alliance.

Armstrong, S (2012) *The Quantification of Fear Through Prison Population Projections*. Available at SSRN: http://ssrn.com/abstract=1991866.

Ashworth, A (2010) *Sentencing and Criminal Justice*, 5th edn, Cambridge: Cambridge University Press.

Ashworth, A and Redmayne, M (2010) *The Criminal Process*, Oxford: Oxford University Press.

Ashworth, A and Roberts, J (2012) 'Sentencing Theory, Principle and Practice', in M Maguire, R Morgan and R Reiner (eds), *The Oxford Handbook of Criminology*, 5th edn, Oxford: Oxford University Press.

Bail for Immigration Detainees (BID) (2013) *Transforming Rehabilitation: A Revolution in the Way we Manage Offenders. Response from Bail for Immigration Detainees, February 2013*, London: Bail for Immigration Detainees.

Bandyopadhyay, S (2012) *Acquisitive Crime: Improsionment, Detection and Social Factors* (Civitas report), Birmingham: Department of Economics, University of Birmingham.

Barak-Glantz, I (1981) 'Toward a Conceptual Schema of Prison Management Styles', *The Prison Journal*, 61(2), pp. 42–60.

Barton, A, Corteen, K, Scott, D and Whyte, D (eds) (2006) *Expanding the Criminological Imagination*, Cullompton: Willan.

Bauman, Z (1989) *Modernity and the Holocaust*, Cambridge: Polity Press.

Bauman, Z (2000) 'Social Issues of Law and Order', in D Garland and R Sparks (eds), *Criminology and Social Theory*, Oxford: Oxford University Press.

Bauman, Z (2004) *Wasted Lives: Modernity and its Outcasts*, Cambridge: Polity Press.

Bean, P (1981) *Punishment: A Philosophical and Criminological Inquiry*, Oxford: Martin Robertson.

Beccaria, CB (1764; 1986) *Essays on Crimes and Punishment*, Indianapolis, IN: Hackett.

Beck, U (1992) *The Risk Society*, Cambridge: Polity Press.

Bhui, HS (ed.) (2009) *Race and Criminal Justice*, London: Sage.

Blair, A (2004) 'Foreword: Prime Minister', in HM Government, Cutting Crime, Delivering Justice: A Strategic Plan for Criminal Justice 2004–8, London: HMSO.

Bosworth, M (1999) *Engendering Resistance: Agency and Power in Women's Prisons*, Aldershot: Ashgate.

Bosworth, M (2010) *Explaining US Imprisonment*, London: Sage.

Bottoms, A (1977) 'Reflections on the Renaissance of Dangerousness', *Howard Journal*, 16(2), pp. 70–97.

Bottoms, A (1990) 'The Aims of Imprisonment', in D Garland (ed.), *Justice, Guilt and Forgiveness in the Penal System*, Edinburgh: University of Edinburgh.

Bottoms, A (1995) 'The Philosophy and Politics of Punishment and Sentencing', in C Clarkson and R Morgan (eds), *The Politics of Sentencing Reform*, Oxford: Clarendon.

Bottoms, A, Rex, S and Robinson, G (eds) (2004) *Alternatives to Prison: Options for an Insecure Society*, Cullompton: Willan.

Bowker, L (1977) *Prisoner Subcultures*, Lexington, MA: DC Heath.

Bowling, B and Phillips, C (2002) *Racism, Crime and Justice*, London: Longman.

Box, S (1987) *Recession, Crime and Punishment*, London: Macmillan.

Box, S and Hale, C (1982) 'Economic Crises and the Rising Prisoner Population', *Crime and Social Justice*, 17, pp. 20–35.

Boyle, J (1977) *A Sense Of Freedom*, London: Pan.

Bradley, Lord (2009) *The Bradley Report: Lord Bradley's Review of People with Mental Health Problems or Learning Disabilities in the Criminal Justice System*, London: Department of Health.

Braithwaite, J and Pettit, P (1990) *Not Just Deserts: A Republican Theory of Criminal Justice*, Oxford: Clarendon.

Brownlee, I (1998) *Community Punishment: A Critical Introduction*, London: Longman.

Bryans, S and Jones, R (eds) (2001) *Prisons and the Prisoner*, London: HMSO.

Burgess, A (1962) *A Clockwork Orange*, London: Penguin Essentials.

Canton, R (2011) *Probation: Working with Offenders*, Cullompton: Willan.

Carlen, P (1983) *Women's Imprisonment: A Study in Social Control*, London: Routledge.

Carlen, P (ed.) (2002) *Women and Punishment: The Struggle for Justice*, Cullompton: Willan.

Carlen, P and Worrall, A (2004) *Analysing Women's Imprisonment*, Cullompton: Willan.

Carrabine, E (2004) *Power, Discourse and Resistance: A Genealogy of the Strangeways Prison Riot*, Aldershot: Ashgate.

Carter, P (2004) *Managing Offenders, Reducing Crime: A New Approach,* London: Home Office (the 'Carter Review').

Cavadino, M and Dignan, J (2006) *Penal Systems: A Comparative Approach,* London: Sage.

Cavadino, M, Dignan, J and Mair, G (2013) *The Penal System: An Introduction,* 5th edn, London: Sage.

Centre for Social Justice (2009) *Locked Up Potential: A Strategy for Reforming Prisons and Rehabilitating Prisoners, A Policy Report by the Prison Reform Working Group, Chaired by Jonathan Aitken,* London: Centre for Social Justice.

Chigwada-Bailey, R (2003) *Black Women's Experience of Criminal Justice,* Winchester: Waterside.

Christie, N (1993) *Crime Control as Industry: Towards Gulags, Western Style?* London: Routledge.

Christie, N (2000) *Crime Control as Industry: Towards Gulags, Western Style?* 2nd edn, London: Routledge.

Clarke, J and Newman, J (1997) *The Managerial State: Power, Politics and Ideology in the Remaking of Social Welfare,* London: Sage.

Cleaver, E (1968) *A Soul on Ice,* New York: Dell.

Clemmer, D (1948) *The Prison Community,* New York: Holt, Reinhart and Winston.

Codd, H (2008) *In the Shadow of the Prison,* Cullompton: Willan.

Cohen, S (1985) *Visions of Social Control: Crime Punishment and Classification,* Cambridge: Polity Press.

Cohen, S (2001) *States of Denial: Knowing About Atrocities and Suffering,* Cambridge: Polity Press.

Cohen, S and Scull, A (eds) (1983) *Social Control and the State,* Oxford: Blackwell.

Cohen, S and Taylor, L (1972; 1981) *Psychological Survival: The Experience of Long-Term Imprisonment,* 2nd edn, Harmondsworth: Penguin.

Cohen, S and Taylor, L (1978) *Prison Secrets,* London: RAP/NCCL.

Committee for the Prevention of Torture (2009) *Report to the Government of the United Kingdom on the Visit to the United Kingdom carried out by the European Commission for the Prevention of Torture and Inhuman or Degrading Treatment or Punishment from 18 November to 1 December 2008,* Strasbourg: CPT.

Corston, J (2007) *The Corston Report: A Report by Baroness Jean Corston of a Review of Women with Particular Vulnerabilities in the Criminal Justice System,* London: Home Office.

Coyle, A (2005) *Understanding Prisons,* Milton Keynes: Open University Press.

Crawley, E (2004) *Doing Prison Work: The Public and Private Lives of Prison Officers*, Cullompton: Willan.

Creighton, S and Arnott, H (2009) *Prisoners: Law and Practice*, London: Legal Action Group.

Creighton, S, King, V and Arnott, H (2005) *Prisoners and the Law*, 3rd edn, Haywards Heath: Tottel.

Cressey, R (1959) *The Prison*, New York: Anchor Press.

Crewe, B (2009) *The Prisoner Society: Power, Adaptation and Social Life in an English Prison*, Oxford: Oxford University Press.

Crewe, B and Bennett, J (eds) (2012) *The Prisoner*, London: Routledge.

*Daily Express* (2011*)* 'Cameron orders Ken Clarke to scrap soft sentences', 21 June.

*Daily Mail* (2012a) 'War on "holiday camp" jail perks as Prison Minister calls for privileges to be earned through hard work and good behaviour', 28 October.

*Daily Mail* (2012b) 'Chris Grayling gets tough: New Justice Secretary ditches Ken Clarke's plan to cut jail numbers', 18 September.

Davies, M, Croall, H and Tryer, J (2010) *Criminal Justice: An Introduction to the Criminal Justice System in England and Wales*, 4th edn, London: Pearson-Longman.

Davis, AY (2003) *Are Prisons Obsolete?* New York: Seven Stories Press.

Davis, AY (2005) *Abolition Democracy*, New York: Seven Stories Press.

Davis, AY (2012) *The Meaning of Freedom and Other Difficult Dialogues*, San Francisco, CA: City Light.

de Haan, W (1990) *The Politics of Redress: Crime, Abolition and Penal Abolition*, London: Sage.

de Haan, W (1991) 'Abolition and Crime Control: A Contradiction in Terms', in K Stenson and D Cowell (eds), *The Politics Of Crime Control*, London: Sage.

Delgado, R and Stefancic, J (2001) *Critical Race Theory: An Introduction*, New York: New York University Press.

Di Georgi, A (2006) *Rethinking the Political Economy of Punishment: Perspectives on Post-Fordism and Penal Politics*, Aldershot: Ashgate.

Dick, PK (1956) *The Minority Report, The Collected Short Stories of Philip K Dick*, vol. 4, London: Gollancz.

Dick, PK (1977) *A Scanner Darkly*, London: Gollancz.

Dilulio, JJ (1990) *Governing Prisons: A Comparative Study of Correctional Management*, London: Free Press.

Dostoevsky, F (1860) *House of the Dead*, Harmondsworth: Penguin.

Drake, D (2011) *Prisons, Punishment and the Pursuit of Security*, London: Palgrave.

Durkheim, E (1893; 1984) *The Division of Labour in Society*, London: Macmillan.

Durkheim, E (1912; 2001) *The Elementary Forms of Religious Life*, Oxford: Oxford University Press.

Easton, S (2011) *Prisoners' Rights: Principles and Practice*, London: Routledge.

Easton, S and Piper, C (2008) *Sentencing and Punishment: The Quest for Justice*, 2nd edn, Oxford: Oxford University Press.

Elias, N (1939; 1984) *The Civilising Process*, two vols, Oxford: Blackwell.

Ellis, T and Savage, S (2011) *Debates in Criminal Justice: Key Themes and Issues*, London: Routledge.

Emery, FE (1970) *Freedom and Justice within Walls: The Bristol Prison Experiment*, London: Tavistock.

Emsley, C (1996) *Crime and Society in England 1750–1900*, London: Longman.

Emsley, C and Knafla, LA (eds) (1996) *Crime History and Histories of Crime: Studies in the Historiography of Crime and Criminal Justice in Modern History*, London: Greenwood Press.

Farrall, S (2002) *Rethinking What Works with Offenders: Probation, Social Context and Desistance from Crime*, Cullompton: Willan.

Farrall, S and Calverley, A (2006) *Understanding Desistance from Crime: Theoretical Directions in Resettlement and Reintegration*, Maidenhead: Open University Press.

Feeley, M (2002) 'Entrepreneurs of Punishment: The legacy of privatisation', *Punishment and Society*, 4(3), pp. 321–44.

Feeley, M and Simon, J (1992) 'The New Penology: Notes on the Emerging Strategy of Corrections and its Implications', *Criminology*, 30, pp. 449–74.

Feeley, M and Simon, J (1994) 'Actuarial Justice: The Emerging New Criminal Law', in D Nelken (ed.), *The Futures Of Criminology*, London: Sage.

Field, S (2012) *Prison Law Index: The Definitive Annual A–Z Index of Prison Law Cases and Materials*, 2nd edn, Stockport: prisons.org.uk.

Finch, E and Fafinski, S (2012) *Criminology Skills*, Oxford: Oxford University Press.

Fitzgerald, M and Sim, J (1982) *British Prisons*, 2nd edn, Oxford: Blackwell.

Flew, A (1954) 'The Justification of Punishment', in HB Acton (ed.) (1969) *The Philosophy of Punishment*, London: Macmillan.

Flynn, N (1998) *Introduction to Prisons and Imprisonment*, Winchester: Waterside.

Flynn, N (2010) *Criminal Behaviour in Context: Space, Place and Desistance from Crime*, London: Routledge.

Foucault, M (1977) *Discipline and Punish: The Birth of the Prison*, Harmondsworth: Penguin.

Fox, C and Albertson, K (2010) 'Could Economics Solve the Prison Crisis?', *Probation Journal, The Journal of Community and Criminal Justice*, 57(3), pp. 263–80.

Frauley, J (ed.) (2014) *C. Wright Mills and the Criminological Imagination*, Aldershot: Ashgate.

Garland, D (1990) *Punishment and Modern Society: A Study in Social Theory*, Oxford: Oxford University Press.

Garland, D (2001) *The Culture of Control: Crime and Social Order in Contemporary Society*, Buckingham: Open University Press.

Garland, D and Young, P (eds) (1983) *The Power to Punish: Contemporary Penality and Social Analysis*, Oxford: Heinemann Education.

Gattrell, VAC (1994) *The Hanging Tree*, Oxford: Oxford University Press.

Gelsthorpe, L and Morgan, R (eds) (2007) *Handbook of Probation*, Cullompton: Willan.

Geltner, G (2008) *The Medieval Prison: A Social History*, Princeton, NJ: Princeton University Press.

Genders, E and Player, E (2007) 'The Commercial Context of Criminal Justice: Prison Privatisation and the Perversion of Purpose', *Criminal Law Review*, pp. 513–29.

Gilmore, J, Moore, JM and Scott, D (eds) (2013) *Critique and Dissent*, Ottawa: Red Quill.

Gladstone, H (1895) *Report from the Departmental Committee on Prisons (1895)*, C. 7702, London: Parliamentary Papers.

Godfrey, B and Lawrence, P (2005) *Crime and Justice 1750–1950*, Cullompton: Willan.

Goffman, E (1959; 1990) *The Presentation of Self in Everyday Life*, London: Penguin.

Goffman, E (1961; 1991) *Asylums: Essays on the Situation of Mental Patients and Other Inmates*, London: Penguin.

Golash, D (2005) *The Case Against Punishment*, New York: New York University Press.

Goldson, B (ed.) (2000) *The New Youth Justice*, Lyme Regis: Russell House.

Goldson, B and Muncie, J (eds) (2006) *Youth Justice*, London: Sage.

Green, P (2009) *Do Better Do Less: The Report of the Commission on English Prisons Today*, London: Howard League for Penal Reform.

*Guardian, The* (2005) 'A system in chaos', 23 June.

Hall, S, Critcher, C, Jefferson, T, Clark, J and Roberts, B (1978) *Policing the Crisis: Mugging the State and Law and Order*, London: Macmillan.

Halliday, J (2001) *Making Punishments Work: Report of a Review of the Sentencing Framework for England and Wales*, London: Home Office Communication Directorate (the 'Halliday Report').

Hannah-Moffat, K (2001) *Punishment in Disguise: Penal Governance and Federal Imprisonment of Women in Canada*, Toronto: University of Toronto Press.

Harding, R (1997) *Private Prisons and Public Accountability*, Milton Keynes: Open University Press.

Harper, G and Chitty C (eds) (2005) *The Impact of Corrections on Re-offending; A Review of 'What Works'*, Home Office Research Study 291, 2nd edn, London: Home Office.

Hay, D (1975) 'Property, Authority and the Criminal Law', in D Hay, P Linebaugh, JG Rule, EP Thompson and C Winslow (eds) *Albion's Fatal Tree*, Harmondsworth: Penguin.

Heidensohn, F (1985) *Women and Crime*, London: Macmillan.

Heidensohn, F (ed.) (2006) *Gender and Justice*, Cullompton: Willan.

Helyar-Cardwell, V (ed.) (2012) *Delivering Justice: The Role of the Public, Private and Voluntary Sectors in Prisons and Probation*, London: Criminal Justice Alliance.

Herrnstein, R and Murray, C (1994) *The Bell Curve: Intelligence and Class Structure in American Life*, New York: Free Press.

HM Chief Inspector of Prisons (1998) *Annual Report 1997–8*, London: HMSO.

HM Chief Inspector of Prisons (1999) *Suicide is Everyone's Concern: A Thematic Review*, London: HMSO.

HM Chief Inspector of Prisons (2005) *Parallel Lives*, London: HMSO.

HM Chief Inspector of Prisons (2012) *Annual Report 2011–12*, HC613, London: HMSO.

HM Chief Inspector of Prisons (2013a) *Annual Report 2012–13*, London: HMSO.

HM Chief Inspector of Prisons (2013b) *Report of an Unannounced Inspection of HMP Thameside 14–17 January 2013*, London: HMCIP.

HM Government (1991) 'Custody, Care and Justice: The Way Ahead for the Prison Service in England and Wales' (White Paper), London: HMSO.

HM Inspectorate of Probation (2013) *Annual Report 2012–13, Independent Inspection of Adult and Youth Offending Work*, Manchester: NM Inspectorate of Probation.

HM Prison Service (1993) *HM Prison Service Corporate Plan 1993–6*, London: HMSO.

HM Prison Service (1995) *Annual Report and Accounts Apr 1994–Mar 1995*, London: HMSO.

HM Prison Service (1998) *Prison Service Strategic Framework*, London: HMSO.

HM Prison Service (2000) *The Human Rights Act: What Does It Mean for the Service?* London: HM Prison Service.

HM Prison Service (2003a) *Annual Report and Accounts Apr 2002–Mar 2003*, London: HMSO.

HM Prison Service (2003b) *Prison Service Action Plan*, London: HM Prison Service.

HM Prison Service (2003c) *Re-Introduction of Disinfecting Tablets, Prison Service Instruction (PSI) 53/2003*, London: HM Prison Service.

HM Prison Service (2005) *Annual Report and Accounts Apr 2004–Mar 2005*, London: HMSO.

Hobhouse, S and Brockway, AF (1922) *English Prisons Today*, London: Longmans, Green.

Home Office (1979) *Report of the Committee of Inquiry into the United Kingdom Prison Service*, London: HMSO (the 'May Report').

Home Office (1990) *Crime, Justice and Protecting the Public*, London: HMSO.

Home Office (1996) *Protecting the Public: The Government's Strategy on Crime in England and Wales*, London: HMSO.

Home Office (2002) *Justice for All*, London: HMSO.

Home Office (2004a) *Reducing Crime, Changing Lives: The Government's Plans for Transforming the Management of Offenders*, London: HMSO.

Home Office (2004b) *Reducing Reoffending: National Action Plan*, London: HMSO.

Home Office (2004c) *Cutting Crime, Delivering Justice: A Strategic Plan For Criminal Justice 2004–8*, London: HMSO.

Home Office (2006) *Respect Action Plan*, London: HMSO.

Honderich, T (2006) *Punishment: The Supposed Justifications Revisited*, London: Pluto Press.

Hood, R (1992) *Race and Sentencing*, Oxford: Oxford University Press.

House of Commons Justice Committee (2013) *Women Offenders: After the Corston Report, Second Report of Session 2013–14, HC 92*, London: The Stationary Office.

Howard League for Penal Reform (2010) *Barbed: What Happened Next?* London: Howard League for Penal Reform.

Howard League for Penal Reform (2011) *Submission to the Leveson Inquiry: Culture, Practice and Ethics of the Press*, London: The Howard League for Penal Reform.

Hucklesby, A and Hagley-Dickinson, L (eds) (2007) *Prisoner Resettlement: Policy and Practice*, Cullompton: Willan.

Hudson, B (1993) *Penal Policy and Social Justice*, London: Macmillan.

Hudson, B (2003) *Understanding Justice*, 2nd edn, Milton Keynes: Open University Press.

*Huffington Post* (2013) 'Venezuela Prison Riot: More than 60 reportedly killed', 27 January.

Hunt, A and Wickham, G (1994) *Foucault and the Law*, London: Pluto Press.

Ignatieff, M (1978) *A Just Measure of Pain: The Penitentiary in the Industrial Revolution, 1750–1850*, Harmondsworth: Penguin.

INQUEST (2013) *Preventing the Deaths of Women in Prison: The Need for an Alternative Approach*, London: INQUEST.

INQUEST (2014) Deaths in Prison (England and Wales) 1990-date. Available at: http://www.inquest.co.uk/statistics/deaths-in-prison (accessed on 12/03/2014).

International Centre for Prison Studies (2013) *World Prison Brief*, London: International Centre for Prison Studies.

Irwin, J (1970) *The Felon*, Englewood Cliffs, NJ: Prentice Hall.

Jacobs, JB (1977) *Stateville: The Penitentiary in Mass Society*, Chicago, IL: University of Chicago Press.

James, AL, Bottomley, AK, Liebling, A and Clare, E (1997) *Privatising Prisons: Rhetoric and Reality*, London: Sage.

Jewkes, Y (2002) *Captive Audience: Media, Masculinity and Power in Prisons*, Cullompton: Willan.

Jewkes, Y (ed.) (2007a) *Handbook of Prisons*, Cullompton: Willan.

Jewkes, Y (2007b) *Media and Crime*, 2nd edn, London: Sage.

Jewkes, Y and Bennett, J (2007) *Dictionary of Prisons and Punishment*, Cullompton: Willan.

Jewkes, Y and Johnson, H (eds) (2006) *Prison Readings: A Critical Introduction to Prisons and Imprisonment*, Cullompton: Willan.

Johnstone, G (2011) *Restorative Justice: Ideas, Values, Debates*, 2nd edn, London: Routledge.

Jones, H and Cornes, P (1973) *Open Prisons*, London: Routledge.

Joyce, P (2006) *Criminal Justice: An Introduction to Crime and the Criminal Justice System*, Cullompton: Willan.

Kafka, F (1919) *In the Penal Colony*, London: Penguin Modern Classics.

Kafka, F (1925) *The Trial*, London: Penguin Modern Classics.

Kant, E (1796–97) *The Metaphysics of Morals*, trans. M Gregor (1991) Cambridge: Cambridge University Press.

Karstedt, S, Loader, I and Strang, H (2011) *Emotions, Crime and Justice*, Oxford: Hart.

Kauffman, K (1988) *Prison Officers and Their World*, Cambridge, MA: Harvard University Press.

Keith, B (2006) *The Zahid Mubarek Inquiry*, Vols 1 and 2, London: HMSO (the 'Keith Report').

King, R and Elliott, K (1977) *Albany*, London: Routledge Kegan Paul.

King, RD and Morgan, R (1980) *The Future of the Prison System*, Farnborough: Gower.

Lacey, N (2008) *The Prisoners Dilemma: Political Economy and Punishment in Contemporary Democracies*, Cambridge: Cambridge University Press.

Learmont, J (1995) *Review of Prison Service Security in England and Wales and the Escapes from Parkhurst Prison on Tuesday 3 January 1995*, London: HMSO (the 'Learmont Report').

Leech, M (1993) *A Product of the System: My Life In and Out of Prison*, London: Victor Gollancz.

Liebling, A (2004) *Prisons and their Moral Performance: A Study of Values, Quality and Prison Life*, Oxford: Oxford University Press.

Liebling, A, Price, D and Shefer, G (2011) *The Prison Officer*, 2nd edn, Cullompton: Willan.

Livingstone, S, Owen, T and MacDonald, A (2008) *Prison Law*, 4th edn, Oxford: Oxford University Press.

Loader, I (2010) 'For Penal Moderation: Notes towards a Public Philosophy of Punishment', *Theoretical Criminology*, 14(3), pp. 349–67.

Lockyer, K (2013) *Future Prisons: A Radical Plan to Reform The Prison Estate*, London: Policy Exchange.

Lombardo, LX (1981) *Guards Imprisoned: Correctional Officers at Work*, New York: Elsevier.

Lygo, R (1991) *Management of the Prison Service: A Report*, London: Home Office.

Maguire, M, Vagg, J and Morgan, R (eds) (1985) *Accountability and Prisons: Opening Up a Closed World*, London: Tavistock.

Mair, G (ed.) (2004) *What Matters in Probation*, Cullompton: Willan.

Mair, G and Burke, L (2011) *Redemption, Rehabilitation and Risk Management: A History of Probation*, London: Routledge.

Martinson, R (1974) 'What Works?' – Questions and Answers about Penal Reform, *The Public Interest*, 35, pp. 22–54.

Maruna, S (2001) *Making Good: How Ex-convicts Reform and Rebuild their Lives*, Washington, DC: American Psychological Association.

Maruna, S and Immarigeon, R (2004) *After Crime and Punishment*, Cullompton: Willan.

Maruna, S and Liebling, A (eds) (2005) *The Effects of Imprisonment*, Cullompton: Willan.

Mathiesen, T (1965; 2012) *Defences of the Weak: Sociological Study of a Norwegian Correctional Institution*, Oxford: Routledge.

Mathiesen, T (1974) *The Politics of Abolition* (40th anniversary edition to be published in 2014), Oxford: Martin Robertson.

Mathiesen, T (1980) 'The Future of Control Systems: the Case of Norway', *International Journal of the Sociology of Law*, 8(2), pp. 149–64.

Mathiesen, T (1990; 2006) *Prison On Trial*, 3rd edn, Winchester: Waterside.

Matthews, R (2005) 'The Myth of Punitiveness', *Theoretical Criminology*, 9(2), pp. 175–201.

Matthews, R (2009) *Doing Time: An Introduction to the Sociology of Imprisonment*, 2nd edn, London: Palgrave.

Mauer, M (1999) *Race to Incarcerate*, New York: The New Press.

McConville, S (1995) 'The Victorian Prison: England, 1865–1965', in N Morris and DJ Rothman (eds), *The Oxford History of the Prison*, Oxford: Oxford University Press, pp. 117–50.

McConville, S (ed.) (2008) *The Use of Punishment*, Cullompton: Willan.

McLaughlin, E and Muncie, J (eds) (2002) *Criminological Perspectives: Essential Readings*, 2nd edn, London: Sage.

McLaughlin, E, Muncie, J and Hughes, G (2001) 'The Permanent Revolution: New Labour, New Public Management and the Modernisation of Criminal Justice', *Criminology and Criminal Justice*, 1, pp. 301–18.

McLennan, RM (2008) *The Crisis of Imprisonment: Protest, Politics, and the making of the American Penal Estate, 1776–1941*, Cambridge: Cambridge University Press.

McVicar, J (1974, 2002) *McVicar by Himself*, London: Artnik.

Melossi, D (ed.) (1999) *The Sociology of Punishment*, Aldershot: Ashgate.

Melossi, D (2008) *Controlling Crime, Controlling Society: Thinking about Crime in Europe and America*, Cambridge: Polity.

Melossi, D and Pavariani, M (1981) *The Prison and the Factory: Origins of the Penitentiary System*, London: MacMillan.

Mills, CW (1959) *The Sociological Imagination*, Oxford: Oxford University Press.

Ministry of Justice (2008) *Race Review 2008: Implementing Race equality in Prisons – Five Years On*, London: National Offender Management Service.

Ministry of Justice (2009) *The Future of the Control Board*, Consultation Paper 14/09, London: Ministry of Justice.

Ministry of Justice (2010) *Breaking the Cycle: Effective Punishment, Rehabilitation and Sentencing of Offenders*, London: The Stationary Office.

Ministry of Justice (2012a) *Punishment and Reform: Effective Community Sentences*, Consultation Paper CP8/2012, London: The Stationary Office.

Ministry of Justice (2012b) *National Offender Management Service Business Plan 2012–2013*, London: Ministry of Justice.

Ministry of Justice (2012c) *National Offender Management Service Annual Report and Accounts 2011–12*, London: The Stationary Office.

Ministry of Justice (2012d) *Offender Management Statistics (Quarterly) October to December 2012*, London: Ministry of Justice.

Ministry of Justice (2013a) *Proven Reoffending Quarterly Bulletin, July 2010–June 2011*, London: Ministry of Justice.

Ministry of Justice (2013b) *Improving the Code of Practice for Victims of Crime, Consultation Paper CP8/2013*, London: Ministry of Justice.

Ministry of Justice (2013c) *Transforming Rehabilitation: A Strategy for Reform*, London: The Stationary Office.

Ministry of Justice (2013d) *Transforming the Criminal Justice System: A Strategy and Action Plan to Reform the Criminal Justice System. Cm 8658*, London: The Stationary Office.

Ministry of Justice (2013e) *Population and Capacity Briefing for Friday 12 July 2013*, London: Ministry of Justice.

Ministry of Justice (2013f) *Ministry of Justice Population Statistics* (published weekly), London: Ministry of Justice.

Ministry of Justice (2013g) *Ministry of Justice CNA and individual prison populations* (figures published monthly), London: Ministry of Justice.

Ministry of Justice (2013h) *Offender Management Statistics Quarterly Bulletin October to December 2012*, London: Ministry of Justice.

Ministry of Justice (2013i) *Story of the Prison Population: 1993–2012 England and Wales*, London: Ministry of Justice.

Morgan, R and Liebling, A (2007) 'Imprisonment: An Expanding Scene', in M Maguire, *The Oxford Handbook of Criminology*, 4th edn, Oxford: Oxford University Press.

Morris, N and Rothman, D (1998) *The Oxford History of the Prison*, Oxford: Oxford University Press.

Morris, TP and Morris, P (1963) *Pentonville: A Sociological Study of an English Prison*, London: Routledge Kegan Paul.

Mountbatten, Earl (1966) *Report of the Inquiry into Prison Escapes and Security Command 3175*, London: HMSO (the 'Mountbatten Report').

Murray, C (1984) *Losing Ground: American Social Policy, 1950–80*, New York: Basic Books.

Murray, C (1997) *Does Prison Work?* London: IEA.

National Audit Office (2010) *Managing Offenders on Short Custodial Sentences. Report by the Comptroller and Auditor General, HC 431 Session 2009–2010*, London: The Stationary Office.

National Audit Office (2012) *Comparing International Criminal Justice Systems, Briefing for the House of Commons Justice Committee, February 2012*, London: National Audit Office.

Nelken, D (2010) *Comparative Criminal Justice: Making Sense of Difference*, London: Sage.

Northern Ireland Prison Service (2012) *Analysis of Northern Ireland Prison Service Population from 1.4.2011 to 31.3.12*, Belfast: Department of Justice.

O'Malley, P (1999a) 'Volatile and Contradictory Punishment', *Theoretical Criminology*, 3(2), pp. 175–96.

O'Malley, P (1999b) 'Governmentality and the Risk Society', *Economy and Society*, 28: 138–48.

Obi, M (2008) *Prison Law: A Practical Guide*, London: The Law Society.

Office for National Statistics (2013) *Release: Crime Statistics, Period Ending June 2013*, London Office for National Statistics.

Oparah, J (2013) 'Why No Prisons?', in D Scott (ed.), *Why Prison?* Cambridge: Cambridge University Press.

Osborne, SP (ed.) (2010) *The New Public Governance? Emerging Perspectives on the Theory and Practice of Public Governance*, Abingdon: Routledge.

Pakes, F (2010) *Comparative Criminal Justice*, 2nd edn, Cullompton: Willan.

Parenti, C (1999) *Lockdown America: Police and Prisons in the Age of Crisis*, New York: Verso.

Patel, Lord (2010) *Reducing Drug-related Crime and Rehabilitating Offenders: Recovery and Rehabilitation for Drug Users in Prison and on Release, Recommendations for Action*, London: Department of Health.

Penfold, C, Turnbull, PJ and Webster, R (2005) *Tackling Prison Drug Markets: An Exploratory Qualitative Study*, London: Home Office online report 39/05.

Phillips, C (2012) *The Multicultural Prison: Ethnicity, Masculinity, and Social Relations among Prisoners*, Oxford: Oxford University Press.

Piacentini, L (2004) *Surviving Russian Prisons*, Cullompton: Willan.

Piper, C (2011) *The English Riots and Tough Sentencing*, London: Brunel Law School.

Pratt, J (2000) 'Emotive and Ostentatious Punishment', *Punishment and Society*, 2(4), pp. 417–39.

Pratt, J (2002) *Punishment and Civilisation*, London: Sage.

Pratt, J (2008) 'Scandinavian Exceptionalism in an Era of Penal Excess, Part 1: The Nature and Roots of Scandinavian Exceptionalism', *British Journal of Criminology*, 48(2), pp 119–37.

Pratt, J (2011) 'Penal Excess and Penal Exceptionalism: Welfare and Imprisonment in Anglophone and Scandinavian societies', in A Crawford (ed.), *International and Comparative Criminal Justice and Urban Governance*, Cambridge: Cambridge University Press.

Pratt, J and Eriksson, A (2012) *Contrasts in Punishment: An Explanation of Anglophone Excess and Nordic Exceptionalism*, London: Routledge.

Prison Reform Trust (1998) *Annual Report 1997–98*, London: Prison Reform Trust.

Prison Reform Trust (2005) *Private Punishment: Who Profits?* London: Prison Reform Trust.

Prison Reform Trust (2012a) *Out For Good: Taking Responsibility for Resettlement*, London: Prison Reform Trust.

Prison Reform Trust (2012b) *Bromley Briefings Prison Factfile June 2012*, London: Prison Reform Trust.

Prison Reform Trust/INQUEST (2012) *Fatally Flawed: Has the State Learned Lessons from the Deaths of Children and Young People in Prison*, London: Prison Reform Trust and INQUEST.

Prison Reform Trust/National AIDS Trust (2005) *Joint Report on the Spread of Contagious Diseases in Prison*, London: PRT/NAT.

Radzinowicz, L (1968) *Report of the Advisory Committee on the Penal System on the Regime for Long-term Prisoners in Conditions of Maximum Security*, London: HMSO (the 'Radzinowicz Report').

Radzinowicz, L and Hood, R (1986) *A History of English Criminal Law, vol. 5, The Emergence of Penal Policy*, London: Stevens and Son.

Ramsbotham, D (2003) *Prisongate: The Shocking State of Britain's Prisons and the Need for Visionary Change*, London: Free Press.

Rawlings, P (1999) *Crime and Power: A History of Criminal Justice 1688–1998*, Harlow: Longman.

Raynor, P and Vanstone, M (2002) *Understanding Community Penalties*, Milton Keynes: Open University Press.

Reiman, J (2007) *The Rich Get Richer and the Poor Get Prison: Ideology, Class, and Criminal Justice*, 7th edn, Boston, MA: Allyn and Bacon.

Rickford, D and Edgar, K (2005) *Troubled Inside: Responding to the Mental Health Needs of Men in Prison*, London: Prison Reform Trust.

*Rio Times, The* (2012) 'Prison System in Brazil Criticized', 15 November.

Robinson, G and Crow, I (2009) *Offender Rehabilitation: Theory, Research and Practice*, London: Sage.

Rodley, N (2009) *The Treatment of Prisoners under International Law*, 3rd edn, Oxford: Clarendon.

Rolston, B, Tomlinson, J, Moore, JM and Scott, D (eds) (2014) *Beyond Criminal Justice*, Bristol: EGSDSC.

Ross, RR and Fabiano, EA (1985) *Time to Think: A Cognitive Model of Delinquency Prevention and Offender Rehabilitation*, Johnson City, TN: Institute of Social Sciences and Arts.

Rothman, DJ (1971) *The Discovery of the Asylum*, Boston, MA: Little, Brown.

Ruck, SK (ed.) (1951) *Paterson on Prisons. The Collected Papers of Sir Alexander Paterson*, London: Frederick Muller.

Ruggiero, V (2010) *Penal Abolitionism*, Oxford: Oxford University Press.

Ruggiero, V and Ryan, M (eds) (2013) *Punishment in Europe*, London: Palgrave.

Ruggiero, V, Ryan, M and Sim, J (eds) (1996) *Western European Penal Systems: A Critical Anatomy*, London: Sage.

Rusche, G (1933) 'Labour Market and Penal Sanction: Thoughts on the Sociology of Criminal Justice', in D Melossi (ed.), (1998) *Sociology of Punishment*, Aldershot: Ashgate.

Rusche, G and Kirchheimer, O (1939; 2003) *Punishment and Social Structure*, London: Transaction.

Rutherford, A (1984) *Prisons and the Process of Justice: The Reductionist Challenge*, London: Heinemann.

Rutherford, A (1993) *Criminal Justice and the Pursuit of Decency*, Oxford: Oxford University Press.

Rutherford, A (1996) *Transforming Criminal Policy*, Winchester: Waterside.

Ryan, M (2005) *Penal Policy and Political Culture*, Winchester: Waterside.

Ryan, M and Ward, T (1989) *Privatization and the Penal System*, Milton Keynes: Open University Press.

Sanders, A, Young, R and Burton, M (2010) *Criminal Justice*, 4th edn, Oxford: Oxford University Press.

Sapsford, R (ed.) (1996) *Researching Crime and Criminal Justice*, Milton Keynes: The Open University.

Scott, D (1996) *Heavenly Confinement? The Prison Chaplain in North East England's Prisons*, London: Lambert Press.

Scott, D (2006) 'Ghosts beyond Our Realm: A Neo-Abolitionist Analysis of Prison Officer Occupational Culture and Prisoner Human Rights', unpublished PhD thesis, University of Central Lancashire.

Scott, D (2007) 'The Changing Face of the English Prison: A Critical Review of the Aims of Imprisonment', in Y Jewkes (ed.), *Handbook on Prisons*, Cullompton: Willan.

Scott, D (2009) 'Punishment', in A Hucklesby and A Wahidin (eds), *Criminal Justice*, Oxford: Oxford University Press.

Scott, D (2013a) 'Visualising an Abolitionist Real Utopia: Principles, Policy and Praxis', in M Malloch and W Munro (eds), *Crime, Critique and Utopia*, London: Palgrave.

Scott, D (ed.) (2013b) *Why Prison?* Cambridge: Cambridge University Press.

Scott, D (2014a) *Caretakers of Punishment: Power, Legitimacy and the Prison Officer*, London: Palgrave.

Scott, DG (2014b) 'Critical Research Values and the Sociological Imagination', in Frauley, J (ed.), *C. Wright Mills and the Criminological Imagination*, Aldershot: Ashgate.

Scott, D and Codd, H (2010) *Controversial Issues in Prison*, Milton Keynes: Open University Press.

Scottish Prison Service (2012) *Corporate Plan 2012–15*, Edinburgh: Scottish Government.

Scottish Prison Service (2013) *Scottish Prisoner Population as at Friday 19 July 2013*, Edinburgh: Scottish Prison Service.

Scraton, P (2007) *Power, Conflict and Criminalisation*, London: Routledge.

Scraton, P and Chadwick, K (1987) '"Speaking Ill of the Dead": Institution-alised Responses to Deaths in Custody', in P Scraton (ed.), *Law, Order, and the Authoritarian State: Readings in Critical Criminology*, Milton Keynes: Open University Press.

Scraton, P and Moore, L (2014) *The Incacertation of Women: Punishing Bodies, Breaking Spirits*, London: Palgrave.

Scraton, P, Sim, J and Skidmore, P (1991) *Prisons Under Protest*, Milton Keynes: Open University Press.

Scull, A (1977) *Decarceration: Community Treatment and the Deviant – A Radical View*, Englewood Cliffs, NJ: Prentice Hall.

Scull, A (1979) *Museums of Madness*, Basingstoke: Palgrave Macmillan.

Scull, A and Andrews, J (2001) *Undertaker of the Mind: John Monro and Mad-Doctoring in Eighteenth-Century England*, Berkeley, CA: University of California.

Scull, A and Lukes, S (2013) *Durkheim and the Law*, 2nd edn, Basingstoke: Palgrave Macmillan.

Sellin, JT (1976) *Slavery and the Penal System*, New York: Elsevier.

Sharpe, J (1990) *Judicial Punishment in England*, London: Faber and Faber.

Shefer, G and Liebling, A (2008) 'Prison Privatisation: In Search of a Business-like Atmosphere?', *Criminology and Criminal Justice*, 8 (3), pp. 261–78.

Shichor, D (1995) *Punishment for Profit: Private Prisons/Public Concerns*, London: Sage.

Shover, N (1996) *Great Pretenders: Pursuits and Careers of Persistent Thieves*, Boulder, CO: Westview Press.

Sim, J (1990) *Medical Power in Prisons: The Prison Medical Service in England, 1774–1989 (Crime, Justice and Social Policy)*, Milton Keynes: Open University Press.

Sim, J (1994a) 'Reforming the Penal Wasteland? A critical review of the Wolf Report', in E Player and M Jenkins (eds), *Prisons After Woolf: Reform Through Riot*, London: Routledge.

Sim, J (1994b) 'The Abolitionist Approach: A British Perspective', in A Duff, S Marshall, RE Dobash and RP Dobash (eds), *Penal Theory and Practice: Tradition and Innovation in Criminal Justice*, Manchester: Manchester University Press.

Sim, J (2009) *Punishment and Prisons: Power and the Carceral State*, London: Sage.

Simon, J (2007) *Governing Through Crime: How the War on Crime Transformed American Democracy and Created a Culture of Fear*, New York: Oxford University Press.

Sivanandan, A (2001) 'Poverty is the new Black', *Race and Class*, 43(2), pp. 1–6.

Smith, DJ (2010) *A New Response to Youth Crime*, Cullompton: Willan.

Smith, N 'Razor' (2005) *A Few Kind Words and a Loaded Gun: The Autobiography of a Career Criminal*, London: Penguin.

Smith, P (2008) *Punishment and Culture*, Chicago, IL: University of Chicago Press.

Smith, P and Natalier, K (2005) *Understanding Criminal Justice*, London: Sage.

Social Exclusion Unit (2002) *Reducing Reoffending by Ex-Prisoners*, London: HMSO.

Solzhenitsyn, AI (1963) *One Day in the Life of Ivan Denisovich*, Harmondsworth: Penguin.

Sparks, R (2001) 'Prisons, Punishment and Penality', in E McLaughlin and J Muncie (eds), *Controlling Crime*, London: Sage.

Sparks, R, Bottoms, AE and Hay, W (1996) *Prisons and the Problem of Order*, Oxford: Clarendon.

Spierenburg, P (1984) *The Spectacle of Suffering*, Cambridge: Cambridge University Press.

Steele, J (2002) *The Bird That Never Flew: The Uncompromised Autobiography of One of the Most Punished Prisoners in the History of the British Penal System*, Edinburgh: Mainstream.

Stern, V (1989) *Imprisoned by Our Prisons: A Programme for Reform*, London: Unwin Hyman.

Stern, V (1997) *A Sin Against the Future*, Harmondsworth: Penguin.

Straw, J (1997) *Prison Reform Trust Lecture 1997*, London: Prison Reform Trust.

Sudbury, J (ed.) (2005) *Global Lockdown: Race, Gender, and the Prison-Industrial Complex*, New York: Routledge.

Sveinsson, K (ed.) (2012) *Criminal Justice v Racial Justice: Over-representation in the Criminal Justice System*, London: The Runnymede Trust.

Sykes, G (1958) *Society of Captives: A Study of a Maximum Security Prison*, Princeton, NJ: Princeton University Press.

Tanner, W (2013) *The Case for Private Prisons*, London: Reform Research Trust.

Tarling, R (1993) *Analysing Offending: Data Models and Interpretations*, London: HMSO.

Taylor, AJP (1968) 'Introduction', *The Communist Manifesto*, Harmondsworth: Penguin.

Telegraph (2012) 'David Cameron to defy Europe on prisoner voting', 24 October.

Thomas, JE (1972) *The Prison Officer*, London: Routledge Kegan Paul.

*Times, The* (1995) 'Labour gives pledge to end prison privatisation', 8 March.

Toch, H (1975) *Men in Crisis: Human Breakdown in Prison*, Chicago, IL: Aldine.

Toch, H (1977) *Living in Prison: The Ecology of Survival*, New York: Free Press.

Tomlinson, M (1996) 'Imprisoning Ireland', in V Ruggiero, M Ryan and J Sim (eds), *Western European Penal Systems: A Critical Anatomy*, London: Sage.

Tonry, M (ed.) (2006) *The Future of Imprisonment*, Oxford: Oxford University Press.

Tonry, M (ed.) (2007) *Crime, Punishment and Politics in Comparative Perspective*, London: University of Chicago Press.

Tonry, M (ed.) (2012) *Retributivism Has a Past: Has it a Future?* Oxford: Oxford University Press.

Tucker, SB and Cadora, E (2003) 'Justice Reinvestment: To Invest in Public Safety by Reallocating Justice Dollars to Refinance Education, Housing, Healthcare and Jobs', *Ideas for an Open Society, Occasional Papers, vol. 3, no. 3*, New York: Open Society Institute.

Tumim, S (1997) *Crime and Punishment*, London: Phoenix.

Uglow, S (2009) 'The Criminal Justice System', in C Hale, K Hayward, A Wahidin and E Wincup (eds), *Criminology*, Oxford: Oxford University Press.

Vagg, J (1994) *Prison Systems: A Comparative Study of Accountability in England, France, Germany and The Netherlands*, Oxford: Clarendon.

van Swaaningen, R (1986) 'What is Abolitionism?', in H Bianchi and R van Swaaningen (eds), *Abolitionism: Towards a Non-Repressive Approach to Crime*, Amsterdam: Free University Press.

van Swaaningen, R (1997) *Critical Criminology: Visions from Europe*, London: Sage.

van Zyl Smit, D and Dunkel, F (eds) (2001) *Imprisonment Today and Tomorrow: International Perspectives on Prisoners' Rights and Prison Conditions*, 2nd edn, London: Kluwer Law International.

van Zyl Smit, D and Snacken, S (2011) *Principles of European Prison Law and Policy*, Oxford: Oxford University Press.

von Hirsch, A (1976) *Doing Justice: The Choice of Punishment*, New York: Hill and Wang (Report of the Committee for the Study of Incarceration).

von Hirsch, A (1986) *Past for Future Crimes: Deservedness and Dangerousness in the Sentencing of Criminals*, Manchester: Manchester University Press.

von Hirsch, A (1993) *Censure and Sanctions*, Oxford: Clarendon.

Wacquant, L (2000) 'The New Peculiar Institution: On the Prison as Surrogate Ghetto', *Theoretical Criminology*, 4(3), pp. 377–89.

Wacquant, L (2001) 'Deadly Symbiosis: When Ghetto and Prison Meet and Mesh', *Punishment and Society*, 3(1), pp. 95–134.

Wacquant, L (2009) *Punishing the Poor: The Neoliberal Government of Social Insecurity*, London: Duke University Press.

Walklate, S (2004) *Gender, Crime and Criminal Justice*, 2nd edn, Cullompton: Willan.

Walmsley, R (2011) *World Prison Populations List*, London: International Centre for Prison Studies.

Ward, T and Maruna, S (2007) *Rehabilitation*, London: Routledge.

Webb, S and Webb, B (1922) *English Prisons Under Local Government*, London: Longman, Green.

Weiss, R and South, N (eds) (1998) *Comparing Prison Systems: Toward a Comparative and International Penology*, Amsterdam: Overseas Publishers Association.

West, DG and Farrington, DP (1973) *Who Becomes Delinquent?* London: Heinemann.

Westmarland, L (2011) *Researching Crime and Justice: Tales from the Field*, London: Routledge.

Wiener, MJ (1990) *Reconstructing the Criminal: Culture, Law and Policy in England 1830–1914*, Cambridge: Cambridge University Press.

Wilson, JQ (1975) *Thinking about Crime*, New York: Basic Books.

Woodcock, J (1994) *Report of the Enquiry into the Escape of Six Prisoners from the Special Security Unit at Whitemoor Prison, Cambridgeshire, on Friday 9 September 1994*, London: HMSO (the 'Woodcock Report').

Woolf, LJ (1991) *Prison Disturbances April 1990: Report of an Inquiry by the Rt Hon Lord Justice Woolf (Parts I and II) and His Honour Judge Stephen Tumim (Part II)*, London: HMSO (the 'Woolf Report').

Woolf, LJ (2002) 'Making Punishments Fit the Needs of Society', *Prison Service Journal*, 142, pp. 6–9.

Worrall, A and Hoy, C (2005) *Punishment in the Community*, Cullompton: Willan.

Wyner, R (2003) *From the Inside*, London: Aurum.

Young, J (2011) *The Criminological Imagination*, Cambridge: Polity Press.

Zehr, H (2005) *Changing Lenses: A New Focus for Crime and Justice*, 3rd edn, Scottdale, PA: Herald Press.

# LIST OF CASES

*Becker v Home Office* [1972] 2 QB 407, [1972] 2 All ER 676
*Dickson v United Kingdom* [2007] ECHR 44362/04
*Edwards v United Kingdom* (2002) 35 EHRR 487
*Ezeh and Connors v United Kingdom* (2002) 35 EHRR 28

*Hirst v United Kingdom* (2004) 38 EHRR 40

*Raymond v Honey* [1983] 1 AC 1, [1982] 1 All ER 756

*Stafford v United Kingdom*, Application no. 46295/99 [2002] ECHR 2002-IV, 115

*Vinter, Bamber and Moore v United Kingdom* [2013] ECHR 66069/09, 130/10 and 3896/10

# INDEX